11.95

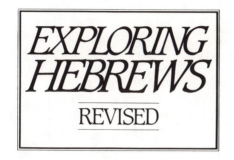

EXPLORING HEBREWS

REVISED

D0162164

EXPLORING HEBREWS
REVISED

by

JOHN PHILLIPS

MOODY PRESS
CHICAGO

© 1977, 1988 by
THE MOODY BIBLE INSTITUTE
OF CHICAGO

Revised Edition

All rights reserved. No part of this book may be reproduced in any form without permission in writing from the publisher except in the case of brief quotations embodied in critical articles or reviews.

Library of Congress Cataloging in Publication Data

Phillips, John, 1927-
    Exploring Hebrews.
      1. Bible. N.T. Hebrews-Commentaries. I. Title.
BS2775.3.P47   227'.87'07   76-39908

ISBN 0-8024-2498-8

1 2 3 4 5 6 7 Printing/VP/Year 92 91 90 89 88

Printed in the United States of America

Contents

Foreword

Exploring Hebrews, by John Phillips, is exactly what the title implies. In his explorations, the author gives us first a comprehensive view of the whole book with special attention to the so-called "warning passages." One thing he suggests in reading the book of Hebrews is omitting these passages in order to bring out the book's main purpose.

In his exposition, the author draws freely on what other expositors have written. He aptly illustrates with personal experiences together with quotations from other sources. At times he uses his imagination to bring out what the letter to the Hebrews could have meant to an honest seeker who may have had questions about the sacrifices mentioned in the Old Testament and their meaning in the light of what our Lord did when He offered Himself without spot to God as the one great sacrifice that not only satisfies God but that meets our every need as well.

In his analysis, the author uses alliteration quite freely to give his readers a framework to use as they study the Scriptures for themselves. To further stimulate profitable study of the letter to the Hebrews, he makes some practical and contemporary applications.

Again and again he sounds the evangelical note. Here and there he bursts forth into notes of worship, causing the reader to sing along with him in praise of the One who is the grand subject of the letter to the Hebrews.

Exploring Hebrews is a book that exalts Christ. Read it, and see for yourself.

CARL ARMERDING

Introduction

The trumpets of the Temple sound long and loud the daily summons to the evening sacrifice, and the priests perform their required washings, attire themselves in their gorgeous vestments, and set out for the house of God, which crowns the hill Moriah like a golden diadem, glittering and flashing in the sun. Again the summons rings forth, and yet again for the third and last time. The officiating priests of the day hasten up the broad steps leading to the outer court. From all over Jerusalem the people, the Levites, and the priests flock toward the Temple as the surrounding hills echo back the trumpet sound.

Through the outer court, the court of the Gentiles, they bustle through pillared cloisters leading to the stately dwellings of the priests and the Temple's ministering officers. On they go toward the inner or holy Temple, looking with pride and admiration on the marble walls, the gold and silver gates, the gleaming gold ornaments of clustering grapes and pomegranates, the cedar roofs and splendid hangings of purple and scarlet, and the altars of rich incense that fill the air with fragrant perfumes.

The sacrificing priest for the day approaches the altar now surrounded by the gathering crowd and takes the appointed animal victim from the hands of the attending Levites. After slaying it in accordance with all the necessary forms, he presents it before the Lord. The fire burns and the smoke ascends while the sacrifice is consumed.

Standing somewhere in the assembled crowd is a Jew, born of the tribe of Levi and of the house of Aaron, thus by every right a priest. But he has become a Christian, so this splendid Temple and its gorgeous ritual, decreed by Holy Writ and by traditions reaching back from century to century, is no longer for him. However, he gazes at it somewhat wistfully, feeling a tug at his heart. Although he knows that the Temple and its functions are mere shadows, and that the substance is Christ, the Temple looks so real and the rituals speak with such authority that the shadow looks like the substance, while the substance seems like the shadow. The epistle to the Hebrews was written for him.

In a house off an alley a few blocks back from the massive wall of Jerusalem is another Jew. In his home there is a prized possession—a copy of the books of Moses, of the prophets, and of the psalms. It has been in his family for years, and he knows most of it by heart. Lately he has been reading it again. He is thinking things through. *Can the blood of bulls and goats really take away sin?* he asks himself. *Of what value are all these rituals? Surely they must speak of something else. There must be a reality behind them all. And is it really Calvary? Can it be that the Christians are right after all?* He opens one of the scrolls. *And what of all these prophecies concerning the Messiah? Ought not Christ to have suffered? How else can Isaiah 53 and Psalm 22 and Psalm 16 be explained? "They pierced my hands and my feet," it says. "Thou wilt not . . . suffer thy holy one to see corruption." What can that mean but resurrection from the dead? And what then? Are the Christians correct when they say that Jesus of Nazareth fulfilled such Scriptures as these?*

He goes from scroll to scroll, finding in each one unexplained ceremonies, unsatisfied longings, unfulfilled prophecies. Deciding to stake everything on the despised and rejected Jesus of Nazareth, he becomes a Christian, makes his faith known, and is cut off from his people. His outraged parents disinherit him, cast him out of the family and outside the camp, hold a funeral for him, and consider him dead. His heart aches for his loved ones, for the close-knit family ties of the Jews. Missing the cheer and comfort of home, missing the rich ritual in which he has been reared, missing the synagogue and its forms, he begins to wonder if he should go back. The epistle to the Hebrews was written for him.

THE AUTHOR

Who wrote this epistle? No one knows. Some say Luke, some say Barnabas, some say Apollos, some say Clement, and some say Paul. Luke, it seems, was a Gentile and, unless he wrote under Paul's tutorship, seems a most unlikely candidate. It has been suggested, of course, that the thoughts were Paul's but the language Luke's. Barnabas was both a Jew and a Levite, but there is no real evidence that he wrote Hebrews. Apollos has been put forward both by Martin Luther and Dean Alford, but none of the early writers suggested him. Clement of Rome can hardly have been the author, because the Roman church rejected Hebrews as canonical for a long time.

What about Paul? Criticisms of Paul's authorship center in the vocabulary, in the language, and in the style of Hebrews, all of which are different from the other Pauline letters. Such differences might be explained by the fact that in all his other letters Paul was addressing Gentiles, whereas in Hebrews his audience was the Jews. Certainly Paul was an instructed scribe, a pupil of the celebrated Gamaliel, and thoroughly conversant with the thought forms of the Hebrew people. That Paul did write an epistle to the Hebrews is evident from 2 Peter 3:15. And is Hebrews really as anonymous as it is said to be? Its last chapter mentions Timothy and has a distinctly Pauline note; moreover, it shows that the writer was well-known to his readers.

Paul is the most likely candidate from every point of view. He was indeed "the apostle of the Gentiles" and delighted to "magnify [his] office" as such. But he never lost sight of the fact that he was an Israelite. His first concern when entering a new field of labor was to find the Jewish community in town and appeal to his countrymen first.

Paul's first recorded sermon, given in the synagogue at Pisidian Antioch (Acts 13:16-41), is based on the history, promises, and hopes of Israel and on the coming and ministry of Jesus the Messiah, as recorded in the gospels. Some have suggested that this sermon was the basis, indeed, for the epistle to the Hebrews. No one can doubt that. Paul knew how to address himself to the Hebrew people just as he knew how to address himself to the Gentiles. "The religion of the nominal Jew was as false as is the religion of the nominal Christian. And while 'the Jew's religion,' which rejected Christ, is denounced in the Apostle Paul's ministry toward Judaisers, the divine religion which pointed to Christ is unfolded in the Epistle to the Hebrews."[1]

The suspicion with which Paul was regarded by the Jews might be a good enough reason for Paul's not signing the letter. Actually, the lack of a signature to the epistle gives it a Melchizedek character—without genealogy, without beginning or ending of days—and it is fitting, in a way, that this book should remain anonymous in view of the high matters of which it speaks.

The Argument

Certain key expressions run through the epistle and are woven into its fabric in golden strands. They bring out on its tapestry the letter's main purpose, which was to urge Jews who had been brought to the doors of salvation to go on and not to draw back. One such key word is *perfection*. It never means "sinlessness" in the New Testament. For the most part, it contrasts the mature Christian experience with the immature one (2:10; 5:9; 6:1; 7:11, 19, 28; 10:14; 12:1-2). The word *eternal* occurs repeatedly, to show that Christianity is a permanent, abiding reality, in contrast with Judaism, which was temporary and passing (5:9; 6:2; 9:12, 14-15; 13:20 [NASB*]; see also the companion words *for ever*, 1:8; 5:6; 6:20; 7:17, 21, 24 [NASB], 28; 13:8). Another key word is *heaven* or *heavens* (1:10; 4:14; 7:26; 8:1; 9:24; 12:25-26). See also *heavenly*, which contrasts Judaism, which

---

* *New American Standard Bible.*
1. Sir Robert Anderson, *The Hebrews Epistle in Light of the Types* (London: James Nisbet, 1911), pp. 9-10.

was earthly, with Christianity, which was heavenly in character (3:1; 6:4; 8:5; 9:23; 11:16; 12:22). An important word is the word *better*, used repeatedly throughout the letter to show that, for all its outward show and splendor, Judaism was a poor second to Christianity. Christ is better than the angels. We have a better covenant, a better sacrifice, a better resurrection. *Let us* is another key expression, used to urge upon us the vital importance of personally appropriating all that is available to us in Christ. And, in contrast, the word *lest* is used to express the dread possibility of missing the real thing altogether, even though the initial responses to the gospel were encouraging (2:1; 3:12-13; 4:1; 12:15-16).

THE APPEALS

Five warning passages appear in Hebrews. Much of the controversy that surrounds the epistle is centered in them. Serious as they are, they can be omitted entirely from the letter without the epistle's meaning being altered. Try reading the epistle through from beginning to end, deliberately skipping the warning passages. You will be astonished at the new smoothness you will detect in the narrative and at the increased ease with which you will be able to follow the letter's main argument. Then go back and read each of the warning passages at a single sitting so that you will receive the full impact of their message. For, undoubtedly, these warning passages are exceedingly important.

When it comes to their interpretation, however, we must examine the warning passages in their respective contexts. That is where the Holy Spirit has placed them, and that is where they belong. When they are examined in the light of their structure and their surroundings, most of the difficulties associated with them disappear. Before beginning our study of Hebrews as a whole, it might be appropriate to briefly isolate the warning passages and get their thrust firmly fixed in our minds.

WARNING NUMBER 1 (2:1-4)

The context preceding Hebrews 2:1-4 has demonstrated that Christ is more than the angels. He is superior in His *majesty* as Son of God and superior in His *ministry* as Son of Man. Because of this we are to pay special heed to the Word of God and even more so since God has now spoken in His Son. The first warning has to do with *disregarding the salvation of God*—that "so great salvation" (2:3) purchased for us by One so superior to the greatest and most glorious of the angels. The punishment is on the *spiritual* side of things. Those who disregard God's salvation are the spiritual losers; they lose out on God's salvation and never have spiritual life.

WARNING NUMBER 2 (3:7–4:13)

The context surrounding Hebrews 3:7–4:13 deals with Israel's failure to enter into the rest provided for them by God. The Old Testament Israelites believed in God to bring them out of Egypt, but they did not believe in God to bring them into Canaan. As a result they lost the blessing of the Promised Land. The warning has to do with *disbelieving the sufficiency of God*. The Israelites were content with half a salvation, so to speak, and that is all they received. The punishment emphasis was on the *temporal* side of things. Those who disbelieved had to be content with a second-class life in the wilderness, and there they died, never having enjoyed the rest of Canaan. Similarly, today there are many Christians who are saved but who live earth-bound lives with no joy, no peace, no rest, and no victory.

WARNING NUMBER 3 (5:11–6:20)

The context of Hebrews 5:11–6:20 has to do with Christ, our great High Priest, and with the amazing ministry He sustains toward His own. Among the Jews were those who, while giving intellectual assent to these truths, nevertheless stood still or turned away altogether. They were choosing in favor of the outworn priesthood of the sons of Aaron and were despising the Melchizedek priesthood of the Son of God. This warning has to do with *discrediting the Son of God* and is much more serious in nature than the preceding ones. The punishment emphasis is on the *eternal* side of things. Those who turn away from Christ are warned of the impossibility of being renewed to repentance. The root of the matter was never really in them, and, by their attitude to Christ, they reveal the true condition of their souls.

WARNING NUMBER 4 (10:26-39)

The greatest and rarest privilege in the Old Testament—offered only to a select few—was to enter once a year into the Temple's Holy of Holies. This is introduced in Hebrews 10:26-39 with a reminder that the veil, which kept all others out from that inner sanctuary, was torn aside when Christ died. Now all believers can come into God's immediate presence. The writer warns his readers that it is possible for them to turn back, to treat the New Covenant with contempt, and to sin willfully against the Holy Spirit. This warning has to do with *despising the spirit of God* and is filled with the most fearful and solemn declarations. The punishment emphasis is on the *judicial* side of things. To despise God's Spirit is to become an apostate. The readers are warned that it is "a fearful thing to fall into the hands of the living God" (10:31).

WARNING NUMBER 5 (12:15-29)

The context of Hebrews 12:15-29 has to do with the great heroes of faith who, in their day and generation, dared to believe God in the face of all kinds of outward pressure. Proof of true regeneration is to be seen in patient submission to God's chastening. God is calling His own to press on. The warning has to do with *disobeying the summons of God.* It is illustrated by the case history of Esau who traded away spiritual and eternal realities for temporary sensual indulgence. He wanted this world's benefits and had no sense of spiritual values. It is illustrated further by a vivid contrast drawn between Sinai and Zion, with great emphasis being placed upon the glorious company into which the true believer is brought. The punishment emphasis is on the *millennial* side of things. Those who fail to respond to God's dealings will be the losers in the kingdom.

Part One
The Superior Person of Christ (1:1–2:18)

I

He Is Superior in His Majesty
as the Son of God (1:1–2:4)*

A. The Expression of the Sonship of Christ by God (1:1-3)
1. He Expounds the Mind of God (1:1-2a)
2. He Executes the Will of God (1:2b-3a)
   a. He Has an Inherited Claim to All Things (1:2b)
   b. He Has an Inherent Claim to All Things (1:2c-3a)
      (1) Because of What He Is (1:2c)
      (2) Because of Who He Is (1:3a)
3. He Expresses the Heart of God (1:3b-c)
   a. As Christ Crucified (1:3b)
   b. As Christ Crowned (1:3c)
B. The Examples of the Sonship of Christ in Scripture (1:4-14)
1. His Excellent Name (1:4-5)
2. His Earthly Fame (1:6-7)
3. His Eternal Claim (1:8-14)
   a. The Glory of Christ's Person (1:8-9)
      (1) Christ's Sovereignty
      (2) Christ's Deity
      (3) Christ's Dynasty
      (4) Christ's Authority
      (5) Christ's Integrity
      (6) Christ's Spirituality
      (7) Christ's Vivacity
   b. The Glory of Christ's Power (1:10)
      (1) He Founded the Earth (1:10a)
      (2) He Fashioned the Heavens (1:10b)

*Note: Points in the chapter outlines may not correspond in every detail to the text as developed.

Part One
The Superior Person of Christ (1:1–2:18)

I

He Is Superior in His Majesty as the Son of God (1:1–2:4)

The book of Hebrews has been called the "orphan epistle" because it lacks the signature of a human author. But God, who delights to be a Father to the fatherless, has adopted this epistle. Instead of beginning with the name of Paul or James or Peter, it begins, "God." It is no wonder that its human author fades into obscurity.

Counting the book of Revelation, there are twenty-two epistles in the New Testament. We can express them in this formula: $9 + 4 + 9$. There are nine letters addressed to Christian churches, four letters addressed to individuals, and nine letters addressed to Jewish Christians.

Comparing the two major groups of nine we note that each group begins with a major theological treatise in which the Old Testament is interpreted in the light of Christ and Calvary.

Romans introduces the first nine epistles. It discusses the relationship of the gospel to Israel's *moral* law. Great appeal is made to the Old Testament *prophetic* ministry.

Hebrews introduces the last nine epistles. Hebrews discusses the relationship of the gospel to Israel's *ritual* law. Great appeal is made to the Old Testament *priestly* ministry.

Each of these two groups of epistles ends with prophecy in which the second coming of Christ is discussed. Thessalonians ends the first group and underlines the effects of Christ's coming on the *church* and the world; Revelation ends the second group and underlines the effect of Christ's coming on the *Jew* and the world.

The shadow of the Temple, still standing on Mount Moriah, lies across this entire epistle. There can be little doubt that the Jews would put up many a stubborn argument against Christian teaching in seeking to dissuade their fellows from embracing Christianity and in their efforts to wean away Jewish converts from their newfound faith.

After all, was not the law given by angel meditation? How dare anyone question Moses and challenge his authority? Was not the Aaronic priesthood divinely ordained? Did not God Himself inaugurate the elaborate system of offerings and sacrifices and ritual cleansing? Did not God Himself command the building of the Tabernacle and give David the blueprints for the Temple? Were not Israel's feast days God-ordained? How dare anyone set aside the Passover and the Day of Atonement? Had not the prophets urged on the building of the second Temple after the end of the Babylonian captivity? How could anyone expunge all these things from the Bible and have anything left but an emasculated book? How could God's Christ possibly be a man who had suffered crucifixion when God's curse rested on all those who died on a tree? How could Jesus be a priest when He was not a Levite of the Aaronic family? Had not the leaders of Israel almost unanimously rejected the claims of Jesus to be the Messiah? And so it went on.

The letter's chief purpose is to demonstrate that Christ and the New Testament truth and the Christian faith stand far above and beyond anything found in the Old Testament or expressed in the Jewish religion. The issue is presented in the opening verse.

The Hebrew faith was codified in the Mosaic law, which was given through the instrumentality of angels. But the Lord Jesus is superior to the angels, both in His majesty as the Son of God and in His ministry as the Son of Man. This theme opens the epistle.

A. THE EXPRESSION OF THE SONSHIP OF CHRIST BY GOD (1:1-3)

Dan Crawford was a pioneer missionary to Africa. He was sitting one day in the doorway of his tent writing a letter. A little black boy stood for a long while staring in astonishment at the strange white man's even stranger occupation. At last he could stand it no longer.

"What are you doing, white man?" he asked.

The missionary explained that he was writing a letter; he was committing his thoughts to paper. The boy digested the information for a moment and then said, "Ah! I know what you're doing. You're putting thoughts in prison."

"Ah, no!" exclaimed the missionary with his ready wit. "You're wrong, lad. I'm not putting thoughts into prison. I'm *setting thoughts free!*"

*1. HE EXPOUNDS THE MIND OF GOD (1:1-2*a)

That is exactly what God did when Jesus came. Throughout the Old Testament era, God communicated to men using spokesmen like Jonah, Jeremiah, David, Daniel, and Moses. But there remained so much more to be said! How could He fully express His heart, His mind, His will? He would send His Son! So we read that "God, who at sundry times and in divers [diverse] manners spake in time past unto the fathers by the prophets, hath in these last days spoken unto us by his Son" (1:1-2*a*).

2. HE EXECUTES THE WILL OF GOD *(1:2b-3a)*

In the person of the Lord Jesus, God found a perfect vehicle of expression. He simply translated Deity into humanity, or, as John puts it, "The Word was made flesh" (John 1:14).

Now the Lord Jesus, as God's Son, has *an inherited claim* to all things. God has had other heirs. Abraham, who was one of them, entered Canaan as heir to everything he saw, yet he wandered all his days as a homeless stranger in the land that was rightfully his. He was buried at last in a cave, the only piece of real estate in Canaan ever deeded over to him by men. Nevertheless, every stock and stone was his, every bird and every beast from the Delta of the Nile to the wide Euphrates.

Thus it was with the Lord Jesus. He lived in this world as a pilgrim and a stranger, heir to it all, yet not having received the promises. Even the tomb in which He was laid to rest was borrowed. But now the will has been publicly read: He is "appointed heir of all things" (Heb. 1:2*b*). The world in its entirety has been given to Him, and, as executor of the divine will, He is coming back to enforce its every clause.

Christ's claim to all things is not only inherited; He has *an inherent claim* to all things. "He made the worlds" (1:2*c*); therefore, as Creator, they belong to Him.

Some years ago I needed a black and white glossy print of the heavens as an illustration in a book, so I went to a planetarium for one. After leafing through several files of photographs, I finally selected one, a magnificent shot of the Orion Nebula. I asked the planetarium director the charge. "There's no charge," he replied. When I expressed surprise, he added with a twinkle in his eye, "We don't own Orion!" He hastily changed the subject when I asked, "Sir, do you know the One who does?" For Jesus made the worlds and lays claim to them all by inherent right.

We are told that He is "the brightness of his [God's] glory, and the express image of his person" (1:3*a*) and that He upholds "all things by the word of his power" (1:3*b*). Underline the words in your Bible: *His* glory! *His* person! *His* power!

When Isaiah was called to the prophetic ministry, he was given a vision of that glory. He saw a throne high and lifted up. He who sat thereon was so glorious that the shining seraphim, the sinless sons of light, hid their faces in their wings before Him. They dared not gaze upon "the brightness of his glory." Saul of Tarsus was won to Christ when that "light . . . above the brightness of the [noonday] sun" (Acts 26:13) burst upon him. He was blinded by "the brightness of his [Christ's] glory."

Moreover, Christ is "the express image" of God's person. The phrase "express image" refers to something "engraved" or "impressed" as, for instance, a coin or seal that bears line for line all the features of the instrument making it. The idea is that of a dye impress. The lines of Deity have been reproduced in Jesus' humanity, so to find out what God is like we need only look at Jesus. We can take the lines of Christ's personality and draw those lines on out into infinity and obtain a perfect concept of God. As J. B. Phillips puts it, Jesus is "God in focus."

He upholds all things "by the word of his power." Our words, at best, are only legislative; His are executive. He speaks and it is done. In creation He said, "Light be!" and light was! This same executive power was evident when He lived on earth. "Lord, if thou wilt, thou canst make me clean" (Matt. 8:2), said a leper to Him one day. "I will; be . . . clean" (v. 3), said Jesus. It was the word of His power. As the Son of God, the Lord Jesus is the executor of God's will as far as the created universe is concerned.

3. *He Expresses the Heart of God (1:3b-c)*

But there is more! He gives expression to all that is in God's heart. He is not only the Creator; He is also the Redeemer. "He . . . purged our sins" (Heb. 1:3*b*). In a single sentence, we are taken from creation to Calvary. Mark the contrast: His glory, His person, His power, and then *our* sins! Who can measure the number or the nastiness of our sins? God has declared that all our *righteousness* is, in His sight, as a filthy rag, so what must He think of our *sins*? The Lord Jesus has made purification for sins by dying on the cross (1:3*b*).

But God never leaves Christ on the cross. In some churches Christ is depicted as a babe in His mother's arms or as a helpless sufferer on a crucifix. Such a concept of Christ is inadequate and misleading.

God reminds us that the Lord Jesus has "sat down on the right hand of the Majesty on high" (1:3*c*). He is now on the throne.

Thus God has given expression to the sonship of Christ as the One who reveals God to us, as the One who has created the entire fabric of the material universe and is its rightful Heir, and as the One who not only died for us but who is now enthroned in heaven.

B. The Examples of the Sonship of Christ in Scripture (1:4-14)

1. *His Excellent Name (1:4-5)*

Since Christ has been made "so much better than the angels," He has "by inheritance obtained a more excellent name than they" (1:4). Several angels are named in the Scriptures. There is *Michael*, whose name means "Who is like God?" and there is *Gabriel*, whose name means "man of God." Another angel's name is given in the Hebrew of Daniel 8:13, *Palmoni*, "the wonderful number-er,"[1] and then there is *Satan*, who is given some forty different names in the Bible, all of which express aspects of his evil nature. But no angelic name can compare with the name *Son* given by God to Jesus.

Michael was glorious *in might* as the commander in chief of the armies of heaven. Although in human affairs supreme power is sometimes usurped by the military, this cannot happen in heaven. Michael's name is a guarantee against that, for who, indeed, is like God? *Gabriel* was glorious *in ministry*, for he was the herald angel, the bearer of messages from God to men. In human affairs, the messenger can sometimes overshadow the message, as when Mark Anthony appeared before Cleopatra with a message from Rome. He so dazzled the queen that she flung herself into his arms and all Egypt at his feet, defying Octavius and all the might of Rome. Gabriel's name is a guarantee against that kind of thing, for he is God's man and none other's. *Lucifer* was glorious *in majesty* for he was "the anointed cherub" (Ezek. 28:14), the highest of all created intelligences. He was "son of the morning" (Isa. 14:12). As one star differs from another in glory, so was Lucifer a star of first magnitude set to shine in solitary grandeur as the herald of the dawn. But the time came when he forgot that the rising sun eclipses the brightest star, and he imagined himself to be the greatest and most glorious being in the universe.

The Lord Jesus has a more excellent name than any angelic being. He is not merely mighty like Michael; He is almighty. He is not just a messenger like Gabriel; He is Himself the Word. He is not only a star like Lucifer; He is the sun.

And what is this "more excellent name" of His? *Son!* Hebrews quotes from Psalm 2:7 (the psalm is messianic and deals primarily with Christ's second coming; v. 7 has primary reference to Christ's resurrection) and 2 Samuel 7:14 (which has reference to Christ's birth[2]) and declares, "For unto which of the angels said he at any time, Thou art my Son, this day have I begotten thee? And again, I will be to him a Father, and he shall be to me a Son?" (1:5). The reference to 2 Samuel takes us to the cradle; the reference to Psalm 2 takes us to the empty tomb and to the second advent. What does all this have to do with Christ's superiority over the angels as Son? Everything! As ministering spirits, they were sent to attend His birth. They were sent again to attend His resurrection, and in a coming day they will attend His return to earth. They are His servants; they cannot be compared with Him.

---

1. See E. W. Bullinger, *Number in Scripture*, 6th ed. (London: Lamp, 1952), p. 20.
2. This reference is to David's exultation in the son just promised to him by God. It is used here as a messianic utterance pointing to Christ's first coming.

2. *HIS EARTHLY FAME (1:6-7)*

The Son has an excellent name, and along with that He has earthly fame. Scripture is now quoted to support this line of truth: "And again, when he bringeth in the firstbegotten into the world, he saith, And let all the angels of God worship him. And of the angels he saith, Who maketh his angels spirits, and his ministers a flame of fire" (1:6-7).

Authorities differ about the position of the word *again* in the sentence. Some follow the King James Version, which puts the emphasis on the Lord's first coming; others follow the *American Standard Version,* which puts the emphasis on Christ's second coming ("And when he again bringeth in the firstborn into the world," v. 6). There is a matter of some two thousand years involved between the two renderings, but no matter! The angels worshiped Him when He stepped off His throne to be born in that Bethlehem barn, awakening the slumbering echoes of the Judean hills with their songs of praise. They will worship Him when He comes again to set up His kingdom on earth.

The point is, they worship Him because they are but creatures, and He is the Son. Worship is His right. Thus the writer of Hebrews brings his readers to the heart of the matter: the Son is to be worshiped as God is worshiped. Once they acknowledge Jesus as God, they cannot possibly go back to the empty shadows of Judaism. Having once acknowledged Him as God, the only possible thing is to go on.

The angels, great as they are, are only ministering spirits whose function it is to rush to do His bidding. There are *messenger* angels such as came to patriarchs like Abraham and Jacob, to prophets like Daniel, to priests like Zacharias, and to people like Elizabeth and Mary. There are *ministering* angels such as those who came to apostles like Peter and Paul, who care for little children, who came to Christ in the wilderness and the Garden, and who are concerned for Christians. There are *martial* angels such as do battle against God's human foes, as for instance Sennacherib, and against God's human foes, as described in Daniel and Revelation. There are *managing* angels who rule the elements, who function in connection with God's creation, and who function in God's court, smiting men like Herod when their impiety passes the final boundary of God's permissive will. But one and all, they are only angels, as far removed from the Son as the finite from the infinite. And they worship Him.

3. *HIS ETERNAL CLAIM (1:8-14)*

The third example from Scripture refers to the Lord's eternal claim. The Lord Jesus is indeed the Son of God as demonstrated by His person, power, permanence, and position.

First, there is *the glory of Christ's person.* "But unto the Son he saith, Thy throne, O God, is for ever and ever: a sceptre of righteousness is the sceptre of thy kingdom. Thou hast loved righteousness, and hated iniquity; therefore God, even thy God, hath anointed thee with the oil of gladness above thy fellows" (1:8-9).

Christ's sovereignty is seen in the reference to the throne. Earthly thrones are symbols of power, but their fortunes vary with the passing of time. Think, for example, of the throne of England. What a checkered history it has had! Its kings have been great and gifted, like Henry II, who planned an empire to rival Charlemagne's and who ruled like a medieval Solomon. Its kings have been men like John, who so outraged the barons that they rammed the Magna Charta down his throat. There have been men like Henry III, who managed to idle away fifty-six years doing nothing; like Henry VI, who so despised the throne that his people believed him more fit for a priest than a king; like Richard II, who killed one king to clear the throne for his father and who thereafter killed kings to clear the throne for himself. Normans, Plantagenets, Tudors, Stuarts, Hanoverians, and Windsors are all names that herald the changing dynasties of a human throne. But above and beyond all such thrones is the one on which sits the Son, a Sovereign indeed.

Christ's deity is mentioned next: "But unto the Son he saith, Thy throne, O God," thus emphasizing Jesus' deity. He sits enthroned at the center of the rush and bustle of all the suns and stars and galaxies of space, over all God, blessed forevermore.

Observe, too, *Christ's dynasty.* His throne is "for ever and ever." Israel had two monarchies that ran side by side for some two-and-a-half centuries. The northern monarchy had nineteen kings and nine dynasties, and all its kings were evil. The southern monarchy had only one dynasty, but at last it disintegrated, too, because of the wickedness and weakness of its kings. Moreover, the royal line came under a divine curse so that God had to go back to David and pick up a secondary line in order to bring His Son into the world as the Messiah. Human dynasties are uncertain affairs at best, but Christ's dynasty will never end.

Then notice *Christ's authority*: "A sceptre of righteousness is the sceptre of thy kingdom." The constitution under which He governs can be summed up in a single word: uprightness! His kingdom is organized around that one principle. Moreover, He loves righteousness.

Christ's integrity is beyond all question. Many a power-seeker has sworn to uphold the constitution of his country—until he has arrived in power. Not so Christ! The authority under which He governs is upheld by His personal integrity. The throne is one of righteousness, and He loves righteousness.

Christ's spirituality comes next: "God, even thy God, hath anointed thee." God's anointing added a spiritual dimension to the ministry or task for which a man was called. Moses anointed Aaron; Samuel anointed David; Elijah anointed Elisha—a priest, a prince, a prophet, each anointed for his office and each anointed by another man. The Lord has been anointed by *God*. There is no higher anointing than that. When He was on earth, He was anointed so that He might redeem; now He is anointed so that He might reign.

Moreover, He was anointed with "the oil of gladness," attention thus being drawn to *Christ's vivacity*. What a prospect for this sad, old world of ours, to be governed by a vibrant, happy, vivacious Man! The "fellows" referred to in the context seem to be those who have previously occupied the throne of David on earth. The happiest of them all was David, a man who had a heart and mind to write half the book of Psalms. Yet not all of David's hymns were happy. Some were bitter complaints, and others were drenched with tears. The word for "gladness" here means "much leaping," and it carries the thought of dancing, exultation, and rejoicing. It is used of the unborn John, who "leaped" in his mother's womb when Mary brought tidings to Elizabeth that the Messiah was soon to be born. Once Jesus was "the man of sorrows," but now He is "leaping" with joy upon His throne. Hallelujah, what a Savior! What a King! What a throne!

We are to think not only of the glory of Christ's person but also of *the glory of Christ's power*. It was He who both founded the earth and fashioned the heavens. We read, "And, Thou, Lord, in the beginning hast laid the foundation of the earth; and the heavens are the works of thine hands" (1:10).

Power indeed! Power to launch into space more worlds than man can count. Power to bring forth from nowhere countless stars and their satellites, power to toss them into prodigious orbits throughout intangible space and with invisible ties to hold them whirling and moving with such mathematical precision that we can predict the visit of a comet or the occasion of an eclipse years in advance.

We are to think of *the glory of Christ's permanence*, for although the suns and stars of space will perish, He will remain unchanged. Motion produces friction; friction produces wear; wear produces disintegration. The whole material universe is like some vast clock slowly running down. Our sun is burning out at the rate of 4,200,000 tons of heat every second. Without any direct, catastrophic intervention from on high, all things will eventually fold in upon themselves. For stars and universes have their life cycles. Astronomers have photographed the rubble and debris of stars that have exploded and vanished from the sky.

"They shall perish; but thou remainest; and they all shall wax old as doth a garment; and as a vesture shalt thou fold them up, and they shall be changed: but thou art the same, and thy years shall not fail" (1:11-12).

A billion, billion years from now the Lord will still be sitting upon His throne, deathless in His energy and force, presiding over the destinies of yet unborn worlds and ages. What a contrast with the decaying and obsolete Judaism from which the Hebrew converts had made their way! Everything there was temporary, preliminary, and probational. These Hebrew believers had found the Christ, the Son, the deathless, ageless, changeless Son of God.

We are to consider *the glory of Christ's position*. "To which of the angels said he at any time, Sit on my right hand, until I make thine enemies thy footstool? Are they not all ministering spirits, sent forth to minister for them who shall be heirs of salvation?" (1:13-14).

No angel has ever been invited to share God's throne. Satan, the only one who tried to grasp that throne, was hurled ignominiously out of heaven. Angels, even the greatest and mightiest of them, are the servants of those whom Christ redeems.

So then, Christ is superior in His majesty as the Son of God. This truth, expressed by God, is exemplified in the Word. He is God the Son without peer in the universe. Therefore, there follows the first of the epistle's warning passages. It is a warning against disregarding God's salvation.

C. THE EXPERIENCE OF THE SONSHIP OF CHRIST BY MEN (2:1-4)

Note that this section begins with the word *therefore*. The word *therefore* in the Bible generally sums up the whole of the preceding argument. Since Jesus is God's unique Son, it is imperative that we accept, at its full face value, the salvation He has *procured for us*. How can we logically do anything else?

1. WE MUST APPROPRIATE THE GOSPEL (2:1-3a)

We must appropriate the gospel by paying good heed to it. It is possible to "slip" (2:1) from the truth. The word for "slip" means to float passively past, a picture of indolence and criminal neglect. Enormous privileges are extended to men in the salvation offered by the Son. To do nothing about them, to float indolently past them, is to incur God's judgment.

I was drafted into the British army and placed in the Royal Engineers Corps during World War II. One of our training lectures concerned the defusing of booby-trapped mines. Later we were given a field exercise to defuse some booby-trapped mines fitted with a small blank charge set to detonate harmlessly but with a loud noise if a mistake were made. We listened with rapt attention to the instructor, for the time would soon come when the ability to defuse a live bomb without error on the battlefield would be literally a matter of life or death. We watched every move the instructor made, studied every illustration, mastered the mechanics of every known type of booby trap, asked urgent questions about aspects of the training that we did not understand. Our lives depended on it. Indolence and carelessness would have been the height of folly.

Matters of far greater significance hinge upon the salvation provided by the Son. "Therefore we ought to give the more earnest heed to the things which we have heard, lest at any time we should let them slip" (2:1). Thus the warning is *presented to us.*

The claims of the law could not be neglected (2:2). "Every transgression and disobedience received a just recompense of reward" (2:2*b*). His Hebrew readers would appreciate his analogy. The law of Moses, given through the administration of angels, carried with it not only precepts and principles but dire punishments as well.[3] Again and again throughout their history, the Hebrew people felt the weight of God's displeasure for their rebellion and sin. At times retribution was swift; at other times it seemed to slumber; but it always came.

If there was no escape under the law, then, when God's revelation was yet incomplete: "How shall we escape, if we neglect so great salvation" (2:3)? If when Israel had but the types and shadows to illustrate salvation; if, even with that candle alone to light them, they were held accountable for neglect, how can we hope to escape if we neglect the full light of day that has been brought to earth by the Son?

To neglect a remedy is as serious a matter as to deliberately reject it. Here, for instance, is a man who has a bad pain. He ignores it. He doesn't like doctors or taking medicine. His pain gets worse so, finally, urged on by his wife, he goes to the doctor.

"You have tuberculosis," says the doctor. "Go home, and go to bed. You are a very sick man. You need plenty of rest and plenty of fresh air. And you must take this medicine!"

The man goes home, ignores the doctor's instructions, and neglects the medicine. He gets worse and dies. It is his own fault. He neglected the remedy provided for him.

Here is another man. He feels guilty. He has sinned against God and is thoroughly miserable. He doesn't like church, and he doesn't like preachers, so he denies that there's anything wrong with him. But the convicting work of the Holy Spirit continues. Urged on by his wife, he goes to church and hears the gospel. It is nasty medicine to him. He is told he is a sinner under sentence of death. He is urged to come to Christ who alone can save sinners. But he goes home and neglects God's remedy. At last he dies and goes to a lost eternity. It is his own fault.

---

3. The death penalty was appended for at least one form of transgression under each of the Ten Commandments. The first commandment (Ex. 22:20; cf. Deut. 6:13-15), second (Deut. 27:15), third (Lev. 24:15-16), fourth (Num. 15:32-36), fifth (Ex. 21:15; Deut. 21:18-21), sixth (Ex. 21:12; also manslaughter under certain conditions, Ex. 21:29), seventh (Lev. 20:10), eighth (Ex. 21:16), ninth (Deut. 18:16), tenth (if it found expression in stealing, adultery, etc.). In addition, the death penalty was appended to the Mosaic law for numerous other offenses: for profaning God's altar (Ex. 28:43), for profaning the Tabernacle vessels (Num. 4:15, 20), for rebelling against constituted authority (Deut. 17:12), for uttering false prophecy (Deut. 18:20), for witchcraft (Ex. 22:18), for bestiality (Ex. 22:19), for incest (Lev. 20:11-12), for homosexuality (Lev. 20:13), and so on.

He neglected the remedy provided for him. He neglected what the author of this letter calls "so great salvation."

2. WE MUST APPRECIATE THE GOSPEL (2:3b-4)

Think, first, how the gospel has been *conveyed to us.* "Which at the first began to be spoken by the Lord" (2:3*b*) is how the writer of Hebrews puts it. All Old Testament teaching was revitalized by Him, and all New Testament truth was revealed by Him, at least in embryonic form. He took the law of Moses (such statements as "Thou shalt not kill" and "Thou shalt not commit adultery," for example) and, with His resounding, "But I say unto you," lifted the commandments to dizzy new heights so that murder was unmasked in hatred and adultery in lust. He clothed the truth with flesh and blood, living it out every moment of every day. He offered men salvation in exchange for faith in Himself. We must appreciate the gospel because of the unique way it was conveyed to us.

The gospel has not only been conveyed to mankind by the Son; it has been infallibly *confirmed for us* in two unique ways. First, it has been confirmed by *the truthful witness of the disciples.* It was "confirmed unto us by them that heard" (2:3*c*). For three-and-a-half years these men walked and talked with Jesus, drank in His words, treasured His teachings, learned from His example, and were won by His "infallible proofs" (Acts 1:3). "We have not followed cunningly devised fables," wrote Peter (2 Pet. 1:16). "That which was from the beginning . . . we have heard . . . we have seen [i.e., with the physical eye] . . . we have looked upon [i.e., looked at for a long time until the significance is understood], and our hands have handled, of the Word of life; (for the life was manifested, and we have seen it, and bear witness, and shew unto you that eternal life, which was with the Father, and was manifested unto us)," declared John (1 John 1:1-2).

The gospel has been confirmed also by *a threefold witness of God* Himself. "God also bearing them witness, both with signs and wonders, and with divers miracles, and gifts of the Holy Ghost, according to his own will" (2:4). The "signs and wonders" were to convince the Jew, for "the Jews require a sign" (1 Cor. 1:22). The "divers miracles" were to convince the Gentiles. And the "gifts of the Holy Ghost" were to confirm the message to the Christian.

Christ, in His superior majesty as the Son of God, has "abolished death, and hath brought life and immortality to light through the gospel" (2 Tim. 1:10). Because of who He is and what He has done, and because of the truths embodied in Himself, there is no escape for those who neglect salvation through Him. Thus the writer brings the Hebrews to the crossroad of faith.

II

He Is Superior in His Ministry as the Son of Man (2:5-18)

A. Christ's Sovereignty as Man (2:5-9*a*)
  1. The Sovereignty Bestowed on Mankind Reviewed (2:5-8*b*)
     a. The Destiny of Man (2:5)
     b. The Dignity of Man (2:6)
     c. The Distinction of Man (2:7-8*b*)
        (1) The Probation Involved (2:7*a*)
        (2) The Process Involved (2:7*b*-8*a*)
        (3) The Potential Involved (2:8*b*)
  2. The Sovereignty Bestowed on Mankind Revoked (2:8*c*)
  3. The Sovereignty Bestowed on Mankind Revived (2:9*c*)
B. Christ's Sufferings as Man (2:9*b*-10)
  1. The Marvelous Truth of His Coming (2:9*b-c*)
     a. The Position Involved (2:9*b*)
     b. The Purpose Involved (2:9*c*)
  2. The Marvelous Triumph of His Cross (2:10)
     a. His Sufferings Were Fitting (2:10*a*)
     b. His Sufferings Were Fruitful (2:10*b*)
     c. His Sufferings Were Fundamental (2:10*c*)
C. Christ's Sympathy as Man (2:11-18)
  1. We Are Related to Him (2:11-13)
     a. In Terms of Sanctification (2:11)
     b. In Terms of Scripture (2:12-13)
  2. We Are Rescued by Him (2:14-15)
     a. What He Accepted (2:14*a*)
     b. Who He Accosted (2:14*b*)
     c. What He Accomplished (2:15)

3. We Are Reconciled Through Him (2:16-18)
    a. He Understands Our Nature (2:16)
    b. He Understands Our Need (2:17-18)
        (1) In an Explicit Way (2:17)
        (2) In an Experiential Way (2:18)

II

He Is Superior in His Ministry as the Son of Man (2:5-18)

As man, the Lord Jesus in His sovereignty, His sufferings, and His sympathy meets all the needs of men. As the Son of God, He might seem remote and unapproachable, but as the Son of Man He is the nearest of kin to all mankind. Much is made of this later in the letter, when the discussion turns to the priesthood of the Lord. In the meantime we must know that the Son, for all His dazzling superiority, is near and approachable—just the kind of Savior we need.

A. CHRIST'S SOVEREIGNTY AS MAN (2:5-9*a*)

1. THE SOVEREIGNTY BESTOWED ON MANKIND REVIEWED (2:5-8b)

This section of the epistle begins with *the destiny of man* and a review of the sovereignty originally bestowed by God on mankind. For example, the angels, great and glorious as they are, must one day yield before men. "For unto the angels hath he not put in subjection the world to come, whereof we speak" (2:5). Man's destiny eclipses that of the angels. The heavens themselves are to pass under the rule of man, and man is to judge both the cosmos and the angels (1 Cor. 6:2-3). The existing earth is under the control of angels, but the coming world and the very universe are for man to rule.

To what end do all the worlds of space exist? "Has God any pleasure in dead matter? Is He not the God of the living? Can inanimate matter praise Him, the Lord of all life (Ps. 30:9)? If only our small earth . . . carries organic life . . . then the fiery splendour of the millions of suns, which yet illuminate nothing, were only 'a vast meaningless and purposeless firework in the dead universe,' and all the stars and heavenly bodies were only burning or burned-out craters!"[1]

No less wonderful than his destiny is *the dignity of man*, for "one hath somewhere testified, saying, What is man, that thou art mindful of him? Or the son of man, that thou visitest him?" (Heb. 2:6; cf. Psalm 8:4). Throughout the

---

1. Eric Sauer, *The Dawn of World Redemption,* trans. G. H. Lang (London: Paternoster, 1951), p. 28.

Old Testament era God visited men. He visited Adam in the Garden of Eden. He visited Abraham, Hagar, Jacob, Moses, Joshua, Gideon, Samson's parents, Elijah, Daniel, and the three young Hebrews in the fiery furnace. He visited with Israel in the wilderness and tramped the hot sands of Sinai in their company. He dwelt among them in the glory cloud in the Promised Land. Best of all, He has now visited men in the Person of the Lord Jesus. It is a fact of eternal astonishment that God's delights should be with the sons of men.

Suppose you were to lift the telephone some morning and were told that the president of the United States or the queen of England had decided to visit in your home. What an honor that would be, and with what astonishment you would receive the announcement. "Why me?" you would want to know. It is a fact of even greater surprise that God visits men, loves them, delights in their company, desires their love and friendship, and wishes to abide permanently in their hearts. These great truths must never be allowed to become commonplace; they are a source of wonder in heaven among the angels.

Next comes a statement about *the distinction of man* (2:7-8*b*). For although sin has interrupted God's original intentions with the human race, it has by no means thwarted them. Note *the probation involved* in God's plan for men. Man was placed in a perfect environment, given a specific task and a specific trust, with all things put under his feet. He was monarch of all he surveyed. He was to "tend" and "keep" the Garden for God.

Man was created to stand between the world of the beasts and the world of the angels. He is higher than the beasts and a little lower than the angels, but only for the probationary period. Right now we do not have the powers of an angel; we cannot in a single night selectively slay every firstborn creature within the boundaries of a great nation. We do not have the properties of an angel; we cannot appear and disappear at will. We do not have the position of an angel, dwelling in eternal light before God's throne. But for all that, man is only a *little* lower than the angels, and that, too, only for now.

Note also *the process involved* in God's plans for man. Man has been "[crowned] . . . with glory and honour" (2:7*b*) and has been set over the works of God's hands with all things put in subjection to Him. Unfortunately, the Fall has marred and misdirected much of man's dominion. Just the same, man's inventive genius has enabled him, to a large extent, to subdue the earth. Had man's powers not been impaired by the Fall and his efforts thwarted by the curse, no doubt he would have extended the paradise of Eden over all the earth.

Note further *the potential involved* in man's dominion. God says of man that there is "nothing that is not put under him" (2:8*b*). Man's capacity is greater than he imagines. Nobody has used more than 2 percent of his mental capacity—not even a Beethoven or an Einstein. God has endowed man with vast potential. Had Adam not sinned, doubtless his authority would have been enlarged. His empire would have extended from the Garden to the globe, from the globe eventually to the galaxy. Doubtless, too, in the new creation all will be restored on a greater, grander scale than ever, and man in Christ will come fully and finally into the full potential of his powers, now so severely limited by sin.

2. THE SOVEREIGNTY BESTOWED ON MANKIND REVOKED (2:8c)

Thus the writer of Hebrews reviews the sovereignty bestowed on man, but that sovereignty has been largely revoked because of man's rebellion against God. "But now we see not yet all things put under him" (2:8c), he confesses. Man's noblest achievements go awry. There are still diseases he cannot eradicate, deserts he cannot reclaim, ecological imbalances he cannot restore, growing depletions in vital raw materials he cannot replenish. But, worst of all, man cannot control himself, and the greatest of his discoveries cannot prevent the waging of war.

3. THE SOVEREIGNTY BESTOWED ON MANKIND REVIVED (2:9a)

But all is not lost. The sovereignty bestowed on man has been gloriously, permanently, effectively revived, for "we see Jesus" (2:9a). In Him everything is restored. In Him God has provided a second Man, One worthy of the trust forfeited by Adam. Christ's sovereignty will not be merely over a garden or even a globe, but over all the galaxies of space and over glory itself.

Thus our attention is drawn back to Christ and to His sovereignty as man. The dominion Adam recklessly threw away has been picked up by the Man Christ Jesus.

B. CHRIST'S SUFFERINGS AS MAN (2:9b-10)

1. THE MARVELOUS TRUTH OF HIS COMING (2:9b-c)

It evokes no wonder that man should be made a little lower than the angels, but that God's eternal Son should be made lower than the angels will be an endless theme of astonishment throughout the universe. Note, first, *the position involved*. He stepped off the throne of the universe to be "contracted to the span of a virgin's womb." If the universe is filled with awe at the position He took, what can be said of *the purpose involved?* It was "for the suffering of death" (2:9c). Death is a dreadful thing, dreadful in its fearful expectation. We shrink from the darkness of the tomb, the terror of the great unknown. He shrank from death in Gethsemane for the opposite reason; He knew what to expect. Death is dreadful in its fatal execution, as the body, wracked with pain, fights its losing battle to survive. It is dreadful in its final experience—the dissolution of body and soul and, for the one who rejects Christ, the horrors of an eternity of woe. Christ tasted all of that.

2. THE MARVELOUS TRIUMPH OF HIS CROSS (2:10)

His sufferings were fitting, "for it became him" (2:10*a*) to be made perfect through sufferings. Later on, the writer of Hebrews builds heavily on that, because Christ's priesthood is possible only because He knows human life in all its joys and sorrows, all its temptations and trials.

His sufferings were fruitful, for as a result of them He brings "many sons unto glory" (2:10*b*). Believers have an astounding place in the family—they are sons! They have an equally astounding place in the future—they will be in glory. Heaven, after all, is a prepared place for a prepared people. The Lord's finished work on Golgotha prepared the people; in glory today He is preparing the place.

But *His sufferings were fundamental* also, for they made the Author of our salvation perfect. The Lord Jesus did not need to be made perfect *morally*, for He was always that. As the unbroken tablets of the law were placed in the Ark of the Covenant, so did the unbroken law of God reside in Christ. But He did need to be made perfect *ministerially*. How else could He enter into human life except by suffering? His sufferings are the foundation upon which all His present ministry rests.

C. CHRIST'S SYMPATHY AS MAN (2:11-18)

It is only a step from a consideration of Christ's sufferings as man to a consideration of His sympathy as man. He has entered fully into human life, and His great heart beats for the sons of men.

1. WE ARE RELATED TO HIM (2:11-13)

"For both he that sanctifieth and they who are sanctified are all of one: for which cause he is not ashamed to call them brethren" (2:11). This truth is stated, first, *in terms of sanctification*. He does not have to be ashamed of us. Christ's sanctifying work on the cross is so perfect that God sees us in Him, as perfect as He is. No doubt, as far as our state is concerned, there is much of which we need to be ashamed. But, as far as our standing is concerned, it is perfect. Such is the magnificence of Christ's work that He can bring us into the presence of the angels, into the presence of the Father Himself, and say, "These are my brethren."

A beautiful illustration of this is given in the Old Testament. Joseph's brethren behaved scandalously toward him. They hated him, scorned him, opposed him, and finally sold him into Egypt for the price of a slave. For a couple of pieces of silver apiece, they handed him over to the traders, turning their backs upon his tears. Yet, afterward, when they were thoroughly repentant, Joseph was not ashamed to call them brethren. Even though every shepherd was an abomination to the Egyptians, Joseph took them into the very presence of Pharaoh himself and presented them before the throne, and they were accepted by him.

The truth that Christ is not ashamed of us is so astonishing that it is not only explained in terms of sanctification, but it is stated *in terms of Scripture*. Quotations are given from Psalm 22:22 and Isaiah 8:17-18 as proof. Psalm 22 is the great psalm of the cross. The gospels give the facts of the crucifixion; the psalms give the feelings of the crucified. In Psalm 22, the Lord is prophetically seen on the cross, comforting Himself with thoughts of the people who would forever be identified with Him as a result of His death.[2]

Isaiah 8 was written against the background of the impending Assyrian invasion. A son was born into the prophet's family, a son whose name embodied a prophecy of Assyria's success. In a formal, symbolic, and prophetic way, as a sign and as a sermon, the prophet identified this son and his other sons with himself, just as Christ has identified us with Himself. The outward circumstances in Psalm 22 and Isaiah 8 were unpromising, but the eye of faith looked beyond outward appearances to the ultimate triumph.

We look at the Lord's people today in all their frailty and feebleness, but the Lord looks beyond and sees the fulfillment of God's purposes. Hence, He calls us brethren and confesses us openly and joyfully before the great congregation in heaven.

2. WE ARE RESCUED BY HIM (2:14-15)

The Lord's sympathy as man is expressed further by the fact that we are rescued by Him. Note *what He accepted*: "Forasmuch then as the children are partakers of flesh and blood, he also himself likewise took part of the same" (2:14a). The incarnation is a vital part of New Testament truth. The implications of this great truth are depicted in the book of Ruth. The pagan Moabitess was cut off by the Mosaic law from any part in Israel "to [the] tenth generation" (Deut. 23:3). Boaz, "a mighty man of wealth" (Ruth 2:1), took an interest in Ruth and showed her grace and kindness. Ruth told her mother-in-law this, and at once Naomi exclaimed, "The man is near of kin unto us," (Ruth 2:20). The whole book hinges upon this, for Ruth could be redeemed only because of this near of kin relationship. The same is true of the whole human race. At Bethlehem the Lord Jesus put on humanity in order to become "near of kin" to the whole human race, the relationship without which He never could have redeemed. So we note with awe and wonder what the Lord Jesus accepted: flesh and blood.

He accepted flesh and blood so that He could do what we could never do. Note *who He accosted*. He accosted Satan and destroyed him: "that through

2. For a complete exposition of the Psalms in their messianic scope, see John Phillips, *Exploring the Psalms,* 5 vols. (Neptune, N.J.: Loizeaux, 1985-87).

death he might destroy him that had the power of death, that is, the devil"
(2:14*b*). He accosted Satan at His birth as the dragon (Rev. 12:4). He accosted
Satan at His temptation as the prince of this world (He was tempted to perform a
miracle in order to sustain His own life); as the prince of the power of the air (He
was urged to cast Himself down from the Temple); and as the god of this age (He
was asked to fall down and worship Satan). He accosted Satan as the roaring lion
at Calvary, and, like Samson, rent him asunder, bringing all his power to
nothing.

Satan is a defeated and disarmed foe. His sword, "the power of death," has
been torn from his grasp. No Christian need fear death, for Satan has been van-
quished and death is one of the things God actually *gives* to His people (1 Cor.
3:21-22)! *What an unpleasant gift,* we think. *That's one gift we could do without.*
But look at it this way. As a young man in the British armed forces, I was one
time assigned to work in a prisoner-of-war camp. The place was full of German
officers and men, all behind barbed wire. Now, nobody in Britain *wanted* German
prisoners of war, but we had them, and at least they couldn't harm anyone. They
had been defeated and disarmed and placed out of harm's way. It is the same with
death! We may not want it, but it is one of God's gifts to us, and it cannot harm
us. It can only "promote us to glory."

The Lord Jesus has not only accepted flesh and blood and successfully accosted our greatest foe, but look at *what He accomplished*. He has delivered
"them who through fear of death were all their lifetime subject to bondage"
(2:15). Death would still try to frighten us, but, as Spurgeon put it, since death is
"the last enemy" (1 Cor. 15:26), we should leave him till last. We are not given
dying grace for living, only for dying. When the time comes to make our exodus,
we shall pass over on dry ground.

It was part of the genius of John Bunyan to depict his hero, Christian, having a difficult time when it came time to die, for not all saints pass over easily.
But his Christian companion, Hopeful, had a word of encouragement. "Be of
good cheer, my brother," he said. "I feel the bottom, and it is good." Then Hopeful gave away the secret. "You shall find it deeper or shallower as you believe in
the King of the place," he said.[3]

3. WE ARE RECONCILED THROUGH HIM (2:16-18)

One further thing reveals Christ's sympathy for us as a man. We are reconciled through Him. This reconciliation is because *He understands our nature*
from His own human experience. "For verily he took not on him the nature of
angels; but he took on him the seed of Abraham" (2:16). The mention of Abraham
is significant because, after all, this is an epistle to the *Hebrews*, Abraham's de-

3. John Bunyan, *Pilgrim's Progress* (Philadelphia: Universal Book & Bible House, 1933), p. 161.

scendants. The Lord did not take on an angelic nature, but a human nature; He became a member of a human family, specifically, a Hebrew family.

Some years ago the unmarried dean of women of a great Christian school wrote for a Christian magazine an article entitled "If I Were a Mother," based upon her experiences with hundreds of young women over a considerable period of time. Doubtless it was a good article, but it lacked something, for, after all, she *wasn't* a mother! Motherhood has all kinds of feelings and fears and frustrations that no one other than a mother can ever know—except academically. The Lord Jesus is no academic Savior. He understands our nature because He has entered human life.

Moreover, *He understands our need* and understands it *in an explicit way* (2:17-18). "Wherefore in all things it behoved him to be made like unto his brethren, that he might be a merciful and faithful high priest in things pertaining to God, to make reconciliation for the sins of the people" (2:17). Thus the writer moves smoothly into the great theme he has been approaching with such care, the theme which, within the space of a chapter or so, dominates the letter: Christ's priesthood.

The Lord Jesus has been made like His brethren so that He can be to us all that we need. We need Someone to intercede for us compassionately. He is merciful. We need Someone to intercede for us continuously. He is faithful. He can take care of our needs in God's presence.

Furthermore, He understands our needs *in an experiential way*, "for in that he himself hath suffered being tempted, he is able to succour them that are tempted" (2:18). A multimillionaire may enter the government and legislate for the poor, but undoubtedly the poor would feel better if the man framing the legislation had been raised in a slum, for he would understand better what it means to be poor and underprivileged.

Christ has experienced temptation. He knows what it is like. Therefore, He is able to give "succour" ("to run up at a cry for help"), and that's the kind of sympathetic Savior we need.

Here, then, is the first major section of Hebrews. The Lord Jesus is superior to all others in His Person. As the Son of God He places His hand upon deity; as the Son of Man He places His hand upon humanity. He stands unique in all of space and time as the one Person in the universe who can satisfy God's claims and man's need.

Part Two
The Superior Provisions of Calvary
(3:1–10:30)

III

We Have a Better Savior
(3:1–8:5)

A. His Preeminence (3:1–4:13)
   1. The Two People to Be Considered (3:1-6)
      a. Whom We Are to Contemplate (3:1-2)
      b. What We Are to Contrast (3:3-6)
         (1) Moses: The Servant (3:3-5)
            (a) Inferior to Christ in His Majesty (3:3-4)
            (b) Inferior to Christ in His Ministry (3:5)
         (2) Messiah: The Son (3:6)
            (a) Superior to Moses in His Person (3:6a)
            (b) Superior to Moses in His People (3:6b)
   2. The Twin Perils to Be Considered (3:7–4:3)
      a. Old Testament Times: The Disaster of Rebellion Against God in the Wilderness (3:7-19)
         (1) The Appeal to Scripture (3:7-11)
            (a) A Pertinent Digression (3:7)
            (b) A Pointed Digression (3:8-11)
               i. How Israel Provoked God (3:8-9)
               ii. How God Punished Israel (3:10-11)
                  a. They Did Not Seek Reality (3:10)
                  b. They Could Not See Rest (3:11)
         (2) The Application of Scripture (3:12-19)
            (a) The Exhortation (3:12-15)
               i. To Heed (3:12)
               ii. To Help (3:13)
               iii. To Hold (3:14)
               iv. To Hurry (3:15)

(b) The Example (3:16-19)
    i. The Number of the Sinners (3:16)
    ii. The Nature of the Sentence (3:17)
    iii. The Naming of the Sin (3:18-19)
       a. Disobedience (3:18)
       b. Disbelief (3:19)
b. New Testament Times: The Danger of Rebellion Against God in This World (4:1-3)
   (1) Fear (4:1)
   (2) Failure (4:2)
   (3) Faith (4:3)

3. The True Peace to Be Considered (4:4-13)
   a. Creation Rest (4:4-5)
   b. Canaan Rest (4:6-8)
     (1) The Rest Was Forfeited by Israel (4:6)
     (2) The Rest Was Foreshadowed by David (4:7-8)
   c. Calvary Rest (4:9-13)
     (1) Our Standing: The Rest Experienced (4:9-10)
     (2) Our State: The Rest Exploited (4:11-13)
       (a) A Work to Be Accomplished (4:11-13)
       (b) A Warning to Be Accepted (4:12-13)
          i. God Explores All Motives (4:12)
          ii. God Exposes All Mankind (4:13)

B. His Priesthood (4:14–8:5)
  1. Christ Is a Real Priest (4:14–5:3)
   a. His Name (4:14)
     (1) A Conquering Name (4:14*a*)
     (2) A Confessional Name (4:14*b*)
   b. His Nearness (4:15-16)
     (1) He Knows Our Nature (4:15)
     (2) He Knows Our Needs (4:16)
   c. His Nature (5:1-3)
     (1) He Is Able to Function for Us (5:1)
     (2) He Is Able to Feel for Us (5:2-3)
  2. Christ Is a Rightful Priest (5:4–6:20)
   a. The Choice of This Priest (5:4-10)
     (1) His Exaltation (5:4-6)
       (a) Chosen by God (Aaron) (5:4)
       (b) Chosen as God (Christ) (5:5)
       (c) Chosen for God (Melchizedek) (5:6)

      (2) His Experience (5:7-8)
         (a) The Sufficiency of God (5:7)
         (b) The Sufferings of Men (5:8)
      (3) His Exploits (5:9-10)
         (a) Personal (5:9*a*)
         (b) Perpetual (5:9*b*)
         (c) Positional (5:10)
  b. The Challenge of This Priest (5:11–6:20)
      (1) To Those Who Are Weak (5:11–6:3)
         (a) They Must Face Their Immaturity (5:11-14)
            i. The Mental Problem (5:11)
            ii. The Moral Problem (5:12-14)
               a. They Are Behind in Their Duty (5:12)
               b. They Are Behind in Their Development (5:13-14)
         (b) They Must Forsake Their Immaturity (6:1-3)
            i. The Demand (6:1*a*)
            ii. The Details (6:1*b*-2)
               a. Forsake Inadequate Old Testament Principles (6:1*b*)
               b. Forsake Inadequate Old Testament Practices (6:2*a*)
               c. Forsake Inadequate Old Testament Prospects (6:2*b*)
            iii. The Determination (6:3)
      (2) To Those Who Are Wicked (6:4-8)
         (a) Their Full Enlightenment (6:4-5)
            i. They Had Seen the Truth (6:4*a*)
            ii. They Had Savored the Truth (6:4*b*-5)
               a. They Had Tasted Its Spiritual Character (6:4*b*)
                   1. The Heavenly Gift
                   2. The Heavenly Ghost
               b. They Had Tasted Its Spiritual Content (6:5)
                   1. The Perfection of the World of God
                   2. The Powers of the World to Come
         (b) Their Fearful Enmity (6:6)
            i. The Unavoidable Implication (6:6*a*)
            ii. The Unconditional Impossibility (6:6*b*)
            iii. The Unpardonable Impiety (6:6*c*)
               a. Deliberately and Personally Sharing in the Crucifixion
               b. Deliberately and Publicly Shaming of the Christ

(1) The Change in the Priestly Ordinance (7:11-14)
    (a) The Tribal Descent Changed (7:11)
    (b) The Title Deed Changed (7:12-14)
        i. Because of the Requirement of the Old Law (7:12-13)
        ii. Because of the Restriction of the Old Law (7:14)
(2) The Change in the Priestly Order (7:15-19)
    (a) The Inherent Wonder of the New Order (7:15-17)
        i. The Wonder of Its Design (7:15)
        ii. The Wonder of Its Dynamism (7:16)
        iii. The Wonder of Its Durability (7:17)
    (b) The Inherent Weakness of the Old Order (7:18-19)
        i. There Was No Power in It (7:18*a*)
        ii. There Was No Profit in It (7:18*b*)
        iii. There Was No Perfection in It (7:19)
(3) The Change in the Priestly Ordination (7:20-22)
    (a) A Singular Oath (7:20-21)
    (b) A Superior Operation (7:22)
c. The Undying Life of Christ as Priest (7:23–8:5)
  (1) Why He Is Able to Minister to Us (7:23-28)
    (a) He Is a Continuing Priest (7:23-24)
    (b) He Is a Capable Priest (7:25)
    (c) He Is a Consecrated Priest (7:26-28)
        i. In Life (7:26)
        ii. In Death (7:27)
        iii. In Resurrection (7:28)
  (2) Where He Is Able to Minister for Us (8:1-5)
    (a) The Place of Majesty (8:1)
    (b) A Place of Ministry (8:2-5)
        i. The True Place (8:2-3)
        ii. The Typical Place (8:4-5)

Part Two
The Superior Provisions of Calvary
(3:1–10:30)

III

We Have a Better Savior
(3:1–8:5)

It has been nearly 2,000 years now since God tore apart the Temple veil, signifying the end of an era that had lasted 1,500 years. It is difficult for us to imagine the difficulty a Hebrew would have had in accepting the fact that God had written "finished" over all his religious observances, associations, and concepts. A new day had dawned, abruptly and completely. The Jew had to face the revolutionary fact that Christ had eclipsed all others and that Calvary spelled the end of the law.

A. HIS PREEMINENCE (3:1–4:3)

In the long section of the epistle now before us, the writer delves deeply into Old Testament typology to prove that the era closed was merely one of shadows, whereas substance was in Christ and His cross. He mentions Moses and Joshua, Aaron and Melchizedek. He looks at the sacrifices and the sanctuary and examines the covenant. And again and again he makes his point that Christ is a better Savior and Priest, who provides better security than anything offered under the law. He begins by contrasting Christ with Moses.

1. THE TWO PEOPLE TO BE CONSIDERED (3:1-6)

Before plunging into his theme, the writer pauses to address his readers. He calls them "holy brethren" and reminds them that they are "partakers of the heavenly calling" (3:1). These are marks of a Christian. The believer in Christ is given a *holy character*; he is one of the holy brethren. So complete is Christ's work that there is no doubt about that at all. The believer has an assured position in God's family and has received the divine nature. This is not something earned as a reward of accumulated merit but something sovereignly bestowed upon him because of Christ's finished work.

The believer in Christ is also given a *heavenly calling*, in contrast to the calling of the Hebrew people, which was essentially earthly. In the Old Testament everything had to do with a place; in the New Testament everything has to do with a Person. In the Old Testament, to be in the sphere of blessing, the Jew had to be *in the land,* so much so that any time we see the Jew outside the land, he is in the place of punishment and correction and cut off from the blessing associated with the land. In the New Testament, to be in the sphere of blessing we must be "*in the Lord*." For the Hebrew of old it was a matter of being in Canaan; for us today it is a matter of being in Christ. Thus Paul reminds us repeatedly that our sphere is "in the heavenlies" in Christ (see Eph. 1:3, 20; 2:6; 3:10).

a. WHOM WE ARE TO CONTEMPLATE (3:1-2)

From a consideration of the believer's titles, the writer turns at once to a consideration of *Christ's titles*. He is "the Apostle and High Priest of our profession" (3:1*b*). The word *apostle* means "sent one." Moses was Israel's "apostle," the one sent by God to play the part of a kinsman-redeemer to the enslaved people. Aaron was Israel's high priest. An apostle represents God to man; a priest represents man to God. The Lord Jesus combines both functions. He was the Apostle, the "sent One"—sent from heaven to be the true Kinsman-Redeemer to a lost and ruined race—and now He is our High Priest, a theme that is developed at length later in this great section of the epistle.

But if His titles are unique, so is *Christ's truth*. He was "faithful to him that appointed him, as also Moses was faithful in all his house" (3:2). After much persuasion, Moses finally agreed to execute the task imposed upon him by God. He fulfilled his commission magnificently as a redeemer, as a revealer of divine truth, and as a ruler. He was used of God to overthrow Egypt and to lay it in the dust of ignominious defeat; to put Israel under the blood, bring her through the water, and gather her around the table in the wilderness; to impart the law, inaugurate the sacrificial system, build the Tabernacle, lead the people to the borders of Canaan, and smite her many foes. The Jews boasted, "We are Moses' disciples," in their deadly opposition to the Lord Jesus Christ. But if Moses was faithful, so was Christ faithful—in a greater cause and at immeasurably greater cost. The Hebrews are told here to get their eyes off Moses and to get them on Christ instead.

b. WHAT WE ARE TO CONTRAST (3:3-6)

For Christ "was counted worthy of more glory than Moses, inasmuch as he who hath builded the house hath more honour than the house. For every house is builded by some man; but he that built all things is God" (3:3-4).

Moses certainly derived glory in God's house, and God did not hesitate to give it to him. The fact that Moses is mentioned by name upward of seven hundred times in the Bible and that his name appears in every section of the Bible is proof of that.

He was truly one of the cornerstones in God's plans for this world, but it would be ludicrous to magnify a stone, however ornate, important, and key it might be, above the building's designer. Moses was not without *his majesty*, but he was still a servant and inferior to Christ.

The word for "servant" used to describe Moses is not the word used in the New Testament to depict a bondsman or a slave, but one that denotes a position of high honor and trust. He was worthy of that trust. He found the house of Israel in ruins and left it rebuilt and in good order.

He was faithful to the great *trust* given to him by God, and what a trust it was! God trusted him to confront Pharaoh and all the might of Egypt and to lead Israel safely to the frontiers of Canaan. He was faithful to the great *talents* given to him by God, for he laid his great intellectual, organizational, and pastoral gifts at God's feet. He was faithful in the great *tests* given to him, even going so far as to request God to blot his name out of God's book rather than have his ministry to Israel fail.

Yet, in all this, Moses was merely a type of the Lord Jesus, or, as the writer of Hebrews puts it, "a testimony of those things which were to be spoken after" (3:5). Moses was not without *his ministry*; nevertheless, he was a servant and inferior to Christ.

Christ was superior in His person to Moses. Moses is at best described as a servant but "Christ as a son" is "over his own house; whose house are we" (3:6).

Jesus once asked His disciples, "Whom do men say that I the Son of man am?" Some, they said, believed He was Elijah; others believed He was John the Baptist risen from the dead; some believed Him to be Jeremiah; others believed Him to be one of the prophets. Thus the Jews themselves likened Jesus to the greatest men in their nation's history. But this would not do! He was as far above the noblest of Israel as the infinite is above the finite. "But whom say ye that I am?" He asked. "Thou art the Christ, the Son of the living God," answered Peter (Matt. 16:13-16). And with that answer, He was content.

Shortly afterward Peter, James, and John saw Moses and Elijah, two of the most illustrious of the heroes of Israel, conferring with Christ about His decease. Awestruck, Peter suggested that they build three tabernacles, one for the Lord, one for Moses, and one for Elijah. He was instantly rebuked by God. Not for a moment would God have these two servants put on a level of even seeming equality with Christ. "This is my beloved Son, in whom I am well pleased," He said. "Hear ye him" (Matt. 17:1-8). Christ is superior in His person to Moses.

He is also superior in His people. Moses' ministry was to the Hebrew people, to the house of Israel. Christ's ministry is to us, a people introduced as "holy brethren, partakers of the heavenly calling."

The writer presses this point home. "Whose house are we," he said, "if we hold fast the confidence and the rejoicing of the hope firm unto the end" (3:6).

"Hope" relates to the future tense of salvation. God always gives us something to look forward to. We sometimes think of hope as an anemic word. For example, we ask someone, "Are you saved?" and he replies, "I hope so," and we naturally conclude the root of the matter is not in him at all. Yet, in some instances, hope has more to offer than faith. Suppose a mother were to say to a disobedient son, "When your father comes home, I'll tell him about your behavior and ask him to punish you." If you asked this boy, "Is your father coming home soon?" he might say, "I *believe* so," but he is unlikely to say, "I *hope* so." Hope combines both expectation and desire.

The Jews, brought out of Egypt by Moses, had hope of Canaan. It had been promised to them, and it was theirs solely on the ground of faith. They failed to enter into it, however, because of their unbelief. It is the same with believers today. We become part of God's house on the basis of faith alone, but it is possible for us to fail to enter into the practical enjoyment of all that this means.

The writer emphasizes "confidence" and "rejoicing" in connection with our hope. This was particularly applicable to the new Hebrew believers to whom he was writing because of the danger of their drifting back into a dead Judaism. They needed boldness to overcome the opposition facing them, and they needed to glory in the spiritual benefits which were theirs in Christ—benefits far exceeding those offered under the law. For us today there is the danger of settling for a second-class Christian life, one devoid of boldness and glorying, a life daunted by foes and haunted by fears. If we "consider the Apostle and High Priest of our profession," boldness and glorying will follow as a matter of course.

2. THE TWIN PERILS TO BE CONSIDERED *(3:7–4:3)*

The writer now begins the second great warning of Hebrews. The first warning had to do with disregarding the salvation of God; this one has to do with disbelieving the sufficiency of God.

a. OLD TESTAMENT TIMES: THE DISASTER OF REBELLION AGAINST GOD IN THE WILDERNESS (3:7-19)

The writer already has warned the Hebrews of the danger of a second-class Christian experience. He now develops this theme by appealing to Scripture (3:7-11) and by drawing attention to the experiences of Israel in the wilderness. The digression in his discussion is *pertinent*, as is evidenced by the opening words: "Wherefore (as the Holy Ghost saith, To day if ye will hear his voice . . .)" (3:7). The warning comes directly from the Holy Spirit.

Furthermore, it is a *pointed* digression, for the writer draws an exact parallel between an historical incident and present-day experience (3:8-11). We have first *the appeal to Scripture* (3:7-11).

He reminds his readers how *Israel had provoked God* in the wilderness. He says, "Harden not your hearts, as in the provocation, in the day of temptation in the wilderness: when your fathers tempted me, proved me, and saw my works forty years" (3:8-9). The unbelief and complaints of Israel in the wilderness were truly astonishing. They had seen God pour out His plagues upon the land of Egypt, separating, as the judgments proceeded, between the land of Goshen, where the Hebrews dwelt, and the rest of Egypt. They had witnessed the crowning judgment: the slaying of the firstborn in every Egyptian home. The emancipated people had experienced a miraculous deliverance at the Red Sea and had seen the Egyptian army overthrown. But before long they began to criticize and complain, almost driving Moses to distraction. Their rebellion even led to attempts upon Moses' life, and that rebellion was prolonged for some forty years.

There was an inevitable consequence to all this. Israel had provoked God; *God had punished Israel* (3:10-11). They refused to accept the reality of all that He had done and was doing for them. God in turn refused to allow them to enter into Canaan to rest. "They do alway err in their heart; and they have not known my ways" (3:10), He said. These, remember, were people who had experienced God's salvation and had been truly redeemed.

This appeal to the scriptural example is now reinforced with *the application of Scripture* (3:12-19). He begins with *an exhortation*. First, the Hebrews must *heed* what is being said. "Take heed, brethren, lest there be in any of you an evil heart of unbelief, in departing from the living God" (3:12). This part of the exhortation is addressed to those who were not true believers at all. The word for "evil" is a strong one denoting not passive but positive and active evil, the kind of evil, indeed, which is not content unless it is dragging someone else down. The word for "departing" means "to stand off from." It is from this word, in one of its forms, that we derive our English word *apostasy.* The "evil heart of unbelief" was the root; the "standing off" was the fruit; the problem is seen in the one and the proof in the other.

To stand off from the truth being revealed to them in the New Testament was proof that a pernicious unbelief controlled the heart. No matter what profession such a person might make, his behavior proved him to be an active unbeliever. No wonder the readers are urged to "take heed."

They are next urged to *help.* The writer assumes that the majority of his readers are truly saved. To these he says, "Exhort one another daily, while it is called To day; lest any of you be hardened through the deceitfulness of sin" (3:13). Believers who were truly saved must counter by active and continuous exhortations to those in whose hearts active evil was at work.

The truly saved person will soon be evident by the fact that he will *"hold . . . stedfast"* (3:14) to his confidence, firmly, to the end. According to Wuest, this word *confidence* is translated "title deed" in Hebrews 11:1. The word was used by the Greeks for documents kept in the official archives, relating to a person's ownership of a piece of property.[1] The believer's title deeds to salvation are all in Christ, and he is thus as secure as Christ Himself can make him. The true believer will "hold stedfast," in contrast with the mere professor of the faith who will be "departing" (3:12). When a person reverted to Judaism, he left the ground of grace and proved he had never been born of God.[2]

There is an urgency about all this. The readers are urged to *hurry*, as it were, to make sure of their standing in Christ. "While it is said, To day if ye will hear his voice, harden not your hearts, as in the provocation" (3:15). Today! Again and again he rings out the word. God never promises us tomorrow. Now is the time to get eternal matters settled. The issues are too important and the pressures too urgent to tolerate delay.

Having exhorted his readers to examine their status carefully, the writer now goes back to *his example* of the failure of Israel in the wilderness (3:16-19). The failure was truly overwhelming. With the exception of Caleb and Joshua, all the believers failed. The spies brought back the fruit of Canaan all right, but they also brought back an alarming report of the foes in Canaan. Only Joshua and Caleb urged a living faith in God's promises, assuring the trembling Hebrews that the dreadful and diabolical foes in Canaan were really defeated foes. The majority of the host panicked in unbelief and refused to make another forward move (3:16).

Here we have an example of majority rule outvoting divine rule. But having a majority in favor of something does not necessarily make it right. The entire generation in the wilderness rebelled as did that later generation of Jews (covered by the book of Acts) of whom Christ spoke such imperative words of warning (Matthew 23). The rebellion of Israel in the wilderness furnishes us with a sobering illustration of "a sin unto death" (1 John 5:16). "To whom sware he," the writer of Hebrews notes, "that they should not enter into his rest." The time came when those who would not enter into Canaan could not enter in. Because they were disobedient and unpersuadable, they were banished from the land of rest and spent the remainder of their days moving on—as Numbers 33 so graphically portrays—moving on ever pursued by the avenger, Death.

So then, they were condemned to ceaseless wanderings in the wilderness, until they were overtaken at last by death. Unbelief triumphed. They were saved, but they never enjoyed Canaan. They settled for less than God had for them. A people who had trusted God to bring them out of Egypt simply refused to trust God to bring them into Canaan. As a result they lost, not their salvation, but the joy, the peace, and the rest God intended for them in the Promised Land (3:18-

---

1. See Kenneth S. Wuest, *Word Studies in Hebrews in the Greek New Testament* (Grand Rapids: Eerdmans, 1966), 2:77-78, 81.
2. W. E. Vine, *The Epistle to the Hebrews* (Grand Rapids: Zondervan, 1952), p. 37.

19). This Old Testament disaster is now used as the basis for an appeal to the Hebrew believers.

b. NEW TESTAMENT TIMES: THE DANGER OF REBELLION AGAINST GOD IN THIS WORLD (4:1-3)

The true believer in the Lord Jesus can fail as sadly as Israel failed in the wilderness. We are living in a world that is as barren of spiritual things as the Sinai Desert was of the things needed to sustain the Israelites on their way to Canaan. God planned the wilderness experience for Israel as a necessary stage on the way to the Promised Land. The journey from Sinai to Kadesh-barnea was to be brief and each step a maturing process. Canaan could then be subdued quickly by a people ready for conquest. The Hebrews failed to profit from the wilderness experiences and, as a result, were condemned to know nothing better than the wilderness.

What the wilderness was to Israel, the world is to us. God has something better for us than the world. In Christ we have every blessing we need—victory, rest, and rich provision. But, as faith was needed to bring us into an experience of salvation, so faith is needed to bring us into the fullness that there is in Christ.

Many believers have the idea that the failure to enter into all that God has for them in Christ is regrettable but not serious. Three words sum up the situation. The first is *fear*. "Let us therefore fear, lest, a promise being left us of entering into his rest, any of you should seem to come short of it" (4:1). We must not even *seem* to come short of it. A little girl fell out of bed one night. When asked about it the next morning, she replied, "I must have stayed too close to where I got in!" It is a serious thing not to go on in the Christian life; that is the chief burden of this whole epistle. It is true that a Christian, truly saved, cannot lose his salvation, but he can certainly lose his reward. If we live our lives as borderline Christians, we are indistinguishable from the world. It makes good sense, therefore, to press on in the things of God and make our salvation evident to all.

The writer resorts once more to his Old Testament illustration to underline *failure*. "For unto us was the gospel preached, as well as unto them: but the word preached did not profit them, not being mixed with faith in them that heard it" (4:2, margin). The Hebrews at Kadesh-barnea did not identify themselves with Caleb and Joshua, so the good report these faithful men brought did them no good. We can fail in a similar way.

> The land, which we passed through to search it, is an exceeding good land. If the Lord delight in us, then he will bring us into this land, and give it us; a land which floweth with milk and honey. Only rebel not ye against the Lord, neither fear ye the people of the land; for they are bread for us: their defense is departed from them, and the Lord is with us: fear them not. (Num. 14:7-9)

These were the words of the two witnesses. Good tidings indeed! Of course there were battles in Canaan, but the blessings far outweighed the battles and, in any case, the foe had been stripped of all his power. Of course we today have to wrestle against principalities and powers, against the rulers of this world's darkness, and against wicked spirits in high places (Eph. 6:12), but that is nothing compared with "all spiritual blessings in heavenly places in Christ" (1:3) and with "the exceeding riches of his grace" (2:7). Besides, the adversaries we face have all been stripped of their power, for does not God speak to us of

> the exceeding greatness of his power to us-ward who believe, according to the working of his mighty power, which he wrought in Christ, when he raised him from the dead, and set him at his own right hand in the heavenly places, far above all principality, and power, and might, and dominion, and every name that is named, not only in this world, but also in that which is to come. (Eph. 1:19-21)

With such good tidings, what a pity to fail!

The answer to fear and failure is *faith*. "For we which have believed do enter into rest, as he said, As I have sworn in my wrath, if they shall enter into my rest: although the works were finished from the foundation of the world" (Heb. 4:3). Those who believe do enter into rest. Faith is the God-ordained way of appropriating that which God has provided for us. The believer does not work to enter into the fullness there is in Christ; he believes.

3. THE TRUE PEACE TO BE CONSIDERED (4:4-13)

At this point the writer of Hebrews embarks upon a discussion of the nature of the true rest God has in store for His people.

What a blessing it is to be at peace and at rest! We live in such a restless, warring world. The peace and rest offered by the world is a wretched imitation of what God has for us. Two artists once attempted to paint a picture of peace. The first drew an idyllic scene. He painted an ocean, still as a pond, mirroring in its depths every line and curve of a sailboat floating quietly by. Overhead the sky was blue, flecked with light, fluffy clouds. And on the shore children played in the shallows and made castles in the sand. It was a picture of peace.

The second artist's picture was nearer to the truth. He depicted a wild and rocky shore against which angry billows burst in towering clouds of spray. The sky was black with the storm, and the surging waves tossed and heaved. But far up on a rocky crag, hidden in a cleft of the rock and sheltered from the wind, sat a bird, safe and secure in her nest, looking out with a serene and untroubled eye at all the turmoil beneath. It was a picture of peace indeed.

a. CREATION REST CONSIDERED (4:4-5)

God has always wanted men to have rest. The first of three aspects of this theme the writer considers is *creation* rest. "For he spake in a certain place of the seventh day on this wise, And God did rest the seventh day from all his works. And in this place again, If they shall enter into my rest" (4:4-5). Israel's Sabbath was based on this fact (Ex. 20:8-11). But God's Sabbath rest was broken by sin, as the Lord Jesus clearly declared. When the Jews accused Him of breaking the Sabbath, He replied, "My Father worketh hitherto, and I work" (John 5:17). As a matter of fact, the Jews failed to keep the Sabbath the way God had planned. They made it a dreadful burden instead.

Matthew 12:1-8 tells how the disciples plucked ears of corn on the Sabbath day. Edersheim illustrates the rabbinic view of what the disciples did. They *plucked* the ears of corn and were thus guilty of reaping! They *rubbed them* and were therefore guilty of sifting or threshing. He quotes the Talmud: "In case a woman rolls wheat to remove the husks, it is considered sifting; if she rubs the heads of wheat, it is regarded as threshing; if she cleans off the side-adherences, in her hand, it is winnowing." The extremes to which the rabbis went bordered on the insane. It was forbidden to stop, with a little wax, the hole in a cask by which fluid was running out! Nor could a person wipe a wound on the Sabbath! A man could not move a sheaf in his field on the Sabbath, but he could lay a spoon on it and in order to remove the spoon, also remove the sheaf on which it lay.[3]

b. CANAAN REST CONSIDERED (4:6-8)

The second rest discussed by the writer is *Canaan* rest. This rest was forfeited by Israel at Kadesh-barnea. "Seeing therefore it remaineth that some must enter therein, and they to whom it was first preached entered not in because of unbelief: again, he limiteth a certain day, saying in David, To day, after so long a time; as it is said, To day if ye will hear his voice, harden not your hearts. For if Jesus (Joshua) had given them rest, then would he not afterward have spoken of another day" (4:6-8).

The rest was forfeited at Kadesh-barnea but was offered again upon Moses' death when Joshua assumed command of Israel. Joshua's brilliant and God-given victories in Canaan certainly augured well, but not for long. Joshua made three serious strategic blunders. He failed to gain control of the coastline and left the western borders of the land in the hands of the Philistines and the Phoenicians; he made a disastrous covenant with the Gibeonites; and, after two magnificent campaigns in which he utterly smashed the Canaanite coalitions, he failed to

---

3. Alfred Edersheim, *The Life And Times of Jesus the Messiah* (Grand Rapids: Eerdmans, 1971), 2:56.

complete "mopping-up operations" and left a potentially dangerous residue of foes unslain. From these military errors resulted most of Israel's subsequent woes during the dark and apostate days of the judges. Certainly there was no rest.

Then came David, but even his glorious victories did not bring rest to the people although *the rest was foreshadowed*. He was followed by Solomon, whose fatal policy of intermarriage with pagan princesses and of softness toward pagan religions led ultimately to the captivities. David, however, did speak of a rest for the people of God (Ps. 95), a rest no doubt messianic and millennial. So far the Hebrew people have not come into the good of this rest that was foreshadowed and foretold by David.

c. CALVARY REST CONSIDERED (4:9-13)

The writer comes to the rest he has in mind: *Calvary* rest. "There remaineth therefore a rest to the people of God. For he that is entered into his rest, he also hath ceased from his own works, as God did from his" (4:9-10). When Christ died upon the cross of Calvary, He cried, "It is finished!" (John 19:30). He had finished the work God gave Him to do. Today God rests in Christ's finished work and so does the believer. That is one reason Christian believers do not keep the Old Testament Sabbath, for our rest is not in a day but in a Person. We enter into the reality of what Jesus meant when He said, "Come unto me, all ye that labour and are heavy laden, and I will give you rest. Take my yoke upon you, and learn of me; for I am meek and lowly in heart: and ye shall find rest unto your souls. For my yoke is easy, and my burden is light" (Matt. 11:28-30). As far as the believer's *standing* is concerned, he has already entered into rest. His salvation is based upon a finished work.

But often our *state* does not correspond to our standing. Many genuine believers lack assurance of salvation. Many occupy lower ground than God intends by confusing the dispensations or imposing Galatian bondage upon the soul.

The child of God must deliberately appropriate for himself the rest the Lord has wrought. "Let us labour therefore to enter into that rest, lest any man fall after the same example of unbelief" (4:11).

A missionary in Africa offered a ride in the back of his pickup truck to a national who was walking along, struggling beneath the weight of a heavy load. The African gladly accepted the ride. After a few miles the missionary glanced in his rear-view mirror and was astonished to see the black man standing stiffly upright in the back of the truck, still holding his load on his shoulders. The missionary stopped the truck to see why the man was still carrying his load. "I didn't know the truck could carry both me and my load," was the man's reply!

Calvary rest frees us from the burden of our sin. We can rest it all on Christ along with all the other heartaches and problems of life. The writer wants to see this accomplished in his readers. He wants their state to be in keeping with their standing in Christ.

Resting in the finished work of Christ for salvation does not mean cessation of all activity. Perhaps an illustration will help us here.

A man is swept out to sea on a homemade raft. Under pressure of wind and wave, it gives every indication of instant dissolution. The man on board struggles desperately just to keep the raft afloat. His paddle, dug repeatedly into the buffeting waves, does nothing to bring him nearer the shore.

He looks up from his labors and sees a ship has come up alongside. The crew throws him a line and bids him come on board. He at once abandons his raft and his own efforts to save himself and accepts the salvation now offered him. He is saved! He paces the deck of that great ship with solid planking beneath his feet and massive engines driving that vessel on its way. *His standing* is now secure.

He is taken to the captain, who says, "Welcome aboard, friend." After some conversation, he continues, "And now we would like your help. We're shorthanded. The cook could use you in the galley. Would you be willing to help?" That has to do with *his state*. His salvation is sure. Nobody is going to pitch him back overboard if he refuses to help. But his gratitude is such that he is only too willing to help get the necessary work done. Helping out on board has nothing to do with his salvation. He can rest in that even though a hundred tasks beckon to him now that he is saved.

That is surely what the author has in mind when he says, "Let us labour therefore to enter into that rest" (v. 11). The call to service in the Christian life is not a call to bondage but to a labor of love.

We must beware at this point of another mistake. We are not called to serve the Lord in our own strength. The Holy Spirit, indwelling the believer, intends to do the work, giving guidance, supplying the strength, providing power. Calvary rest takes care of that. Serving the Lord is no drudgery; it is a delight.

When George Mueller of Bristol died in 1898, his death was a national event. It is recorded of his funeral that nothing like it was ever seen in the city. Businesses closed to give their employees time off to witness the event. Thousands lined the streets leading to the cemetery. On Bristol Cathedral, flags flew at half-mast, and the bells that tolled away the passing of a giant were muffled in mourning. In all the main streets of Bristol, black shutters were put up to the windows and blinds were drawn. The whole city mourned. Obituary notices appeared in newspapers nationwide. England's *Daily Telegraph* summed up the life of this great Christian: "Mr. Mueller robbed the cruel streets of thousands of victims, the gaols of thousands of felons, the workhouse of thousands of helpless waifs." The *Bristol Times* said, "He was raised up for the purpose of showing that the age of miracles is not past."

Few people labored as long and as arduously in the cause of Christ as George Mueller. When he was seventy years of age he decided to become a missionary. He already had behind him some mighty monuments to a life of faith. Five large orphan houses stood as monuments to his extraordinary vision, zeal, and trust in God. More than ten thousand orphans had been loved, housed, fed, educated, and settled in gainful employment. Day schools and Sunday schools in many lands had benefited from his munificence. Nearly two million Bibles and Bible portions had been circulated through his efforts. Three million books and tracts had been given away. A poor man, solely dependent on God, George Mueller had received and given away the astonishing sum of $7.5 million (probably more like fifty to a hundred times that amount in today's economy).

When he was seventy he decided the time had come for a change. He would be a missionary! Five times within the first eight years of his Christian life George Mueller had offered himself as a missionary candidate to various mission boards. He had always been turned down as unpromising material! Now suddenly the world became his parish. He traveled throughout the United Kingdom, the European continent, the United States, the mainland of Asia, the subcontinent of Australia. He traveled more than 200,000 miles in days when traveling was not as convenient and as comfortable as it is today. He spoke more than six thousand times, despite advancing years. He died at the age of ninety-three and entered into his eternal rest.

What was the secret of this busy life? Rest! He had learned the secret of Calvary rest. He had learned the secret summed up in the lines of the hymn:

> Lord Jesus, Thou has promised rest,
> Then give it now to me.
> The rest of ceasing from myself
> To find my all in Thee.

George Mueller pointed an unwavering finger to the source of his strength. Telling of his daily habit of having a quiet time with God in meditation upon the Word of God and in believing, simple, childlike prayer, he said, "I have always considered it the first business of the day to get my own soul happy in the Lord."

This passage of Hebrews concludes with a warning. God's living Word must be the ultimate test of our profession of faith. That Word explores all motives, the writer informs us. It is "quick, and powerful, and sharper than any twoedged sword, piercing even to the dividing assunder of soul and spirit, and of the joints and marrow, and is a discerner of the thoughts and intents of the heart" (4:12). God's Word cuts right through all profession of faith, stripping away that which is merely natural from that which is truly spiritual.

A person may weep at the Lord's Table or shout his hallelujahs at the testimony meeting; however, his emotions may be carnal just as easily as spiritual. God's Word divides between the soul and the spirit. A man may have a thorough grasp of Bible truth and be a walking encyclopedia of scriptural knowledge and yet not be spiritual. A person may have a strong will and determine that he is never going to indulge again in a questionable habit and carry out his resolve, but that does not prove him spiritual.

It is only the Word of God, brought to bear upon the issues of life, which can reveal what is carnal and what is spiritual. It is a "discerner" (4:12), a critic of the thoughts and intents of the heart. As we read the Word of God, it probes into the inner recesses of our beings and explores all our motives.

It also exposes all mankind. "Neither is there any creature that is not manifest in his sight: but all things are naked and opened unto the eyes of him with whom we have to do" (4:13). The word *opened* literally means "to have the throat exposed" as when, for example, an athlete would seize his opponent and bend back his neck. It pictures a throat exposed to the slash of a sword. What an illustration of man's total exposure and vulnerability to God and His Word!

So, then, the writer of Hebrews again confronts his readers with Christ. He is preeminent, able to do what neither Moses nor Joshua could do: bring His people into genuine rest because He is a superior Savior and because the provisions of salvation available through Calvary are superior to anything found in the Old Testament.

In view of this, it is imperative that we make sure of our salvation, lest we be found to be mere professors of Christianity. We must take to heart the example of the Israelites who, although saved and separated from Egypt and all that this meant typically, never entered into Canaan and thus missed God's rest. God expects His people to avail themselves of all He has for them in Christ. And how can a person be sure of his salvation? By exposing his heart to the piercing sword of God's Word, for sooner or later, that sword will find him out if he is a mere pretender.

B. His Priesthood (4:14–8:5)

Man has always felt his need for a priest, one who could represent him before God. In most pagan cultures priests are the most powerful men in the community, holding a virtual monopoly over learning and manipulating national affairs by their iron control over the consciences, the secrets, the fears, and the superstitions of the people.

In much of Christendom, powerful, priestly castes have arisen in the same tradition—orders that have assumed powers and privileges quite out of keeping with the priestly function as taught in the New Testament. Some of these priesthoods cling to Judaistic traditions, and some, quite frankly, have their real roots in paganism.[4]

In Israel, in Old Testament times, priesthood was a monopoly granted by divine decree to the family of Aaron. The Mosaic law laid down elaborate rituals governing the consecration, behavior, and function of the priests. The rules and rituals related to the Old Testament priests are full of rich symbolic teaching.

No man in Israel could be both king and priest, for the priesthood was to be a counterforce in the nation to offset abuse of power by a monarchy that, in itself, existed to guard the purity of Israel's religious codes. Often, however, both kings and priests were failures, at which times prophets surfaced. A prophet could be a king, a priest, or one of the common people. His work was to speak with authority from God regardless of opposition from "church" or state.

1. CHRIST IS A REAL PRIEST (4:14–5:3)

In the New Testament, priesthood is centered in Christ. This is a revolutionary departure from the Old Testament law, thus calling for special, careful, and detailed handling by the writer of Hebrews. His readers, steeped in the Mosaic law concerning priesthood, would wonder on what legal ground Christ could possibly be a priest. But a priest He is, and such a real and sufficient priest that all the Aaronic privileges and responsibilities are completely abolished and swept away by Him. They are now completely obsolete and redundant. No wonder, faced with such a monumental alteration in the divine order, the writer devotes such a lengthy section of his letter to explaining the correctness, the cause, and the consequences of the change!

When the Lord Jesus lived on earth, His ministry was essentially that of a prophet. He came to reveal God to men in a singularly undiluted and memorable form. When He returns to earth to reign, His ministry will be primarily that of a king. He will conquer all His foes and inaugurate a rule of righteousness. Today, at God's right hand in glory, His ministry is that of a priest.

When Israel fought Amalek in the wilderness, Moses was on the mount while Joshua and the army were in the valley. As long as Moses' hands were upraised, Joshua and his men prevailed. But Moses, after all, was a mere man, and his arms grew tired, for there is no more tiring work in the world than that of intercession and prayer. So Aaron and Hur had to come alongside Moses and help hold up his hands (Ex. 17:8-16). We have a priest in heaven today whose arms never tire. He cannot fail in upholding us in all our weakness before the throne of God.

4. See Alexander Hislop, *The Two Babylons* (Neptune, N.J.: Loizeaux, 1916).

a. HIS NAME (4:14)

First of all, we are given His name. "Seeing then that we have a great high priest, that is passed into the heavens, Jesus the Son of God, let us hold fast our profession" (4:14). His priesthood could not possibly derive from David, so He is not "Jesus the son of David," nor could it even derive from Abraham, so He is not "Jesus the son of Abraham." He is Jesus, the Son of God. The Old Testament records the names of many an illustrious son of Aaron, including those of Jeremiah, Ezra, and Ezekiel. But now a new name is added, one that eclipses them all: Jesus, the Son of God.

The Lord Jesus never functioned as an Aaronic priest while on earth. Expositors differ as to whether or not the Lord was a priest while on earth. Some maintain that He was a priest, that His priesthood dates from the time God acknowledged Him on Earth as His Son (Heb. 5:5), and that this occurred either at His baptism (Matt. 3:17) or at the time of the transfiguration (Matt. 17:5). That Jesus was the Son of God was revealed by the Father to Peter (Matt. 16:16-17) and was known by Nathanael (John 1:49). Those who hold that Christ was a priest while on earth maintain that, even though Christ could not officiate in the Temple as did the Aaronic priests, He certainly exercised His Melchizedek priesthood in John 17 and also when, on the cross, He offered Himself as a sacrifice for sin. Hebrews 7:27 might well bear this out.

Taking the opposite view, Sir Robert Anderson says,

> Not until the mediator of the covenant had "made purification for sins" and had gone up to the mount of God was Aaron appointed high priest; and not until the Son of God had completed the work of redemption and ascended to the right hand of the Majesty on high was He called (i.e. publicly announced) of God to be High Priest after the order of Melchizedek. It is not that the Lord then entered upon high-priestly functions of a new character, but that, while on earth (as the Apostle expressly declares) He *would not be a priest at all.* And on earth it was that his *sacrificial* work in redemption was accomplished. That work, therefore, must have been complete before He entered on His high priestly work.[5]

Never once did He officiate at the brazen altar or wash at the brazen laver. Never did He don the rich high priestly robes and enter the sanctuary to minister at the table, at the lampstand, or at the golden altar of incense. Never once did He lift the veil and pass into the Holy of Holies to stand before the Ark of the Covenant. He was not a priest while on earth. But He has done more than any high priest of Israel ever did. He has "passed into the heavens," the visible firmament, to heaven itself. And He has gone there not merely as a priest, nor yet as a high priest, but as our great High Priest, a title never bestowed on any descendant of Aaron.

5. Sir Robert Anderson, *The Hebrews Epistle* (London: Pickering & Inglis, n.d.).

He is a priest of such a caliber that the writer insists that we "hold fast our profession" now that we know Him. This demand had a particular point for the early Hebrew Christians, for to confess Jesus as their great High Priest called for a sharp break with Judaism. This real priest of ours is "Jesus," therefore He is truly human and can enter fully into human needs. He is "the Son of God" and is therefore truly divine, able to enter fully into the demands of Deity. There never was a priest like this before. To abandon Him for an obsolete and dead Judaism was indeed a serious matter.

b. HIS NEARNESS (4:15-16)

First, we note, He knows *our nature*. "For we have not an high priest which cannot be touched with the feeling of our infirmities; but was in all points tempted like as we are, yet without sin" (4:15). Satan assailed Him in the wilderness with the three temptations that brought about the Fall, with "the lust of the flesh, and the lust of the eyes, and the pride of life" (1 John 2:16). Eve was tempted with the lust of the eyes when she saw that the tree was "pleasant to the eyes," with the lust of the flesh when she saw that it was "good for food," and with the pride of life when she saw that it was "a tree to be desired to make one wise" (Gen. 3:6). The Lord Jesus was tempted with the lust of the flesh when urged to "command that these stones be made bread," with the lust of the eyes when Satan "sheweth him all the kingdoms of the world, and the glory of them," and with the pride of life when urged to cast Himself down from the Temple (Matt. 4:1-11). He fully knows temptation.

It was not simply that the Lord Jesus was able not to sin. It went far beyond that. He was not able to sin. He was "in all points tempted like as we are, yet without sin."

Some years ago a friend of mine visited a South African gold mine. He was taken through the various stages whereby the gold was repeatedly refined, put into the crucible, heated into a molten state, the dross skimmed away. At last the refiner was satisfied. The gold was pure.

But there was one more step. Before it could be stamped with the official seal, it had to go to the assayer. He too put the gold in the crucible and heated it to its melting point. My friend asked: "Why does *he* do that? Is he going to refine it further?" "Oh, no," he was told. "His crucible is not to see if it has any impurities to be removed. His crucible and his fire are to demonstrate that the gold is indeed pure."

The temptations of the Lord Jesus were not intended to see if He could sin. There was never any question about that. His temptations were simply to demonstrate Him sinless, to show that He was pure. The word for "tempted" here is *pēirazō* as in 2:18. It means "to be tried" or "to be tested." The same word is used in Matthew 4:1. It carries with it the idea of being "pierced through." He was tested to see whether sin, as to its origin, process, or results, had anything in Him. Sin did not attract Him; sin repelled Him.

He knows not only our nature but *our needs*. "Let us therefore come boldly unto the throne of grace, that we may obtain mercy, and find grace to help in time of need" (4:16). In Old Testament times the ordinary Israelite could not approach the Holy of Holies where God was enthroned, for that was the sole, annual prerogative of the high priest. But we can approach the throne of grace at any time, as often as we wish, whenever we have a need, knowing that our needs are fully known to our priest and will be met with mercy and grace.

c. HIS NATURE (5:1-3)

Without compassion a priest cannot *function for us*. The Lord Jesus is an ideal priest, because He understands us. He understands human nature, not just academically and theoretically, nor yet simply omnisciently as God, but experientially. No angel can function as a priest for man. Angelic beings might study us and our faults and follies, just as we study plants and animals. But, not having entered into human life by way of birth, they cannot appreciate our problems and needs. That is why Israel's priests had to be "taken from among men" (5:1). When offering gifts and sacrifices, they could appreciate the sinner's experience.

The Lord Jesus cannot only function for us, he can *feel for us*. The Old Testament priest could "have compassion on the ignorant, and on them that are out of the way; for that he himself also is compassed with infirmity" (5:2). But here was the problem with the Old Testament priests. They themselves were sinners, and although that gave them ability to feel for others, it also meant that they had to offer sacrifices for themselves as well as for the people. Christ is a real priest, because He can enter into the pressures and problems of human life, yet without ever having sinned Himself. When Adam gazed upon his fallen bride in the Garden of Eden, he loved her and longed after her and had compassion upon her. His solution to the situation in which he found himself was disastrous, for, stepping down to where she was, he became sinful too. The Lord Jesus has likewise stooped to grapple with the problem of sin, but He has solved it in quite another way (2 Cor. 5:21). So, then, Christ is a real priest because of His name, His nearness, and His nature.

2. *CHRIST IS A RIGHTFUL PRIEST (5:4–6:20)*

The Lord Jesus may be a real priest, He may have true compassion for men because of His own humanity, but is He a rightful priest?

a. THE CHOICE OF THIS PRIEST (5:4-10)

Not everyone could decide to be a priest in Bible times. It was not a profession open to all.

(1) HIS EXALTATION (5:4-6)

The writer of Hebrews faces this issue squarely. "And no man taketh this honour unto himself, but he that is called of God, as was Aaron" (5:4). He is coming to grips now with the crux of the matter.

Only members of Aaron's family could be priests; the Lord Jesus was not of that family. He was born into the tribe of Judah. Despite that fact, His exaltation to the priesthood was authoritative, because the same One who put Aaron in that office has now put Christ there instead. "So also Christ glorified not himself to be made an high priest; but he that said unto him, Thou art my Son, to day have I begotten thee" (5:5). The office of the high priest in Jesus' day was filled by evil and politically ambitious men. Ananias and Caiaphas, for example, were a scandal and a disgrace. Their chief purpose was to uphold their own vested interests and their power. Aaron was chosen by God to be a priest; Christ was chosen as God to be a priest. Since He is the Son of God, He has every right to fill that office and is called to it by God for that very reason.

The writer now shows his hand and reminds the Jews of something they had long forgotten: that there was a priesthood that far exceeded that of Aaron and that was in existence long centuries before Aaron ever was born, the priesthood of Melchizedek. God chose Melchizedek to be a priest long before He chose Aaron. In fact, the first mention of the priest in the Bible relates to the priesthood of Melchizedek (Gen. 14:18-21). This sudden mention of Melchizedek throws a shaft of light into the whole argument of the letter. It would become immediately apparent to the intelligent Hebrew where the argument was leading. At this point, however, the writer does little more than inject the name, but he comes back to it later and builds mightily upon it. So then, Christ was exalted to be a priest as Melchizedek was exalted to be a priest. And, had the writer been composing a psalm instead of a treatise, no doubt he would have inserted a *selah* at this point, meaning, "There, what do you think of that?"

(2) HIS EXPERIENCE (5:7-8)

Having mentioned Christ's exaltation to the priestly office by God, the writer next touches again upon His experience. "Who in the days of his flesh, when he had offered up prayers and supplications with strong crying and tears unto him that was able to save him from death, and was heard in that he feared" (5:7).

He had experienced, as a man, *the sufficiency of God.* Throughout His life-time Jesus made prayer and supplication the habit of His life. At every major crisis He was found praying.[6]

In Gethsemane, when the Lord Jesus came to grips with death, the ultimate horror that faces mankind, He prayed to be saved from it, not indeed from physical death, but to be saved "out from under" death. His prayer was answered in His resurrection. On the cross, Jesus prayed again, using the first verse of Psalm 22. (Perhaps He quoted the whole psalm. It certainly fit His needs at that time.)

Jesus not only experienced the sufficiency of God but also *the sufferings of men.* "Though he were a Son, yet learned he obedience by the things which he suffered" (5:8). A closer and more suitable rendering would be: "Son though he was, yet learned he obedience by the things which he suffered."[7] He was not shielded from suffering. Indeed, since He was truly God as well as truly man, no doubt His sufferings were intensified just as are a doctor's sufferings intensified because he knows full well the ravages and the progress of a disease.

A mad dog is said to have terrorized a village. It had already bitten one person, who had died a horrible death. The village blacksmith finally cornered the dog, holding it at bay while everyone else escaped. He was bitten several times before he finally slew the enraged beast. Returning to his forge, he deliberately chained himself to an iron fixture so that when his own insanity overtook him the other villagers would be safe from his maddened rage. Then he calmly awaited his doom.

The Lord Jesus learned obedience through the things that He suffered. His sufferings were real and intense and ran the whole length of every human woe. He is qualified by His experience to be a priest.

(3) HIS EXPLOITS (5:9-10)

He is an excellent choice as a priest because of His exploits, too. Think of His *personal* exploits. He was "made perfect" (5:9), that is, He was exalted to glory. He always was morally perfect, but these perfections shone as never before in the matchless splendor of His life on earth. Now He has received recognition in glory. The black background against which He walked on earth displays the excellencies of His life just as black velvet brings out the beauty of a diamond.

His exploits were not only personal; they were *perpetual.* He has become "the author of eternal salvation" (5:9) to all who obey Him. He is the cause of salvation; He has brought it into being. It will last as long as He does. Note the emphasis upon *eternal* salvation, for it belies the notion that Hebrews teaches a person can lose his salvation. Salvation is eternal.

6. See G. Campbell Morgan, *The Cries of the Christ* (Old Tappan, N.J.: Revell, 1903).
7. Vine, p. 50.

A person who is "saved" falls into sin soon afterward and, according to some, loses his salvation. Before he can be "saved again," he dies and goes to a lost eternity. What was he saved from? The penalty of sin? No, because he lost his salvation and is now eternally lost. Was he saved from the power of sin? Evidently not, because he sinned to such an extent that he lost his salvation. Was he saved from the presence of sin? No, because he is not in heaven but in hell, lost forever. He wasn't saved from anything, so he wasn't saved at all. The dire warning passages of Hebrews do not teach that a truly saved person can lose his salvation. Salvation, once accepted, is eternal.

The reference in this verse to obedience does not alter this truth. Vine says that the word *hupakouō* means "to listen, and then to obey the word spoken. The primary reference is to the response to the gospel."[8]

Then, too, the exploits of Christ are *positional*. He is "called of God an high priest after the order of Melchisedec [Melchizedek]" (5:10). That one name, Melchizedek, swept away 1,500 years of Jewish ritual and religion. When Rip Van Winkle fell asleep in the American colonies, King George III ran the country; when he awoke, George Washington was in power. He almost lost his head by shouting for the wrong George! There was a new order in the country. The name *Washington* swept away an entire political system. Similarly, the name *Melchizedek* was a revolutionary name. It swept away an entire system of religion and replaced it with something far greater.

At this second mention of the name *Melchizedek,* all within a few sentences, the intelligent Hebrew reader would begin to pace the floor with a thousand tumultuous thoughts racing through his mind. Aaron! Melchizedek! A ritual priest! A royal priest! A priest installed by the law of Moses! A priest installed before Moses was born!

So then, Christ is not only a real priest, He is a rightful priest. He has been chosen as priest. But before the significance of Melchizedek can be developed, the writer has a challenge, a third warning, to insert: "Don't discredit the Son of God!" The warnings are becoming more serious and sobering, for with increased truth comes increased responsibility.

b. THE CHALLENGE OF THIS PRIEST (5:11–6:20)

This third warning is serious. The writer has already developed much of his Christology and is about to press home the significance of the Melchizedek priesthood of the Lord Jesus. He anticipates reactions to this teaching and digresses at length to warn against any drawing back from the truth as it is in Christ. At stake is an eternal salvation. His warning is in three parts. First, he has a warning to

8. Ibid, p. 51.

those who are *weak*; then, a warning to those who are *wicked*, resentful, and antagonistic to the truth; and finally, a warning to those who are *wise*.

(1) TO THOSE WHO ARE WEAK (5:11–6:3)

The first challenge of the rightful priest is to those who are weak. The wavering Hebrew believers must *face their immaturity*. Especially, they must face their *mental* immaturity. The writer deliberately digresses from a discussion of Melchizedek. The problem is not that his subject is too abstruse but that his readers are mentally unready to grapple with it. The word he uses is "dull" or "sluggish" (5:11). Some of his hearers were doubtless afraid to face the truth of Melchizedek because of the practical implications that would follow.

In addition to their mental problem is *a moral* problem (5:12-14). The Hebrew believers are *behind in their duty*. They should be ready and able to teach others the principles of Christianity, but instead they need someone to teach them the first principles of the oracles of God. They were in need of milk, not solid food. "Ye ought to be teachers" (5:12), he says. The word *ought* implies moral obligation. We cannot escape personal responsibility and accountability for the truth we have.

They were *behind in their development* as well as in their duty. They were still babes. Spiritual babyhood is fostered by ritualism. An elaborate ritual was acceptable in Old Testament times because that was the infancy stage of divine revelation, but with the coming of Christ the nursery should have been left behind. The Hebrew believers had to put away the cramping and inhibiting rituals of their former faith. They had made no progress in spiritual things because they were still tied to the apron strings of the old dispensation. By then they should have developed enough moral judgment to be able to discern and accept the truth when they heard it. It was high time they faced their immaturity (5:13-14).

The writer also demands that they *forsake their immaturity*. "Wherefore let us cease to speak of the first principles of Christ, and press on unto perfection" (6:1a, author's paraphrase). This is to be a once-for-all action.

The Hebrew Christians must abandon the Temple sacrifices, together with its attending rituals and its accompanying priesthood. They have far better provisions for their need in Calvary, and a far better priest in Christ. Some of the Hebrews were looking back speculatively to the Temple as though there could be coexistence between Judaism and Christianity. Not so! The Old Testament contained only "the beginning word of the Christ."[9] The substance found in Christ must not be forsaken for the mere shadows found in the Levitical ritual.

To eliminate all doubt, the writer elaborates. They were to forsake *Old Testament principles as inadequate*. "Not laying again the foundation of repentance

---

9. See Wuest, 2:110.

from dead works, and of faith toward God" (6:1*b*). "Repentance from dead works" was an Old Testament truth preached by John the Baptist. "Repentance toward God" is New Testament truth (Acts 20:21). Similarly, "faith toward God" was an Old Testament requirement; what is required now is faith in our Lord Jesus Christ (20:21).

The Hebrew believers were to lay aside *Old Testament practices* as inadequate: "of the doctrine of baptisms, and of laying on of hands" (6:2*a*). The "baptisms" referred to are "the washings," the ablutions, which formed such a prominent part of Levitical ritual. These were only symbolic, at best, and they have been replaced by the reality: "the washing of regeneration" (Titus 3:5). The "laying on of hands" was another prominent feature of Levitical sacrifices. The offerer was required to identify himself with his sacrifice by laying his hands upon it (Lev. 1:4). Since Christ has done away with the offerings at Calvary, such a ritual is not only obsolete but also an insult to God. We now lay hold of Christ.

The Hebrews were to lay aside *Old Testament prospects as inadequate*: "of resurrection of the dead, and of eternal judgment" (6:2*b*). Resurrection, in the Old Testament, was believed and taught, but only in a most elementary and basic way. Since Christ has been raised from the dead, all such teaching has been placed on a higher plane, and the believer's hope of sharing in that resurrection has been brought fully to light. Why grope with the candle of Old Testament revelation when one has the blazing sun of New Testament truth? Eternal judgment was likewise taught in the Old Testament, but that is all past for the believer in Christ. The believer has a much better prospect than that!

So having confronted the Hebrews with the demand that they forsake their immaturity and furnished them with the details of what is involved, the writer expresses his own determination. "And this will we do, if God permit" (6:3). As far as he is concerned, he has no intention of going over these rudimentary things. He wants to press on to new and better and higher truth. However, he realizes that he may be hindered in this by their spiritual dullness.

Thus the writer exhorts the weak. Their immaturity is disgraceful and even dangerous. They must make up their minds to go on.

(2) TO THOSE WHO ARE WICKED (6:4-8)

This passage of Scripture, one of the most controversial in the New Testament, should be read over and its structure, as outlined at the beginning of this section, noted. The subjects of this terrible warning are those who, having once made the initial responses to the gospel, deliberately returned to Judaism. Essentially, such a sin would be possible only to Jews and especially to Jews of the first century who were living while the Temple was still standing. In a secondary sense, however, the warning has an application to those today who are drawn by the gospel message and who make a profession of faith, only to renounce it in order to return to a dead religious system. This is apostasy.

(a) THEIR FULL ENLIGHTENMENT (6:4-5)

The writer, having warned the weak that they are, so to speak, on thin ice, and having urged them to get off onto solid ground, now turns his attention to those of his readers who were deliberately planning on going back into Judaism.

They had come a significant way toward real faith in Christ but not far enough. They had *seen the truth* and seen it in a clear and unmistakable way. They were "once enlightened" (6:4*a*)

D. L. Moody used to tell of a man who came under conviction of sin and who was brought under the sound of the gospel. When he became ill, Moody visited him in the hospital. The man was afraid he was going to die and, although he would not accept Christ then and there, promised the evangelist that should he get well he would come to revival meetings and accept Christ. He recovered from his illness but failed to honor his pledge. Moody went to see him, but again the man procrastinated and shrugged off the warning that he was on dangerous ground.

Shortly afterward he became ill again, and this time his condition was terminal. Moody called on him once more to urge him to accept Christ. The man said, "It is too late." Moody pleaded with him, pointing him to Scriptures that emphasize God's grace. But the man said, "I had my chance, and now it's too late." Moody offered to pray for him, but the stricken man only said, "It is too late."

Moody tells how he knelt by the man's bedside and attempted in vain to pray. "The heavens seemed as brass," he said. Finally he left, having had no success at all, either in talking to the man or in praying for him. Shortly afterward the man was buried in a Christless grave. He had been enlightened but had rejected the truth. This was the peril these early Hebrew inquirers faced.

They had not only seen the truth; they had actually *savored the truth*. They had "tasted of the heavenly gift, and were made partakers of the Holy Ghost" (6:4*b*). In other words, they had tasted the *spiritual character* of the truth in Christ. A person may put the pot on the stove and throw in the ingredients for soup. As the meat and vegetables begin to simmer, he may put in his spoon and taste it and decide it needs a little more seasoning or that it has too much salt. But there is a great deal of difference between tasting the soup and filling a bowl and enjoying it to the full.

Some had taken the first tentative taste of what Christ has to offer the soul. They had "tasted of the heavenly gift." Think of that gift! God has given us the Scriptures, He has given us His Son, He has given us His Spirit, and He gives us salvation. These Hebrews had been "once enlightened" (6:4a); the word means "once for all." Their eyes had been opened to what God offered in Christ. This could not be repeated if they drew back.

Moreover, they had been made "partakers of the Holy Ghost" (6:4c). The initial work of the Holy Spirit is to convict of sin, of righteousness, and of judgment to come, and to make Christ real to the soul (John 16:7-11). These Hebrews had been brought to the place of repentance and to an enlightened understanding that Christ was all He claimed to be: God's answer to their every need. But to be "a partaker" of the Holy Spirit is not to be a possessor of the Holy Spirit. To recognize the truth in Christ is not to be a Christian. At this point a person can still draw back.

Those of whom the writer is speaking had not only tasted something of the spiritual character of what was offered them in Christ; they also had tasted something of its *spiritual content*. They had "tasted the good word of God" (6:5a). The types of the Tabernacle, the preaching of the prophets, the songs of the psalmists —all these were fulfilled in Christ. New Testament truth does not contradict Old Testament truth but completes it. All the tributaries and rivers of the Old Testament pour their united floods at last into the ocean of Christ. This had been seen by these Jews. They had tasted the good word of God.

Furthermore, they had tasted "the powers of the world to come" (6:5b). Many of the Hebrews to whom this epistle was addressed had seen the miracles wrought by Christ and His apostles. They had seen the evidence of conversion in the transformed lives of thousands of their fellow Jews who had embraced the gospel and received Christ as Savior. In these lives the "powers of the world to come" already were evident.

(b) THEIR FEARFUL ENMITY (6:6)

Although not saved, these people had been fully enlightened to the truth in Christ. It was now a question of choice on their part. Would they go on and become true, born-again believers, or would they draw back and repudiate what they had both seen and heard? The wicked made the wretched choice and turned their backs upon Christ.

The writer mentions the *unavoidable implication* evident in this reaction to the gospel. They fell away (6:6a). The word is used only here in the Greek translation of Ezekiel 14:13 and 15:18 where Israel's apostasy is described. They become apostates.

Solemnly, the writer then underlines the *unconditional impossibility*. It is impossible "to renew them again unto repentance" (6:6b). There is no such thing as being saved and then lost and then saved again. Those who repudiate Christ prove that they never have been saved at all, and they sear their souls so that the initial work of repentance can never again be wrought in their hearts. Like Pharaoh, they harden their hearts beyond the possibility of ever having them softened again.

They are actually guilty of the *unpardonable impiety* of deliberately and personally sharing in the crucifixion. Forgiveness was offered to those who nailed Christ to the cross. He prayed, "Father, forgive them; for they know not what they do" (Luke 23:34). But no forgiveness is offered to those who "crucify to themselves the Son of God afresh" (Heb. 6:6c). This is not a sin of ignorance but of willful, knowing wickedness. To endorse the crucifixion of Christ with eyes wide open to who He is has to be apostasy indeed, for they are not only guilty of deliberately and personally sharing in the crucifixion, they are also guilty of a deliberate and public shaming of the Christ. As the writer puts it, they "put him to an open shame" (6:6c).

(c) THEIR FINAL END (6:7-8)

Having described their full enlightenment and their fearful wickedness, the writer reveals their final end. He does so by means of an illustration taken from nature. A piece of ground has received its full measure of rain and should be productive. There is no reason it should not bear useful fruit. But, instead, the land bears thorns and thistles. Worthless, it is fit only for the fire.

Dr. Harry Ironside told of a farmer who fell heir to a large tract of land in the barren lands of the West. Deciding to give it a trial, he fenced off a few acres and plowed, planted, and cultivated them. But, at harvest time, the land produced nothing but scrub and sagebrush. There was no sense in trying anymore, for the nature of the soil was fully revealed. It is the same with the apostate. Of what avail would it be to bring him back to repentance? The character of his soul is already revealed as obdurate and unresponsive to divine truth. For him, nothing is left but fire.

Truly this is a most solemn warning. The issues at stake when a soul is confronted with Christ are the most serious imaginable. To trifle with God's grace is to offer the final insult to God. To reject His Son is an unpardonable sin.

(3) TO THOSE WHO ARE WISE (6:9-20)

This rightful priest of ours, having issued His challenge to the weak and to the wicked, now has something to say to the wise among the epistle's readers.

(a) THE EXHORTATION (6:9-12)

First, the fruit of salvation should be *clearly discerned* in the believer's life. This fact is, first of all, bluntly declared: "But, beloved, we are persuaded better things of you, and things that accompany salvation, though we thus speak" (6:9). The writer has a settled conviction that his readers are not apostates but genuine believers. There is evidence of this in their lives.

The fruit that gave the writer his assurance is described: "For God is not unrighteous to forget your work and labour of love, which ye have shewed toward his name, in that ye have ministered to the saints, and do minister" (6:10). One way a person demonstrates the reality of his salvation is in the love he has for other Christians (1 John 3:14).

It is a good thing when the fruit of salvation can be discerned; it is better still when that fruit is being *continually developed.* The writer tells his readers to keep on doing what they are doing and to get a firm grasp on the hope that is theirs. What that hope is, he is about to describe.

In the meantime, they must imitate the example of others, who, faced with all kinds of opposition and difficulty, nevertheless by faith and patience entered into the good of all that God had for them. God's promises have a *trust* element in them that is to be grasped by faith and a *time* element in them that is to be grasped by patience. Later in the letter the writer devotes a whole chapter to displaying the victories of those "who through faith and patience inherit the promises" (6:12).

(b) THE EXPECTATION (6:13-20)

Having exhorted the wise among his readers to make their calling and election sure, the writer now tells them that their God is prepared to help them. God has pledged Himself to see them safely home. The writer emphasizes *the significance of this pledge* and, by way of illustration, reminds his readers of Abraham's experience.

"For when God made promise to Abraham, because he could swear by no greater, he sware by himself, saying, Surely blessing I will bless thee, and multiplying I will multiply thee" (6:13-14). This was particularly apt because of the great reverence in which Abraham was held by the Hebrew people. He was the founding father of their race. Abraham received the pledge of God through faith and patience. He pressed on in faith and had the promise confirmed to him by a most emphatic oath made to him by God (Gen. 22:16-18).

Recall the circumstances. Abraham had just come through the most severe of all the tests of his faith and had proved himself willing even to offer up Isaac in sacrifice. The Lord rewarded him with a pledge confirmed by an oath. "In blessing I will bless thee, and in multiplying I will multiply thy seed." This figure of speech is a *polyptoton*, used for special emphasis. Literally God was saying, "I will surely bless," or, "I will richly bless." To these Hebrews, facing all kinds of severe tests themselves, this quotation was particularly appropriate. The pledge used as an illustration was significant. Abraham received what God had pledged, and so would they.

The pledge given to Abraham was not only significant; the writer emphasizes *the sacredness of this pledge*. When men wish to give emphasis to a pledge, they swear or take out an oath. The custom is universal and immemorial, and it usually settles the matter in hand.

In His kindness and in His understanding of human frailty, God, who cannot lie, nevertheless accommodated Himself to human weakness by confirming His word with an unbreakable oath.

Human unbelief is a pernicious thing. How hardly we take God at His word! How refreshing it must be to God when we are willing to take His word at face value without insisting on signs or proofs. David Livingstone's favorite text was Matthew 28:20, "Lo, I am with you alway, even unto the end of the world." His biographers tell us that whenever he was confronted with some special danger or difficulty, he would write the text afresh into his journal, appending the words: "It is the word of a Gentleman of the strictest and most sacred honour, and that's an end of it!"

God is jealous that His word be trusted. David rightly says, "I will worship toward thy holy temple, and praise thy name for thy lovingkindness and for thy truth: for thou hast magnified thy word above all thy name" (Ps. 138:2). Yet, in condescension to human frailty, He "helps our unbelief" by confirming His word with an oath. And, as the writer of Hebrews says, "It was impossible for God to lie" (Heb. 6:18*a*).

Just as God pledged Himself to Abraham, so He has pledged Himself to us, and His pledge is as secure as the very Word of God. In Old Testament times, God provided certain cities throughout Israel, known as cities of refuge. A man guilty of accidental manslaughter could flee to any of these cities and there be safe from the avenger. We have such a city in God's Word and in the hope that is set before us. In the Old Testament the man guilty of manslaughter was unconditionally set free upon the death of the high priest. Surely this is the significance of what the writer of Hebrews now says as he emphasizes *the security of this pledge*. "We might have a strong consolation, who have fled for refuge to lay hold upon the hope set before us" (6:18*b*). The great High Priest had died; our guilt is gone; we are forever free. God's pledge to the manslayer was secure; His pledge to us is secure.

It is so secure that the writer can say of our hope that we have it "as an anchor of the soul, a hope both sure and stedfast, and which entereth into that within the vail [veil]" (6:19). A vessel, drifting before the wind toward a lee shore, throws out an anchor. Down, down it goes until it grips the unseen solid rock below. The hawser tightens, and the anchor holds. The vessel is safe. Our hope is an anchor cast upward to the inner sanctuary of heaven, where it lays hold of

Christ and cannot be moved. Life is the sea, the soul is the ship, hope is the anchor, Christ is the hidden rock within the veil.

How blessed are these verses touching upon the eternal security of the believer and coming after such a dire warning to the willful drifter away from Christ! How secure is our pledge! Before leaving the subject and pressing on with his main line of discussion, the writer would have us know not only the *what* and the *where* of our security, but the *why* as well. Still pointing upward to the heavenly Temple and to the Holy of Holies in that Temple, he says, "Whither the forerunner is for us entered, even Jesus, made an high priest for ever after the order of Melchisedec [Melchizedek]" (6:20).

The security of the manslayer in Israel was purchased by the death of the priest. But Jesus, as our great High Priest, has done something no human priest could ever do. He has gone into the Holy of Holies in heaven, and, furthermore, He is there as our "forerunner." The word signifies "one who comes to a place where the rest are to follow." He has gone in; we are going in too. It's a case of "follow the leader," and the result is as sure as the Leader can make it.

Thus, the writer finishes his digression and brings us back to Melchizedek. He is now ready to continue his treatise. He has shown that Jesus is a *real* priest, as evidenced by His name, His nearness, and His nature. He has shown us that Jesus is a *rightful* priest, chosen of God and with a tremendous challenge to men. Now he is going to show that Jesus is a *royal* priest as well.

3. CHRIST IS A ROYAL PRIEST *(7:1–8:5)*

a. THE UNDOUBTED LORDSHIP OF CHRIST AS PRIEST (7:1-10)

Melchizedek is mentioned only twice in the Old Testament. After Abraham's resounding victory over the invading eastern kings and his deliverance of Lot and the people of Sodom, we read:

> And the king of Sodom went out to meet him after his return from the slaughter of Chedorlaomer, and of the kings that were with him, at the valley of Shaveh, which is the king's dale. And Melchizedek king of Salem brought forth bread and wine: and he was the priest of the most high God. And he blessed him, and said, Blessed be Abram of the most high God, possessor of heaven and earth: and blessed be the most high God, which hath delivered thine enemies into thy hand. And he gave him tithes of all. (Gen. 14:17-20)

The other reference is a brief prophetic reference made by David: "The Lord hath sworn, and will not repent, Thou art a priest for ever after the order of Melchizedek" (Ps. 110:4).

(1) THE PREROGATIVE OF MELCHIZEDEK (7:1)

The writer of Hebrews is now going to prove that the Lord's right to the priesthood is based upon the same right as Melchizedek's. Melchizedek belonged to an order of priesthood unique in the Bible and far older than that of Aaron. The writer begins by discussing Melchizedek himself to underline the undoubted lordship of Christ as priest. For Melchizedek's priesthood was so powerful, so overwhelming, so indisputable, that Abraham acknowledged it instantly, completely, and without question.

First, attention is drawn to the prerogative of Melchizedek. "For this Melchisedec, king of Salem, priest of the most high God, . . . met Abraham returning from the slaughter of the kings, and blessed him" (7:1). Melchizedek had the double rank of king and priest. No Hebrew could unite these offices in his person; the only one who tried to do so was smitten with leprosy for his presumption (2 Chron. 26:1-21).

Israel's kings descended from the tribe of Judah and the house of David; the priests, on the other hand, descended from the tribe of Levi and the house of Aaron. Melchizedek was a king-priest. As a king, he had power with men; as a priest, he had power with God. It was his priestly character that surfaced upon his meeting with Abraham. He came not to demand tribute, but to bless, to reveal to Abraham a new name for God, and to strengthen him in a new life (Gen. 14:19-23).

(2) THE POWER OF MELCHIZEDEK (7:2)

Next, the power of Melchizedek is mentioned. "To whom also Abraham gave a tenth part of all; first being by interpretation King of righteousness, and after that also King of Salem, which is, King of peace" (7:2). At this time Abraham was at the zenith of his influence and power. He had just defeated a powerful and overwhelmingly victorious coalition of eastern kings and was returning flushed with the spoils of war. His name rang throughout the Middle East. But Abraham recognized immediately in Melchizedek a power far greater than his, and he at once acknowledged Melchizedek by giving to him his tithes and his titles.

The name *Melchizedek* simply meant "King of righteousness," and he was king of Salem (Jerusalem), the name that meant "peace." Righteousness and peace met in Melchizedek, making him an outstanding type of Christ. For in Christ, righteousness and peace have met finally and forever. At Calvary, through Christ, God has provided men with an enduring means of righteousness and with an endless measure of peace. How much of this Abraham apprehended we are not told, but evidently he acknowledged the superiority of Melchizedek's sovereignty.

(3) THE PERSON OF MELCHIZEDEK (7:3)

Mention is next made of the person of Melchizedek. He was, so to speak, "without father, without mother, without descent, having neither beginning of days, nor end of life; but made like unto the Son of God . . . a priest continually" (7:3). The person of Melchizedek is introduced suddenly and startlingly into the Genesis narrative and removed from it again with equal mystery and significance. He is not mentioned again until Psalm 110. Genesis is preeminently a book of genealogies, yet Melchizedek is brought forward without any. He appears, as it were, from nowhere. Genealogically speaking, he was without father or mother. Moreover, he has no revealed history. All of a sudden, there he is; then he is gone. There is no record of either his birth or his death, so, symbolically, he had neither beginning nor ending of days.

Melchizedek is deliberately introduced into the Genesis narrative in this peculiar way by the Holy Spirit. He is to be a type of Christ. He was "made like unto the Son of God." We have no idea who the historical Melchizedek was. Some believe he was Shem; others believe he was one of the Christophanies of the Old Testament. But no matter who he was, as to his person, he is a highly typical figure whose history was designedly placed into the Genesis record for the very purpose made of it by the writer of Hebrews.

(4) THE PREEMINENCE OF MELCHIZEDEK (7:4-7)

This preeminence is first shown in *what he expected of Abraham*. "Now consider how great this man was, unto whom even the patriarch Abraham gave the tenth of the spoils. And verily they that are of the sons of Levi, who receive the office of the priesthood, have a commandment to take tithes of the people according to the law, that is, of their brethren, though they come out of the loins of Abraham" (7:4-5). Melchizedek evidently expected Abraham to give him tithes, and he simply accepted them as his right when they were given. Abraham gave him "the spoils" or "the pick of the spoils," or, as one version renders it, "the top of the heap."

Under the law of Moses, Levi and the priests, by virtue of their office, received tithes from the other tribes. But Israel's priests, long centuries even before they were born, gave tithes to Melchizedek in the person of Abraham. Therefore, Melchizedek was greater than Aaron, and Melchizedek's priesthood was superior to Aaron's priesthood.

Furthermore, Melchizedek's preeminence is evident in *what he extended to Abraham*. He blessed Abraham and, adds the writer of Hebrews, "without all contradiction the less is blessed of the better" (7:7). The priestly tribe and family, while still in Abraham's loins, were blessed by Melchizedek and consequently were inferior to him. Melchizedek's lordship and preeminence cannot be contradicted.

(5) THE PERMANENCE OF MELCHIZEDEK (7:8)

Melchizedek's permanence is then discussed. "And here men that die receive tithes; but there he receiveth them, of whom it is witnessed that he liveth" (7:8). The two words *here* and *there* illuminate the argument. "Here" refers to the Levites, whose office was continued from generation to generation by natural succession. One man died and another took his place. "There" refers to Melchizedek, who had neither predecessor nor successor in his office. "He liveth," says the writer of Hebrews. There was no end to his priestly reign.

(6) THE PRIMACY OF MELCHIZEDEK (7:9-10)

Finally, the primacy of Melchizedek is emphasized. "And as I may so say, Levi also, who receiveth tithes, paid tithes in Abraham, for he was yet in the loins of his father when Melchisedec met him" (7:9-10). The entire Aaronic priesthood is thus shown to be of a lesser order than that of Melchizedek. Christ was a priest, not after the inferior order, but after the order of Melchizedek; hence the undoubted lordship of Christ as priest.

The writer of Hebrews is inexorably pursuing his goal, forcing his readers to see how much more they have in Christ than they ever had in Judaism and the Levitical ritual. Why go back to an inferior priesthood when, in the Lord Jesus, they have a supreme and sovereign priest acknowledged, in type if not in actual fact, by no less a person than Abraham himself, the founder of their race? Who would want a high priest drawn from among Aaron's sons when they can have something far better in Christ?

b. THE UNDENIABLE LEGALITY OF CHRIST AS PRIEST (7:11-22)

The priesthood in Israel came to its full flower in the days of David. True, the Temple was not yet built, but David was making preparation for it, and there was great expectancy. David himself was busy writing half the songbook of Israel. He threw the whole weight of his influence behind the nation's religious life. The priests and Levites had his unqualified support in their work. He arranged the priesthood into twenty-four courses so that each man could have an opportunity to minister.

(1) THE CHANGE IN THE PRIESTLY ORDINANCE (7:11-14)

After David, things were never the same. Even Solomon, who built the Temple and showed great initial promise, eventually drifted off into materialistic and idolatrous pursuits.

(a) THE TRIBAL DESCENT CHANGED (7:11)

Yet, it was while the Levitical priesthood was at the height of its prosperity that it received its first hint of a change. Many questions must have been raised at the prophetic word of David in Psalm 110 regarding a dynastic change in the priestly ordinance. It was an inspired utterance in which the existing priesthood was weighed and found wanting and a new one named to eventually take its place. There is no doubt that the writer of Hebrews had this in mind as he began this new thrust in his argument.

(b) THE TITLE DEED CHANGED (7:12-14)

But how could the priesthood be changed? The title deeds of the priesthood were all made out to Aaron and were confirmed as such in the law. But laws can be changed by those properly constituted to do so. Every nation's legal code needs revision as time goes on, and Israel's was no exception. Of course, not just anybody could change the law of Moses; but the One who gave it could. That He intended to do so He declared prophetically in Psalm 110.

The reason for the change was to enable Christ to be a priest legally. "For the priesthood being changed, there is made of necessity a change also of the law. For he of whom these things are spoken pertaineth to another tribe, of which no man gave attendance at the altar. For it is evident that our Lord sprang out of Juda; of which tribe Moses spake nothing concerning priesthood" (Heb. 7:12-14). Thus the title deed to the priesthood, long in the hands of Aaron and the Levites, had to be changed. The requirements and the restrictions of the Mosaic law made that imperative.

(2) THE CHANGE IN THE PRIESTLY ORDER (7:15-19)

With the change in the ordinance came the consequent change in the priestly order. Aaron was replaced by Melchizedek, to whom, in any case, he was an inferior, as the writer has already shown.

(a) THE INHERENT WONDER OF THE NEW ORDER (7:15-17)

There is a wonder in this new order that should excite the imagination of every instructed believer, a wonder of design, dynamism, and durability.

How wonderfully God designed the Melchizedek priesthood and hid it away in His Word from the very beginning of His dealings with the Hebrew people! The seed of this new and superior priesthood was planted in the days of Abraham, and the patriarch himself was brought into subjection to it and, with him, all his unborn race. The seed came into full flower in the days of David when the rival Aaronic priesthood was at its zenith, and the flower was quietly displayed by David in the prophetic greenhouse of Psalm 110. It has now come to full fruit in the person of Christ (7:15).

And what an amazing priesthood it is. Its dynamism is drawn, not from the law but from life. A cold, formal, mechanical law kept the Aaronic priesthood in place (7:16).

But Christ is a priest because of the untrammeled, unhindered, unlimited power and vitality of an endless life! The Aaronic priests grew feeble, took to their beds, and died. Christ has conquered death and all its powers and lives forever in the power of an endless life. It is this that gives His priesthood not only its dynamism but its durability. He is "a priest for ever after the order of Melchisedec" (7:17).

(b) THE INHERENT WEAKNESS OF THE OLD ORDER (7:18-19)

In stark contrast with the inherent wonder of Christ's priesthood is the inherent weakness of Aaron's. There was neither power nor profit in his priesthood. Although his priesthood was elaborate, gorgeous, and surrounded with rich and symbolic ritual, it was, after all, only a shadow priesthood. It had the capacity to satisfy neither God nor man.

It was a bankrupt and unprofitable system at best, unable to make anything perfect. Yet God, by His very nature, demands perfection. As Isaac Watts wrote:

> Not all the blood of beasts
> On Jewish altars slain;
> Could give the guilty conscience peace
> Nor wash away one stain.

That is how weak and unprofitable the Aaronic priesthood was! God has "annulled" it and replaced it with something better, something that really works: Christ's priesthood. How ridiculous it would be for an enlightened Hebrew to consider for a moment going back to the rags and tatters of the Levitical system when he could have the reality in a perfectly garbed Christ!

(3) THE CHANGE IN THE PRIESTLY ORDINATION (7:20-22)

The ordination of Christ to the priesthood was quite different from the ordination of the sons of Aaron. No Old Testament priest was inducted into office with an oath. Theirs was a purely hereditary function. Moreover, they had no pledge from God that their order would continue forever. Remember, when the writer of Hebrews was penning his epistle, the Temple was still standing in Jerusalem, and the priests were still going through the meaningless motions of an obsolete ritual. A few short years later the Romans would come, destroy the Temple, and deport people and priest alike. For many centuries the Levitical functions have literally ceased. That was God's way of forcing upon the attention of the Hebrew people the total redundancy of their priesthood and ritual.

In contrast to all this, Christ was inducted into office by a *singular oath*, for God Himself has sworn that Christ's priesthood will last forevermore.

In addition, the Lord Jesus has *a superior operation* as priest. He has become "a surety of a better testament" (7:22). He is personally pledged to see that His priesthood works. The old, Mosaic covenant barred Christ from the priesthood, but that is all done away with now, and a New Covenant, focusing everything on Christ, has taken its place. The writer will have more to say about that covenant when he finishes hammering home the truths concerning Christ as priest.

He has one more truth to present along this line. He has demonstrated the undoubted lordship and the undeniable legality of Christ as priest. He rounds out his argument by underlining the undying life of Christ as priest.

c. THE UNDYING LIFE OF CHRIST AS PRIEST (7:23–8:5)

A sick person has a family doctor, familiar with his case and his entire medical history, having attended him since birth. But the doctor dies, so the patient must start all over again with a new doctor.

A businessman has a lawyer who knows his affairs and has represented him since the day he first incorporated his business. He has won many a legal battle for him, but the lawyer dies and the businessman must start over again with someone new.

A country has a democratic or republican form of government. Every few years the entire leadership is disrupted and changed so that the actual running of national affairs becomes the business of bureaucrats and petty officials. Leadership is thrust into new and inexperienced hands.

A sinner has deep and continuing needs. Under the Levitical system, he can come to the altar and find there a priest to help him in his hour of need. But the priest to whom he comes, the priest who knows him, understands him, sympathizes with him, and cares for him has died, so the sinner, with all his secret faults, must find another one, someone who is a stranger to him. He must start all over again.

(1) WHY HE IS ABLE TO MINISTER TO US (7:23-28)

How wonderful it would be to have a great physician, an advocate, a king, a priest who would never die! That is exactly what we have in Christ.

The Lord Jesus is able to minister so well for us because He is *a continuing priest*. As the writer of Hebrews puts it, "And they truly were many priests, because they were not suffered to continue by reason of death: but this man, because he continueth ever, hath an unchangeable priesthood" (7:23-24).

And what *a capable priest* He is. Many a man has been forced to place his affairs into the hands of an incompetent person, with disastrous results. Nothing could be worse than to be shut up to the services of one man, with no hope of a change, only to find that man totally unfit for his duties. Imagine having to submit permanently to the inefficient, bumbling practices of an unskilled doctor! Imagine having to trust the far-reaching concerns of a giant corporation to the hands of a dullard attorney! Imagine having to trust the affairs of a nation to a shortsighted, opportunist, pigheaded politician. Imagine having to trust your soul's welfare to the careless attention of an incompetent, disqualified priest! The Lord Jesus is a capable priest, more capable, indeed, than any other who has ever aspired to such office. "Wherefore he is able also to save them to the uttermost that come unto God by him, seeing he ever liveth to make intercession for them" (7:25). He is the only priest we need.

He is not only continuing and capable, He is also *a consecrated priest*. He showed it in His life; "for such an high priest became us, who is holy, harmless, undefiled, separate from sinners, and made higher than the heavens" (7:26). No other priest ever had a testimony like that! Godward, He was holy, fully satisfying all the righteous claims of a holy God. Manward, He was guileless, free from all malice and craftiness and duplicity. Selfward, He was undefiled, without any taint of sin. His whole life was consecrated to the ministry for which He had come into the world and for which He has now ascended higher than the heavens. He mingled with sinners, but he was separate from them. Now He is enthroned, never again to be assailed by evil men.

He proved Himself to be a consecrated priest in His death. "Who needed not daily, as those high priests, to offer up sacrifice, first for his own sins, and then for the people's: for this he did once, when he offered up himself" (7:27).

The reference strikes at the roots of the dogma of the Mass. In the Mass, Christ is offered daily as "an unbloody sacrifice." The whole concept is unscriptural. The Lord's death on the cross of Calvary is of such eternal significance that, although He intercedes daily, He never has to renew the sacrifice. The Old Testament priests had to, but not Christ, our priest. This is one of the superior provisions of Calvary. That is why we have a better Savior. That is why, as priest, the Lord Jesus has no peer.

He is a consecrated priest in eternity. "For the law maketh men high priests which have infirmity; but the word of the oath, which was since the law, maketh the Son, who is consecrated for evermore" (7:28). The Old Testament priests were "infirm" ("constitutionally weak") but not so Jesus! He is "consecrated" a High Priest forever. The endless ages of eternity will come and go, and He will still be there, the Son, our priest. That is why He is able to minister for us so superlatively well. He is a continuing, capable, and consecrated priest.

(2) WHERE HE IS ABLE TO MINISTER FOR US (8:1-5)

And now the writer would sum up all that has been said of Christ as a priest and present the crowning reason that all lesser priests must fade away before Him as the moon before the rising sun.

Think of where He ministers for us: in *the place of majesty* itself. "Now of the things which we have spoken this is the sum: we have such a high priest, who is set on the right hand of the throne of the Majesty in the heavens" (8:1).

Such a high priest! We can picture, perhaps, a man from Moab visiting the camp of Israel on the annual Day of Atonement. He sees a man in gorgeous vestments wearing a mitre on his head and a priceless, gem-studded breastplate on his heart. His rich robes sweep down to the ground and are hemmed with bells and pomegranates. The man from Moab speaks to a nearby Hebrew. "Who's that?" he says.

"That is Aaron," he is told. "He is our high priest, brother of Moses. When we were redeemed from bondage in Egypt, Aaron was Moses' prophet before the throne of Pharaoh; now he is our priest before the throne of God."

The Moabite is impressed. He looks at the crowds. It seems as though every man, woman, and child in the vast camp is present. "Is this some special kind of a day?" he asks.

"Yes," he is told, "this is the annual Day of Atonement. On this day of the year, by divine decree, we are ceremonially cleansed from our sins as a people."

The Moabite looks around. "I see some animals tethered over there," he says. "There is a bullock and a couple of goats, as well as some rams. I suppose these are going to be sacrificed."

His informant enlightens him. "On this day and only on this day in the whole year, our high priest will be permitted to go into the Tabernacle yonder. He will go in through that curtained doorway, pass through the Holy Place, pass an inner curtain we call the veil, usually kept closely drawn, and stand in the Holy of Holies, in the immediate presence of God. Do you see that fiery, cloudy pillar yonder? It is called the Shekinah. It is the visible token that the living God is in residence. It rests upon the mercy seat, between the cherubim, upon the sacred ark, inside the veil.

"The high priest will go in there. Then he will come out and he will take those two goats. He will slay one of them and go back into the Holy of Holies with its blood, which he will sprinkle on and before the mercy seat. Then he will come back out again and take the remaining goat. He will confess all our sins over the head of that goat. Then it will be given into the hand of a ritually clean man who will lead it out into the desert, bearing our sins, there to be left to die abandoned and alone. Thus our sins are cleansed and carried away for another year."

"That's very interesting," says the Moabite, "but what's that big bullock for? He seems like a fine animal. It's the biggest bullock I have ever seen."

"Oh, I forgot to tell you about that. The bullock is for the priest. Before he can do anything about our sin, he has to do something about his own. That's what the bullock is for."

The Moabite looks astonished. "Two small goats to take care of all the sins of this vast crowd," he says, "and a great big bullock for the sins of the priest! Why is that?"

"Well, you see," says his friend, "sin in us is bad enough, but sin in him is far more serious. His sin looms larger in God's sight than all of ours."

Israel had such an high priest. It was all very disappointing. We want something better than that. We want a priest who is *holy*. We want a priest who is sinless, spotless, and undefiled, one who is separate from sinners. One who is as good as God is good, absolutely good. We want *such* an high priest, One who is holy. And we have "such an high priest."

Another man chimes in. "That's all very well," he says, "but there is something very cold about goodness in the abstract. To be perfectly honest, the thought of someone who is absolutely holy is rather a frightening one to me. Someone who is always right, never wrong; well, I find that rather formidable."

"What kind of a priest do you want, then?" says the man from Moab.

"Well, of course, I would like my priest to be holy, but I do wish he could also be *human*, one who is touched, so to speak, with the feelings of our infirmities. I don't want a sinful priest—God forbid! But I should like to have a sympathetic priest, one who is human enough to know our frame."

"I see what you mean," says the Moabite.

"Yes," continues the newcomer, "I want a priest who knows what it is like to live in this sinful world, who knows what it's like to be tempted and tried."

He warms to his theme. "I want a priest who lives in a home like mine, with a crowd of relatives, some of whom aren't very nice, a poor home where life is a struggle. Anyone who is going to be a priest ought to have to know what it's like to get up at five o'clock in the morning, to sweat at hard manual labor on starvation wages. He ought to have to rub shoulders with the world, get into the mainstream of life where men curse and tell lies, where things can be brutal and ugly. He needs to know what it's like to be crowded, misunderstood, contradicted, slandered, cheated, betrayed. He should have to face cruelty, be hurt, know what it is to suffer, to have a body wracked with pain. He should know what it's like to be isolated, vulnerable, hated by those able to do injury. This is a mean world we live in. He ought to experience what it's like. I want such an high priest. One who is human as well as holy."

The man from Moab has become thoughtful. "You know," he says, "I agree. But I want something even more. I would like to have a priest who is *helpful* —not just good and kind and very human. You know, in my country we have gods who are made of wood and stone. I have often prayed to them, but it doesn't help very much. They can't see, they can't hear, they can't speak, or know, or feel. It's really very silly. A human priest, if he was just a human priest, would be rather like that."

"What do you mean?" asks the Israelite.

"It's hard to explain," says the man from Moab, "but you see all these people? Suppose they all began to ask questions and make requests of that high priest of yours. How many could he hear at once? How many could he help? Think of it—three million people all asking him for something at once. All he would hear would be a babel of noise."

"I see what you're getting at," says one of the Hebrews. "You want a priest who is God as well as man, and who has the attributes of Deity—omnipotence, omniscience, omnipresence—One who can hear you and me and Isaac here and all these people and all your people. Good point!"

"Yes," says the Moabite, "give me a priest who is helpful, who is able to help because he controls all the factors of space and time."

And that is what we want—"such an high priest." We want One who can represent us truly at the throne of God, where the action is, where ultimately all accounts will have to be settled.

We want a priest Who is holy, human, helpful. We want a priest Who can satisfy every demand of the law, every righteous claim of God, One who can silence Satan and solve problems. We want *such an high priest*. And, blessed be God! We have One!

> Guilty, vile and helpless, we,
> Spotless Lamb of God was He,
> Full atonement, can it be?
> Hallelujah, what a Savior!

Lifted up was He to die,
"It is finished," was His cry;
Now in heaven exalted high!
Hallelujah, what a Savior!

When a person approaches even a human throne he kneels before it and awaits permission to stand. The Lord Jesus has approached the highest, loftiest throne in the whole universe and, instead of kneeling before it, has seated Himself there, at God's right hand as an equal. "Such an high priest!" Surely that should be our echoing exclamation when we think of One who can do a thing like this. To think that there is One in glory who is able to do a thing like that! And to think that He has a heart that beats for His own! Whoever would want some other priest, no matter of what order, upheld by no matter what system, when he can have a great High Priest like that?

Now that place of majesty where our priest is enthroned is also *a place of ministry*. It is the true place of ministry. He is "a minister of the sanctuary, and of the true tabernacle, which the Lord pitched, and not man. For every high priest is ordained to offer gifts and sacrifices: wherefore it is of necessity that this man have somewhat also to offer" (8:2-3). Later in the letter the writer comes back to this theme and gives a brief description of the Tabernacle and its spiritual significance. Here he mentions it in passing and only because it crowns his argument.

After all, the Tabernacle Moses built was a mere model of the heavenly tabernacle. The Old Testament priests ministered in the model, but Christ ministers in the true tabernacle in heaven. The high priest in the Old Testament could only approach God after having made the appropriate sacrifices. These were constantly repeated as the years came and went. Christ, too, has approached God with the appropriate sacrifices—the sacrifice to end all sacrifices, the sacrifice of Himself.

In contrast with the true place, the heavenly tabernacle where Christ ministers as our priest, is the shadowy, typical Tabernacle pitched by Moses on earth. The only purpose of that model in the wilderness and the elaborate service associated with it was illustrative. The entire fabric of worship connected with it was intended to be a shadow of the ultimate reality in heaven. The whole Levitical ritual was meaningless if divorced from Christ. Meaningless! So meaningless that, were He on earth, Christ could not be a priest at all according to the Levitical rule (8:4-5).

In the Old Testament it was not until Moses, the mediator of the covenant, had made purification of sins and gone up the mount to God (Ex. 24) that Aaron was appointed high priest and his sons set apart to minister in the priestly office (Ex. 28). There was no priesthood in Egypt at all. Similarly, it was not until the Lord Jesus had completed the work of redemption and ascended on high that He was called of God a High Priest after the order of Melchizedek. While on earth He was not a priest at all, as Paul here states. Israel was redeemed and baptized unto Moses in the cloud and in the sea and set apart by the blood of the covenant as a holy people before ever Aaron was made a priest. The priest, in Israel, was appointed to maintain the people in the blessings that were already theirs.

All this is equally true of us. God saves us in our sins as and where we are. He also saves us from our sins, sets us apart for Himself, and gives us access to Himself without the intervention of any priest. If people would understand this, they would soon see through the pretensions of man-made priests.

Yet He *is* a priest; He is a great High Priest. He is a real priest, a rightful priest, a royal priest with a lordship, a legality, and a life unsurpassed. Thus the writer concludes this section of his letter. The superior provisions of Calvary have provided us with a better savior, one who is both preeminent and a priest. But if Calvary has provided us with a better savior, it also has provided us with a better security. This is the next great theme of the epistle.

IV
We Have a Better Security
(8:6-13)

A. It Is an Improved Covenant (8:6)
B. It Is an Imperative Covenant (8:7-8)
C. It is an Important Covenant (8:9-12)
    1. Mindful (8:9)
    2. Meaningful (8:10)
    3. Memorable (8:11)
    4. Merciful (8:12)
D. It Is an Implemented Covenant (8:13)

IV

We Have a Better Security
(8:6-13)

There are a number of covenants in the Bible; two of them are in view in this section of the Hebrew epistle. The covenant referred to as "the first covenant" is the conditional and temporary Mosaic covenant, the covenant of the law. The promises of that covenant were conditioned upon the fulfillment of its terms by the Hebrew people. It offered life to those who kept the law (Ex. 19:1-8). It contained the commandments (20:1-26), in which were expressed the righteous will of God; it contained "judgments" (21:1-24) governing Israel's social life; and it contained "ordinances" (24:12–31:18) dealing with the religious life of Israel. These three elements made up "the law." The religious system of Israel was embraced by this covenant. The commandments were a "ministration of condemnation" and of "death" (2 Cor. 3:7, 9). The ordinances provided Israel with a high priest to represent the people before God and the sacrifices to cover their sins until such time as Calvary could take them away.

The covenant referred to as "the New Covenant" stands in complete contrast to the Mosaic covenant, for its promises are better and its terms unconditional. The writer of Hebrews is about to demonstrate that we have a better security under the New Covenant than was ever offered Israel under the Old.

A. IT IS AN IMPROVED COVENANT (8:6)

First, we have an improved covenant. The Lord Jesus, our great High Priest has "obtained a more excellent ministry" and is also "the mediator of a better covenant, which was established upon better promises" (8:6). When Moses presented Israel with "the first covenant," the people foolishly abandoned the ground of grace and put themselves under the law. "All that the Lord hath spoken we will do," they said, and Moses "returned the words of the people unto the Lord" (Ex. 19:8). It was the answer of complete ignorance. Before long they were making the golden calf and exposing themselves to such wrath that, had not Moses assumed the role of mediator, their whole history would have ended then and there (32:1-

14). Instead of that kind of a covenant, we have an unconditional one, an improved one, indeed, in which God has assumed all the commitments. It is a covenant that cannot fail because the Lord Jesus, who fulfilled to the letter every last demand of the Mosaic covenant, has undertaken to administer and mediate the new one.

B. IT IS AN IMPERATIVE COVENANT (8:7-8)

The provision of a New Covenant was absolutely imperative for two reasons. First, the Old Covenant was poor, "for if that first covenant had been faultless, then should no place have been sought for the second" (8:7). The Old Covenant was not faulty in itself, inasmuch as it did fulfill the purpose for which it was intended: to quicken the conscience and to convict of sin. But it was faulty inasmuch as it simply could not take away sin or give the guilty conscience peace.

Second, a New Covenant was promised. The writer quotes from Jeremiah 31:31-34, where God promised a New Covenant to Israel. Understand what he is saying. Christian believers are included in the good of this covenant, but it is not, in essence, a promise to build a church. It is a New Covenant with *Israel*. It made the church and Christianity possible, but the New Covenant itself was made with Israel and with Judah. The New Covenant began at Calvary and runs on through the millennial age and thence to eternity. The church, as such, is a mystery that began at Pentecost and runs on to the rapture and thence to eternity. The writer of Hebrews introduces the subject of the New Covenant here, not to prove that the church is fulfilling that covenant, but to prove scripturally to the Hebrews that the Old Covenant was temporary and that a new one was promised. Therefore, they should not be surprised at the setting aside of the Old Covenant.

C. IT IS AN IMPORTANT COVENANT (8:9-12)

It is a particularly *mindful* covenant because it takes fully into consideration the failure under the first one. "We will" is what characterized the first covenant; "I will" is what marks out the new one.

It is a particularly *meaningful* covenant. "For this is the covenant that I will make with the house of Israel after those days, saith the Lord; I will put my laws into their mind, and write them in their hearts: and I will be to them a God, and they shall be to me a people" (8:10). The phrase "after those days" is clear enough. The Jeremiah prophecy is to be fulfilled, as far as Israel is concerned, after the whole period of the nation's unbelief is over. Then, during the millennial age, God will engrave His Word upon their minds and hearts, upon the understanding and the emotions, upon the whole man. There is to be at that time a full conversion of the Hebrew remnant, and a God-people relationship will be established and made effective by Him. Since the New Covenant is based upon Calvary, however, the church can and does benefit from it (Matt. 26:27-29).

It is a particularly *memorable* covenant. It will be unforgettable. The Old Covenant recognized the abysmal ignorance of the people. Teachers were needed to expound its truths. In its very essence it was rudimentary, especially adapted to a people in the kindergarten of the school of God. The New Covenant will be based upon an intuitive knowledge of God possessed by all who enter the millennial kingdom (8:11).

Moreover, it is a particularly *merciful* covenant. "For I will be merciful to their unrighteousness, and their sins and their iniquities will I remember no more" (8:12). It is a covenant based upon that full and final solution of the sin question made possible by Calvary.

D. It Is an Implemented Covenant (8:13)

"In that he saith, A new covenant, he hath made the first old. Now that which decayeth and waxeth old is ready to vanish away" (8:13). So much so, indeed, that only a faint shadow of the Old Covenant remained, even as the writer penned his letter, in the obsolete and outworn Temple services, soon themselves to come to an abrupt and prolonged end.

In view of the importance of this New Covenant, we need to understand its relationship both to Israel and to the church. Five clear references to the New Covenant are in the New Testament (Luke 22:20; 1 Cor. 11:25; 2 Cor. 3:6; Heb. 8:8; 9:15). There are also six other incidental references to it (Matt. 26:28; Mark 14:24; Rom. 11:27; Heb. 8:10-13; 12:24). The important thing to clarify is the relationship between the New Covenant—appealed to by the writer of Hebrews—and the promise of the New Covenant in Jeremiah 31:31-34.

Several important considerations call for our attention. First, the blood shed on Calvary is the basis of all the blessings of the believer in the present age. Believers now, therefore, participate in the *soteriological* aspect of that covenant. Jesus said, "This is my blood of the new testament" (Matt. 26:28, margin). The blood shed on Calvary was that required by the promised New Covenant of Jeremiah, and it was shed for the remission of sins. It is in this aspect of the New Covenant that Christian believers have their share. Although the New Covenant was not made with us, it is ministered to us.

Second, the New Covenant was made with Israel and with Judah, not with the church. The reference to Jeremiah's prophecy of the New Covenant by the writer of Hebrews is clearly *eschatological*. The New Covenant with the Hebrew nation was instituted at Christ's death, but it is not yet in force as far as Israel, as a nation, is concerned. It will be ratified with Israel at the time of the Lord's return when "all Israel shall be saved" (Rom. 11:26-27). This time element is important, for both in Jeremiah and here in Hebrews 8 it points to Israel, not the church.

In Hebrews 8 the writer is making full use of the word *new* in Jeremiah's prophecy and is proving that this one word alone automatically made the Mosaic covenant old. Hebrews 8 does not say that the New Covenant with Israel is in force today.

The Christian believer participates in the spiritual promises of the New Covenant but not in the earthly blessings it also entails. We enjoy those provisions of the covenant that promise salvation, the forgiveness of sins, and the ministry of the Holy Spirit. We have no share in those clauses concerning the land, rest from persecution, and material prosperity. In other words, the soteriological clauses in the New Covenant are *inclusive* and embrace the church as well as Israel and all believers; the eschatological clauses are *exclusive* and belong primarily to the nation of Israel, as distinct from the church, though they also embrace, to some extent, Gentile believers in the end times who will share in Israel's millennial blessing.[1]

---

1. Charles Fred Lincoln says, "The blood of the New Covenant shed upon the cross of Calvary is the basis of all blessings for the believer in the present age. . . . He benefits in the New Covenant as a fellow-citizen of the saints and of the household of God (Eph. 2:19), and not as a member of the commonwealth of Israel (Eph. 2:12)" ("The Covenants," Doctoral diss., Dallas Theological Seminary, 1942, pp. 202-3, as cited by J. Dwight Pentecost, *Things to Come* [Grand Rapids: Zondervan, 1958], p. 123).

V

We Have a Better Sanctuary
(9:1-12)

A. The Human Tabernacle (9:1-10)
   1. Its Sacred Furnishings (9:1-5)
      a. The Definition (9:1)
      b. The Description (9:2-5)
         (1) The Holy Place (9:2)
            (a) The Lampstand: For Enlightenment (9:2a)
            (b) The Loaves: For Enablement (9:2b)
         (2) The Holiest Place (9:3-5)
            (a) The Holy Compartment (9:3)
            (b) The Hidden Contents (9:4-5)
                i. The Golden Censer: For Prayer (9:4a)
               ii. The Ark of the Covenant: For Provision (9:4b)
              iii. The Cherubim: For Protection (9:5a)
               iv. The Mercy Seat: For Pardon (9:5b)
   2. Its Salient Features (9:6-7)
      a. A Daily Limitation (9:6)
      b. A Day-of-Atonement Limitation (9:7)
   3. Its Supreme Function (9:8-10)
      a. Designed as a Parable (9:8-10a)
      b. Discarded as a Parable (9:10b)
B. The Heavenly Tabernacle (9:11-12)
   1. Its Majesty (9:11)
      a. Served by a Greater Priest (9:11a)
      b. Situated in a Greater Place (9:11b)
   2. Its Ministry (9:12)
      a. Secured by a Greater Price (9:12a)
      b. Supported by a Greater Plan (9:12b)

V
We Have a Better Sanctuary
(9:1-12)

In this section the writer of Hebrews compares the earthly sanctuary, given to the Hebrew people, with the true, heavenly sanctuary now opened up for the people of God. Because of the provisions of Calvary, we have a better sanctuary. Israel's earthly sanctuaries, both the Tabernacle and the Temple, were indeed ordained of God but were rudimentary, illustrative, temporary, and suited only for those still in their spiritual infancy. These earthly shrines were given by God only until such time as a higher and more spiritual revelation could be given. Calvary has made such a higher revelation possible.

The writer of Hebrews, in dealing with the sanctuary, resorts to the Tabernacle in the wilderness as the basis for his contrast with the heavenly sanctuary. We might wonder why he chose the Tabernacle rather than the Temple. The Tabernacle was God's provision for His people during their wilderness journey from Egypt to the Promised Land. The Temple was David's idea and, although accepted by God, seems to have been somewhat of an innovation. The types of the Tabernacle are suited to us, as a pilgrim people, redeemed by the blood of the Lamb and making our way home through the hostile environment of this world. The types of the Temple are more suited to the nation of Israel and the millennial reign of Christ.

All the picture books have now been put away. God is calling His people today to a more mature faith based upon spiritual rather than temporal things. To still want the earthly models when access has been provided to the heavenly realities is a serious matter.

Bishop Lightfoot of Durham once wrote: "It [the kingdom of Christ] has no sacred days or seasons, no special sanctuaries, because every time and every place alike are holy. Above all it has no sacerdotal system. It interposes no sacrificial tribe or class between God and man. . . . The only priests under the Gospel, designated as such in the New Testament, are the saints, the members of the Christian brotherhood. As individuals all Christians are priests."[1]

A. The Human Tabernacle (9:1-10)

Sir Robert Anderson says,

> While the old covenant had an earthly sanctuary and a human priesthood, the sanctuary of the new covenant is heaven itself, and the Great Priest who ministers there is no other than the Son of God. . . . So exclusive are the prerogatives of the sons of Aaron, that while on earth not even the Lord Jesus Christ could share them. What a staggering fact it is that, during His earthly ministry, the Son of God Himself could not pass within the veil which screened the antechamber to the holy shrine! . . . The very existence of this antechamber—the "first tabernacle" of Hebrews—gave proof that "the way into the holiest of all was not yet made manifest." An earthly place of worship is proof that the heavenly place of worship is still closed.[2]

Drawing the obvious parallel to efforts in Christendom to set up great shrines and cathedrals with specially consecrated, sacrificing priests, Sir Robert Anderson says, "These great facts of the Christian revelation sweep away the whole structure of the false cult of Christendom. The cult would have us believe that every man upon whose head a bishop's consecrating hands have been placed is a sacrificing priest, with powers and privileges higher than those which pertained to the divinely appointed priests in Israel." Since "an earthly place of worship is proof that the heavenly place of worship is still closed," argues Sir Robert, "the Apostle therefore warned the Hebrew Christians that to set up such a place of worship, with an earthly priesthood, was apostasy, for it denied the efficacy of the work of Christ. And by this test the false religion of Christendom, with its earthly shrines and its earthly priesthood, is proved to be outside the pale of true Christianity." The argument applies with equal force to Mormonism.[3]

1. ITS SACRED FURNISHINGS (9:1-5)

Even though the earthly Tabernacle was a temporary provision for a people still in the picture-book stage of divine revelation, nevertheless it had of necessity "ordinances of divine service, and a worldly sanctuary" (9:1).

---

1. J. B. Lightfoot, *Commentary on St. Paul's Epistle to the Philippians* (Grand Rapids: Zondervan, 1957), p. 181. This is a remarkably enlightened statement from one who was an ordained Church of England priest and a bishop in a segment of the Christian church that places emphasis on special days, cathedrals, liturgy, priests, and the like.
2. Sir Robert Anderson, *The Hebrews Epistle in the Light of the Types* (London: James Nisbet, 1911), pp. 57-58.
3. Ibid.

It was "worldly" in the sense that it was of this world rather than of heaven; it was temporary and impermanent, as is everything else in this world. This truth is enforced here by the use of the Tabernacle rather than the Temple as the basis for comparison. The Tabernacle was a temporary structure suited for Israel's wilderness wanderings on the way from Egypt to Canaan. The Temple was more permanent, although even it had a varied and checkered history and was actually temporary. Even its types refer to a temporary era, namely, the Millennium.

The writer has introduced his theme by making mention of the Tabernacle and its service, so now he touches on some of the basic elements of Tabernacle typology. He does not elaborate on all its typical aspects, just those that make his point.

First he mentions some of the sacred furnishings in *the Holy Place*. The Tabernacle of Israel was made up of three areas. First there was *the outer court*, surrounded by a linen wall suspended on brazen pillars. Access was gained through a gate of colored curtains. Inside the gate was the great brazen altar behind which stood the brazen laver. Then came the Tabernacle itself, covered with four layers of draperies and skins. It was made of boards overlaid with gold and was entered by way of a "door" made of drapes. The Tabernacle was divided into two compartments by a curtained veil. The first compartment was called *"the Holy Place"* and contained a lampstand, a table on which were placed twelve loaves of "shewbread," and a golden altar for burning incense. Beyond the veil was the *"Holy of Holies,"* or "The Holiest of all," as it was sometimes called. Here stood the sacred Ark of the Covenant containing a pot of manna, Aaron's miraculous rod, and the unbroken tables of stone upon which the law was inscribed. The ark was covered with a golden lid called the mercy seat and was overshadowed by golden figures of the cherubim.

The "candlestick," or *lampstand,* as it is more generally called, cast light upon the Holy Place and its contents. Everything was rich and beautiful. All the furniture was made of acacia wood overlaid with pure gold. The visible curtains that comprised the door, the ceiling, and the walls were of fine linen dyed scarlet, blue, and purple. The veil that led into the Holy of Holies was the same. The floor, however, was the desert sand, a significant reminder that the priests were still on earth and that there was nothing permanent about their position. The function of the lampstand was obvious; it was for *enlightenment* so that the priests could see to perform their functions, for no natural light illuminated their work. The golden lampstand itself had a central stem and six branching stems, each stem being surmounted by a vessel to contain the oil that enabled the lamps to burn. The writer of Hebrews does not tarry over the spiritual significance of all this.

Next he mentions the table. The lampstand stood on the priest's left as he entered the Holy Place, whereas the table was at his right. (Interestingly enough, the various pieces of Tabernacle furniture were positioned so as to form a cross.) On the table were twelve *loaves* of bread called the shewbread, one for each of the tribes of Israel. These loaves were changed weekly. The priests ate the loaves and thus, symbolically, feasted upon Christ and received strength and *enablement* for their labors. Again, the writer of Hebrews ignores this typology.

Next the writer mentions the veil and takes us beyond into the *Holy of Holies* itself. He will come back later in the epistle to elaborate on the spiritual significance of the veil.

The Most Holy Place was a perfect cube, both in the Tabernacle and in the Temple. It was "all glorious within" and was lighted by the mysterious Shekinah cloud that rested upon the mercy seat. The Most Holy Place is a type of the Lord Jesus in His inner and hidden beauties only occasionally glimpsed by men but fully appreciated by God. The writer of Hebrews has nothing to say about that. He is touching only lightly on all these things. His purpose is to sketch an outline of the Tabernacle for his readers. He will shade in none of its colors; he will give it little body, for, after all, was it not all transitory and temporary?

Next the writer mentions the golden censer, and here the expositor runs into one of the major problems connected with the epistle. Why is the golden altar of incense ignored, and why is mention made of a *golden censer,* and why is that censer said to be in the Holy of Holies?

The ordinary censers used in connection with the tabernacle worship were made of brass (copper) and had to do symbolically with prayer. The use of brass (copper) suggests, no doubt, the poverty and limited value of our own unaided prayers.

On the great Day of Atonement the high priest used a golden censer. A detailed description of the ritual connected with the Day of Atonement is given later in this chapter. We need to note something here, however, of considerable interest. In the normal, daily course of events, the priest would burn the incense on the *golden altar* that stood in the Holy Place near the veil. The clouds of perfume would arise and fill the Holy Place and filter into the Holy of Holies. But on the Day of Atonement the ritual was different. Once a year, on this day, the high priest would take the golden censer and fill it with live coals from the great brazen altar of sacrifice that stood in the outer court. Then he would carry the censer with its glowing coals into the Holy Place. He would pass right by the golden altar, for, on this one day of the year, it had no function. A higher and more significant ritual was being enacted. As he passed the barrier of the veil and went on into the Holy of Holies, the high priest would throw incense onto the burning coals in the golden censer in his hand. Clouds of incense would rise, filling the Holy of Holies, symbolic, surely, of the rich and effective prayers of Christ Himself. Thus the high priest came into God's presence.

That is why, here in this epistle, the most Holy Place is said to contain the golden censer. No matter where it was ordinarily kept, its place of use was in the most Holy Place on the Day of Atonement.

Next the writer mentions the *Ark of the Covenant* and its contents. If the censer symbolized prayer, the contents of the ark symbolized God's *provision* for His people in the wilderness. It contained a pot of manna, the bread from heaven upon which Israel feasted in the wilderness. God is concerned about the *physical* needs of His people. It contained Aaron's rod that budded—a dead stick that, at the appropriate time, had miraculously produced flowers and fruit. God is concerned with the *spiritual* needs of His people. It contained the tables of the covenant, the law of Moses, those great precepts and principles for governing Israel's daily conduct, written by the finger of God. God is concerned with the *moral* needs of His people.

All this was in the ark, which in itself spoke of Christ, symbolizing the great fact that only He can meet fully our physical, spiritual, and moral needs. In Him all our needs are supplied.

Above the ark were the wrought, golden figures of the *cherubim.* These spoke of *protection;* in particular, they guarded God's redemptive rights. They faced inward and downward, forever gazing, so to speak, upon the blood that was on the *mercy seat* on top of the ark.

Associated with the cherubim, beaten out of the same piece of gold, was the lid of the ark, called the *mercy seat.* Upon this mercy seat rested the Shekinah cloud, the visible manifestation of God's presence in the midst of His people in Old Testament times. The mercy seat speaks of *pardon.* Even Israel's high priest could not stand for a moment in that holy presence except when he brought with him a basin of blood from a freshly slain sacrifice. That blood he sprinkled on and before the mercy seat. Thus, and only thus, was he allowed to appear before God.

2. *ITS SALIENT FEATURES (9:6-7)*

Having described the sacred furnishings of the human sanctuary, the writer turns his attention to the salient features connected with it.

The whole emphasis is on the limitations that were inherent in the sanctuary functions of Israel's priests. The ordinary priests were faced with limitation daily. Not once were they allowed, upon pain of instant death, to lift the veil even to so much as peer within the Holy of Holies. They had no access there whatever, for it was forbidden by God that they ever attempt to draw near.

The same limitation was brought home to the high priest dramatically on the Day of Atonement, the only day of the year when he could enter beyond the veil. His ministry beyond the veil was brief and prescribed. As soon as it was accomplished he had to leave God's presence and face the barrier of the veil for another year just as his brethren did.

Since few Christians these days understand Bible typology, we are going to digress at this point to study in further detail the symbolism connected with the all-important Day of Atonement in Israel (Lev. 16). The day was set aside as an annual "feast" (Lev. 23). It was the day when national guilt was reviewed, dealt with, and put away, ceremonially and symbolically. The ritual connected with the day was complex but significant. The Jews still commemorate *Yom Kippur*, but they have discarded the Levitical ritual that made it meaningful.

In Leviticus 16 we have, first of all, *prevalent guilt* (vv. 1-10). This is evident from the enumeration of the various animals that were to be sacrificed.

First a bullock was selected to be used as a sin offering for the high priest. A ram was also set aside to be sacrificed, later, by the high priest as a burnt offering.

At this point, the high priest took off his garments of glory. He remained divested of these until the sacrificial rites of the day had been accomplished. This reminds us at once of the Lord Jesus, who laid aside His glory when He came down here to make atonement for our sin. Nor did He assume that outward glory of His until after the work was finished.

The high priest then had to wash his flesh in water, for here he stood in contrast with Christ who was sinless, holy, and undefiled. After his bath, the high priest put on linen garments. In the typology of the Old Testament, linen is a picture of the righteousness of Christ.

He now selected two goats that were set aside to be used later in making atonement for the guilt of the nation. He also set aside a ram to be used as a national burnt offering. The difference between the sin offering and the burnt offering in the Old Testament is important. In both offerings the sinner placed his hands upon the head of the victim. What happened symbolically, however, was quite different. In the sin offering, all the vileness of the sinner was figuratively transferred to the substitute; in the burnt offering all the virtue of the substitute was transferred symbolically to the sinner. All of that pointed to what we have in 2 Corinthians 5:21: "For he hath made him to be sin for us, who knew no sin, that we might be made the righteousness of God in him."

Having selected the various animals to be used in the ceremony, the high priest presented the two goats before the door of the Tabernacle, where he cast lots to see which goat would be slain and which would become the scapegoat.

All this by way of preparation to show that guilt and sin were prevalent everywhere, even among a redeemed people on their way to the Promised Land. Truly our hearts are "deceitful above all things and desperately wicked" (Jer. 17:9).

Then came *personal guilt* (16:11-14). The high priest now had to take care of his own guilt. He took the bullock and slew it as a sin offering. This was by far the largest animal sacrificed that day. Sin is sin, no matter who the sinner is. But sin in the high priest loomed larger in God's sight than sin in anyone else. Sin in one of the Lord's chosen and consecrated servants is always a more weighty matter than sin in anyone else.

The high priest then took the censer and filled it with burning coals from the altar. He filled his hands with incense. He took the blood of the bullock. Thus protected, he ventured inside the veil of the Tabernacle into the Holy of Holies.

All was beauty and glory within. The Ark of the Covenant was there, covered with gleaming gold and containing objects of great spiritual significance. The mercy seat was there, all of gold. The figures of the cherubim were there, wings overshadowing the mercy seat, faces turned inward and downward as though forever occupied with the blood-sprinkled mercy seat. The Shekinah glory cloud rested there, visible token of God's presence among His people. The light of another world filled that place. The place itself was a perfect cube, its walls curtains of blue, scarlet, and purple fine-twined linen.

As the high priest entered the Holy of Holies, he put incense on the coals in his censer so that thick clouds of perfume filled the place and hid him from view. Thus shielded with that which spoke symbolically of the fragrance of Christ and of Christ's intercessory prayers, he approached the mercy seat. He dipped his finger into the bowl of blood he carried and sprinkled the blood on and before the mercy seat. He did this seven times to symbolize the perfect efficacy of the blood of Christ. Apart from that blood, it would have been death to enter into the Holy of Holies and to stand before a thrice-holy God.

He then retired from the Holy of Holies assured that he was accepted because of the blood. Thus personal guilt was taken care of, and henceforth the high priest could function, on this day, as a type of Christ.

The next stage of the ceremony dealt with *public guilt* (vv. 12-23). The high priest slew the goat for the sin offering and, alone once more, took its blood into the Holy of Holies and sprinkled it as he had done the blood of the bullock. The Levitical ritual emphasizes the aloneness of the priest in this ceremony: "And there shall be no man in the tabernacle . . ." (v. 17). The work of the cross was done by Jesus alone. It was the loneliest work ever performed in the universe.

The high priest again retired from the Holy of Holies, not to go back again for a whole year. He took the blood from the bullock slain for his sins and the blood of the goat slain for the people and put it on the horns of the altar—the Holy Place, the Tabernacle, and the altar all had to be "reconciled" by this blood because of the contaminating nature of human sin.

Now came the central, the most public, and the most impressive part of the ceremony. The high priest took the remaining goat, and it became what was called the scapegoat. The high priest laid his hands upon the head of the goat and confessed over it "all the iniquities of the children of Israel, and all their transgressions in all their sins, putting them on the head of the goat" (v. 21). *All* their iniquities, transgressions, and sins! How God hates sin.

Finally the terrible transaction was finished. The goat stood there bearing, symbolically, in its body, the sin of all.

Now came "a fit man." He took the goat and led it outside the camp, past the furthest tent, on out into the wilderness. On and on, farther and farther, until the camp of Israel was left far behind. Now it was a blur on the distant skyline, now it disappeared altogether below the horizon. On and on they went, the sin-bearer and the fit man. At last, "in a land not inhabited," the man let the creature go and retraced his steps. The goat watched him disappear, bleated, looked around. There was not a blade of grass, not a drop of water. The merciless sun beat down upon the head of the sin-bearer. Its strength was dried up like a potsherd. There was no eye to pity, no arm to save. It died alone, bearing the sin of all.

In the typology of the Old Testament, an unnamed man, as for instance the fit man in this ritual, is usually a type of the Holy Spirit. It was "through the Eternal Spirit" that the Lord Jesus offered Himself without spot unto God. Perhaps nothing in all the Bible more graphically illustrates the horrors of Calvary than that goat standing alone, wilting beneath the weight of a nation's sin. When finally the Holy Spirit withdrew and Jesus was left utterly alone on the cross to cry, "Eli, Eli, lama sabachthani . . . My God, my God, why hast thou forsaken me?" (Mark 15:34), He knew the full horror and weight of our sin.

Two goats were needed to adequately symbolize what took place at Calvary. Often God has to use two types to symbolize one Christological concept. Thus it took both Aaron and Melchizedek to typify Christ's priestly work; it took both David and Solomon to portray Christ's royal power; it takes both the wilderness and Canaan to portray the believer's pilgrimage and position. Here it took two goats—the one symbolized Christ whose blood was shed; the other symbolized Christ who bore our sins.

One would think that with the disappearance of the scapegoat, the work of atonement would be finished. But Leviticus goes on to show us *persisting guilt* (vv. 23-28). The high priest now reentered the Tabernacle—not the Holy of Holies but the Holy Place. Here he took off the linen garments he had worn when making atonement and once again bathed himself. Then he put on his garments of glory again and came forth in splendor from the Tabernacle. The sufferings of Christ and the glory to follow are always linked together in Scripture. Never again will Christ appear in weakness. His next appearing will be in glory and in power.

The high priest now offered his ram for a burnt offering and then offered the nation's ram the same way. The burnt offering was all for God. It symbolized God's satisfaction in the finished work of Christ. It was a worship offering. It is called "a sweet savor offering" because it expressed the Godward side of Calvary and spoke of God's appreciation of His Son. The fat of the burnt offerings was burned upon the altar, the fat symbolizing Christ's inward richness, something only God Himself could fully appreciate. It was forbidden for the Hebrews to ever eat the fat.

At this point, the fit man returned to the camp, having left the scapegoat in the wilderness. He had to wash his clothes and bathe, for even this secondary contact with the scapegoat was ceremonially defiling. It was not until he had thus cleansed himself that he could reenter the camp. His work, however, was not yet done. The blood of the bullock used in the high priest's cleansing and the blood of the goat used in the nation's cleansing, together with the skin, the flesh, and the dung, were given to this fit man who once more went back outside the camp. He there burned all that remained of the sin offerings. Nothing was to be left but ashes—and you cannot rekindle a fire from ashes. God's judgment was fully spent. The fit man then returned, bathed again, and came into the camp.

Now, surely, all would be done! But no. Finally we have *preoccupying guilt* (vv. 29-34). The people were called upon to afflict their souls and to keep the remainder of the day as a day of rest, one of God's appointed Sabbaths—all pointing ahead to the time when God would indeed find His Sabbath rest where we today find ours—in the finished work of Christ. Finally the chapter ends, but not before reminding the people that all this was temporary. The whole thing would have to be repeated "once a year."

Thus it went on throughout all the long centuries of the Old Testament era. It was forced upon the attention of the high priest that he, in himself, had no standing in God's presence. High priest though he was, he had no personal merit, no attainments, no acquired right to appear before God. He was allowed in solely on the ground of shed blood.

3. *ITS SUPREME FUNCTION (9:8-10)*

Thus the writer comes to a discussion of the supreme function of the human Tabernacle. The Tabernacle was *designed as a parable*.

> The Holy Ghost this signifying, that the way into the holiest of all was not yet made manifest, while as the first tabernacle was yet standing: which was a figure [parable] for the time then present, in which were offered both gifts and sacrifices, that could not make him that did the service perfect, as pertaining to the conscience; which stood only in meats and drinks, and divers washings, and carnal ordinances (9:8-10*a*).

The Holy Spirit is thus said to have deliberately arranged the Tabernacle as a depository of typical teaching. It was a parable pointing forward to the future, a species of prophecy indeed. It was planned that way. It taught that the way into the Holy of Holies, the way into God's immediate presence, was not yet opened to men. The Tabernacles's physical structure, with its compartments and its veil, proclaimed it; the sacrifices proclaimed it. The gifts and sacrifices were imperfect; they could never make a conscience clean. Moreover, they were imposed and therefore a burden (Acts 15:10, 28).

But if the Tabernacle was designed as a parable, it is equally true that it is now *discarded as a parable*. The writer says that it and its attending rituals were "until a time of reformation" (9:10*b*). The whole argument of the epistle is that such a time of reformation has come.

B. The Heavenly Tabernacle (9:11-12)

In contrast with the earthly sanctuary is the true, heavenly sanctuary that has now completely and permanently replaced the earthly one in the counsels of God.

1. *its majesty (9:11)*

The heavenly sanctuary has a better majesty than the earthly one. *It is served by a greater priest*, for one thing. "But Christ being come an high priest of good things to come" (9:11*a*), that is, a high priest of "good things realized." As a candle fades into total insignificance before the full blaze of the noonday sun, so the Old Testament priesthood fades into nothing before that of Christ. Who needs a candle when standing in the full blaze of day? As the majesty of the sun obliterates whatever majesty a candle might have had in the darkness of the night, so Christ's majesty obliterates that of the Levitical priesthood.

Moreover, the majesty of our sanctuary is evident because of where it is; *it is situated in a greater place*. Israel's sanctuary was on earth, in the wilderness. Ours is in heaven. Theirs was made with human hands; ours is a "more perfect tabernacle, not made with hands, that is to say, not of this building [creation]" (9:11*b*). It is not connected with the material universe at all.

2. *its ministry (9:12)*

Not only does the heavenly tabernacle have a far superior majesty to that which clung to the earthly Tabernacle, it also has an infinitely superior ministry.

Why? Because it is *secured by a better price*. Everything in the Old Testament depended upon the shedding of the blood of bulls and goats. Christ has offered His own blood. It may well be argued, How could the blood of bulls and calves make any difference in the fitness of an individual to approach God? Sir Robert Anderson has the answer to that: "Just in the same way that a few pieces of paper may raise a pauper from poverty to wealth. The bank-note paper is intrinsically worthless, but it represents gold in the coffers of the Bank of England.

Just as valueless was 'that blood of slain beasts,' but it represented 'the precious blood of Christ' "[4] The "paper" atonement of the Old Testament has now been replaced by the genuine bullion of Christ's atonement. *That* is the currency that must now be offered, because God is no longer honoring the old. During the Southern Confederacy many Southern banks carried on business with Confederate notes. Those are all worthless now, except as museum pieces or collector's items. They certainly cannot be used for the payment of current debts. What folly to go back to bankrupt Judaism when we can come to God with the gold coin of Christ's blood!

In concluding this part of his treatise, the writer points out that the superior majesty of the heavenly tabernacle is *supported by a better plan*—it rests not only upon the better coinage now in circulation but also upon the fact that Christ has entered "once [i.e., once for all] into the holy place, having obtained eternal redemption for us" (9:12b). It will never be repeated! This is in vivid contrast with the annual pilgrimage made by the high priest into the Holy Place of the earthly Tabernacle. Christ has gone in once and once only, because that is all that is necessary. His sacrifice will never be repeated or repudiated. The salvation procured by Christ is eternal.

And with that the writer of Hebrews turns to the concluding argument of this section. We not only have a better Savior, a better security, and a better sanctuary, but we also have a better sacrifice.

4. Ibid, pp. 19-20.

VI

We Have a Better Sacrifice
(9:13–10:39)

A. What Was Wrought by Christ's Sacrifice (9:13-28)
  1. The Old Transgressions Are Removed Forever (9:13-14)
    a. The Limited Value of the Law's Offerings (9:13)
    b. The Limitless Value of the Lord's Offering (9:14)
      (1) Witness of the Cross of the Christ (9:14a)
      (2) Witness of the Conscience of the Christian (9:14b)
  2. The New Testament Was Ratified Forever (9:15-28)
    a. A Brief Statement About Our Benefits (9:15)
      (1) Full Cancellation of an Immense Insolvency (9:15a)
      (2) Full Confirmation of an Immense Inheritance (9:15b)
    b. A Broad Statement About Our Benefactor (9:16-28)
      (1) Our Inheritance Is Conveyed to Us by His Death (9:16-22)
        (a) The Need for His Death Is Stated (9:16-17)
        (b) The Need for His Death Is Studied (9:18-22)
            i. In Light of What Moses Did (9:18-19)
           ii. In Light of What Moses Declared (9:20)
          iii. In Light of What Moses Demonstrated (9:21-22)
      (2) Our Inheritance Is Controlled for Us by His Life (9:23-28)
        (a) His Present Appearing: To Deal with Sin's Power (9:23-24)
        (b) His Past Appearing: To Deal with Sin's Penalty (9:25-28a)
            i. The Unremitting Sacrifices Ordered by the Law (9:25-26a)
           ii. The Unrepeated Sacrifice Offered by the Lord (9:26b-28a)
        (c) His Promised Appearing: To Deal with Sin's Presence (9:28b)
B. What Was Sought by Christ's Sacrifice (10:1-18)
  1. The Shadows of the Past Age (10:1-4)
    a. Its Sad Imperfection (10:1-4)
    b. Its Serious Implication (10:3)
    c. Its Simple Impossibility (10:4)

2. The Shape of the Present Age (10:5-12)
   a. The Miracle Connected with the Descent of God's Son (10:5-9)
      (1) A Body: Fashioned by God from Heaven (10:5-6)
      (2) A Book: Fulfilled for God on Earth (10:7-9)
         (a) Christ's Coming Was Foretold (10:7)
         (b) Christ's Cross Was Foretold (10:8)
         (c) Christ's Competence Was Foretold (10:9)
   b. The Miracle Connected with the Decease of God's Son (10:10-12)
      (1) A Cross to Assure Our Sanctity (10:10)
      (2) A Crown to Assure Our Security (10:11-12)
3. The Shores of the Promised Age (10:13-18)
   a. The Expectation of a Perfect Reign for the Christ (10:13)
   b. The Experience of a Perfect Redemption for the Christian (10:14-18)
      (1) A New Condition (10:14)
      (2) A New Confidence (10:15)
      (3) A New Covenant (10:16-18)
C. What Was Taught by Christ's Sacrifice (10:19-39)
   1. A Tremendous Word of Welcome (10:19-25)
      a. The Great Reality (10:19-21)
         (1) The Place of Access (10:19)
         (2) The Price of Access (10:20)
         (3) The Proof of Access (10:21)
      b. The Great Responsibility (10:22-25)
         (1) As Believers (10:22-24)
            (a) Godward: The Purity of Worship (10:22)
            (b) Selfward: The Possibility of Wavering (10:23)
            (c) Manward: The Priority of Works (10:24)
         (2) As Brethren (10:25)
   2. A Terrible Word of Warning (10:26-31)
      a. The Warning Expressed (10:26-27)
         (1) The Characteristics of the Sin (10:26)
            (a) A Deliberate Sin (10:26a)
            (b) A Damning Sin (10:26b)
         (2) The Consequences of the Sin (10:27)
      b. The Warning Explained (10:28-31)
         (1) The Old Testament Sin: Against God's Government (10:28)
         (2) The New Testament Sin: Against God's Grace (10:29-31)
            (a) The Seriousness of the Crime (10:29)
               i. Rejecting the Son of God (10:29a)
               ii. Refusing the Salvation of God (10:29b)
               iii. Repudiating the Spirit of God (10:29c)

(b) The Solemnity of the Consequences (10:30-31)

    i. Formal Judgment (10:30)

    ii. Fearful Judgment (10:31)

3. A Timely Word of Wisdom (10:32-39)

  a. The Believers Should Think About the Past (10:32-34)

    (1) The Persecution That Once Assailed Them (10:32-34*a*)

    (a) The Reason for It (10:32)

    (b) The Reality of It (10:33-34*a*)

      i. To Show the Faith of Christ to Sinners (10:33*a*)

      ii. To Share the Faith of Christ with Saints ((10:33*b*-34*a*)

    (2) The Persuasion that Once Assured Them (10:34*b-c*)

    (a) Concerning Earthly Loss (10:34*b*)

    (b) Concerning Eternal Gain (10:34*c*)

  b. The Believers Should Think About the Present (10:35-36)

    (1) The Danger of Wavering (10:35)

    (2) The Danger of Weakening (10:36)

  c. The Believers Should Think About the Prospect (10:37-39)

    (1) The Coming Return of the Lord (10:37)

    (2) The Constant Review of Our Lives (10:38-39)

    (a) The Abysmal Contrast Described (10:38)

    (b) The Absolute Confidence Displayed (10:39)

VI

We Have a Better Sacrifice
(9:13–10:39)

The Old Testament Levitical system rested squarely upon sacrifice. Every day countless animals were slain to maintain the religious order.

It is worth noting in passing that the Passover is not a subject of discussion in Hebrews. The Passover was for sinners, the other Levitical offerings were for believers; the Passover taught how people could be redeemed from sin's penalty and bondage, the other offerings teach how those redeemed by the blood of Christ can be kept on their wilderness way as "holy brethren, partakers of a heavenly calling" (3:1).

But every offering was but a token of that greater sacrifice to be made, at length, at Calvary. With the death of Christ the entire religious system of the Old Testament became obsolete. This is basic. The Hebrews must grasp it at all costs. Thus the writer of this epistle embarks upon a thorough examination of Christ's death and its far-reaching implications for all men and especially for the Jewish people.

A. WHAT WAS WROUGHT BY CHRIST'S SACRIFICE (9:13-28)

The death of Christ effected a twofold objective. It completely did away with sin, something the Old Testament sacrifices could never do, and it made possible the introduction of a new testament—one far superior to the covenant upon which the old order rested.

Israel left Egypt a redeemed people, but sin is a pernicious and persistent thing, so the Israelite, although redeemed, was nonetheless a sinner, ever liable to fall. His sin did not put him back under either the doom or the bondage of Egypt, but it did bar him from approaching the sanctuary. Provision had to be made for such sin in the sin offerings. Every time an Israelite sinned he had to bring a sin offering.

But there was more to it than that. The Israelite could contract not only sinful defilement, but ceremonial defilement as well. If he touched a dead body or a bone or even so much as entered a house in which a corpse lay, he became ceremonially defiled. To enter the Tabernacle in such a state was to be cut off from the people of God.

But death was everywhere. Ever since the rebellion at Kadesh-barnea, the grim reaper had been hard at work among the unbelieving generation that had come out of Egypt. Some died natural deaths; some died under God's active judgment. But all were under the sentence; none could escape, for death was everywhere. What hope, then, had any Israelite of maintaining his ceremonial cleanliness? None, unless God made special provision for such a need. And that is exactly what God did provide in the unique sacrifice of the red heifer described in Numbers 19.

1. THE OLD TRANSGRESSIONS ARE REMOVED FOREVER (9:13-14)

The writer's Hebrew readers would be familiar with the Old Testament story. The terrible rebellion of Korah, Dathan, and Abiram had occurred only to be followed by a still wider insurrection of the people against the authority of Moses and Aaron. A plague had broken out in which more than fourteen thousand people died. Had it not been for the intercession of Moses, no doubt the plague would have gone on and on. There were corpses everywhere. Defilement was a common, everyday occurrence throughout the entire camp.

a. THE LIMITED VALUE OF THE LAW'S OFFERINGS (9:13)

Then God gave Israel the ordinance of the red heifer, a ceremonial means for removing ceremonial defilement. No special sin offering was required. The unclean person could cleanse himself, first by being sprinkled with "the water of purification" (water that owed its efficacy to the great sin offering), and then by bathing his whole body. A man who touched a corpse might scrub himself with soap and water and become clinically clean, but that would not make him ceremonially clean.

To wash away his ceremonial defilement, the Israelite had to avail himself of the ordinance of the red heifer. First a red heifer, an animal free from spot or blemish, was taken and was given to Eleazar the high priest. It was taken outside the camp and there slain in the high priest's presence. The blood of the sacrifice was then ceremonially sprinkled seven times before the Tabernacle. This action symbolized the complete and never-to-be-repeated putting away of the believer's sin before God. The body of the red heifer was then burned and reduced wholly to ashes, the ashes were placed in water, and the water was stored in a ceremonially clean place outside the camp. The defiled person was required to go outside the camp, thus confessing that his defilement had cut him off from Israel. There, where the ceremonial water was kept, a clean person was to sprinkle the unclean person with the water. The defilement and the cleansing were both ceremonial and symbolic. A symbolic defilement could be removed by a symbolic ritual.

We need to pause here for a moment and recall what the typology of Numbers 19 is all about.

In any of the sin offerings, the blood-shedding was always the act of the person who had sinned. The same principle applies here. No priest was needed; any clean person could perform the ceremony (Num. 19:13). This teaches that the sprinkling and washing are not symbolic of the work of Christ for us; rather, they speak of our own responsibility to keep ourselves in communion with God by faith and repentance.

The Lord refers to this great ordinance in His conversation with Nicodemus, rebuking him for being a master in Israel but knowing not these things (John 3:10). The ordinance is also key to Ezekiel 36 and 37 and the coming restoration, regeneration, and revival of Israel. The ignorance of Nicodemus was culpable. He should have known about being born of water and the Spirit.

It was by resorting to the water of purification, connected with the ashes of the red heifer, that the Old Testament Israelite proved the continuing virtue and value of the sin offering. It is the same with us—except that we have the reality. We have the Word of God, of which water is often a type in Scripture (Titus 3:5). It is by constant application of the Word of God, and by the repentance that it produces, that we, today, prove the power of Christ's sacrifice to keep us in a position of acceptance and access to God.

The writer of Hebrews fastened upon this particular instance (of the red heifer), because it illustrated in a forceful way the essential ceremonial and symbolic function of the law's offerings. They were indeed of only limited value.

The ritual symbolizes the believer's responsibility to seek restoration of communion with God by faith and repentance after having contracted defilement, innocently, perhaps, during the ordinary course of a day. As we have noted, we have the reality of which the water was the type—recourse to the Word of God (Titus 3:5). By the repentance the Word works in us, the death of Christ is shown to keep us in a state of acceptance and access to God. Washing in Scripture always has to do with practical purity.

b. THE LIMITLESS VALUE OF THE LORD'S OFFERING (9:14)

Contrasted to the limited value of the law's offerings is the limitless value of the offering made by Christ on the cross. "For if the blood of bulls and of goats, and the ashes of an heifer sprinkling the unclean, sanctifieth to the purifying of the flesh: how much more shall the blood of Christ, who through the eternal Spirit offered himself without spot to God, purge your conscience from dead works to serve the living God?" (9:13-14).

How much more! The old transgression is removed forever. Real sin is removed by a real savior.

The first witness to this fact is *the cross of the Christ*. The animals offered in Old Testament times had no wills of their own; they had no spirits that could concur with the act of sacrifice. They were offered by the demand of the law with no consent of their own. Moreover, their lives were transitory, with no saving virtue. But Christ offered Himself, with His own consent, assisting and making effective the sacrifice. His consent was not merely that of a fine spirit, such as could be displayed by any man willing to make an extraordinary sacrifice in the cause of his fellowmen. Christ's consent was that of His own divine personality, the consent of the divine Spirit of the godhead that Christ Himself had within His personality.

Along with the witness of the cross to the limitless value of Christ's offering is the witness of *the conscience of the Christian*. It is the common experience of the Christian that Christ's sacrifice does indeed cleanse the conscience. The inner man is renewed and made alive so that he can truly serve God. What a ritual cleansing could never do, God has done through the death of the Lord Jesus. The old transgression is removed forever.

2. THE NEW TESTAMENT WAS RATIFIED FOREVER (9:15-28)

Christ's death has procured changes of immense value for the believer. Not only has it forever removed the old transgressions, but it has forever ratified the new testament (the word *covenant,* as Vine points out, should really read "testament." The difference is evident. A covenant is an agreement, a contract, but a testament is a will).

a. A BRIEF STATEMENT ABOUT OUR BENEFITS (9:15)

First we are given a brief statement of our benefits under that will as believers. It involves, first of all, *full cancellation of an immense insolvency*. "And for this cause he is the mediator of the new testament, that by means of death, for the redemption of the transgressions that were under the first testament" (9:15).

A person is burdened by a crushing weight of debt. He tries every way within his power to extricate himself, but all his efforts are in vain. The mortgages and liens against him are too great and too many. He only sinks deeper and deeper into insolvency. Nothing but ruin stares him in the face. What can he do but declare bankruptcy and hope that somehow or other, at some future time, he might be able to recover his good name and face his creditors with honor? Then, one morning, he discovers that he is the sole beneficiary of the estate of a billionaire who has died, making him the heir and inheritor of enormous holdings!

That is precisely what has happened to us. We are the spiritual heirs of the Lord Jesus Christ, who has died, leaving us, in His last will and testament, all the immense resources of goodness and grace that were His alone! Our insolvency, our vast debt of sin, and our spiritual bankruptcy are gone!

But better still, we have *full confirmation of an immense inheritance*. We have received "the promise of an eternal inheritance" (9:15b). Two tramps were sitting in the gutter of one of the world's great cities. One was crying. "What's the matter with you?" demanded the other. "Haven't you heard?" said the first. "Rockefeller, the millionaire, died last night." His companion looked at him in astonishment. "Well," he demanded, "so what? You weren't related to him, were you?" "No," said the first tramp. "That's why I'm crying."

Who can measure all the provisions of one eternal inheritance that is ours? The material wealth of a billionaire, left to us by human inheritance, cannot be remotely compared with the incalculable spiritual riches bequeathed to us by Christ. The greater part of the New Testament (as, by some happy inspiration, we call the second part of the Bible) has been written to set forth the wealth that has now come our way. Here, in this Hebrews letter, we have but a brief statement of our benefits.

b. A BROAD STATEMENT ABOUT OUR BENEFACTOR (9:16-28)

We also have, however, a broad statement about our Benefactor, and that is how it should be. We need to get our eyes fixed on Him.

(1) OUR INHERITANCE IS CONVEYED TO US BY HIS DEATH (9:16-22)

First we are told how our inheritance is conveyed to us. Like any other inheritance, it is conveyed by the death of the Testator. *The need for this death is stated*: "For where a testament is, there must also of necessity be the death of the testator. For a testament is of force after men are dead: otherwise it is of no strength at all while the testator liveth" (9:16-17). Since Jesus has died, His will is in force; eternal life and all its accompanying blessings are ours.

The writer of Hebrews, having stated this great fact, now digresses. *The need for this death is studied*. The writer goes back again to the Old Testament. He looks at Christ's death first in the light of *what Moses did*. Moses consecrated the Old Covenant, under which the Hebrews had been reared, with the blood of sacrifice (Ex. 24:4-8).

Today we ratify our agreements with our signature. God has verified His agreement with blood. "For when Moses had spoken every precept to all the people according to the law, he took the blood of calves and of goats, with water, and scarlet wool, and hyssop, and sprinkled both the book, and all the people" (Heb. 9:19). Blood and water together speak of justification by Christ and sanctification in the Spirit. Symbolically, Moses emphasized to Israel the need for death and for the appropriation of all that the death signified if the covenant were to be effective.

Having shown us what Moses did, the writer now emphasizes *what Moses declared*. "This is the blood of the testament," said Moses as he sprinkled the book and the people, "which God hath enjoined unto you" (9:20). First the law was read, then it was received by acclamation by the people, and then it was ratified by the sprinkling of blood. The people promised to do their part; God promised to do His. The covenant went into force, and Moses declared to the people that the blood was an essential part of the covenant. There was to be no mistake about that.

Then the writer of Hebrews drew the attention of his readers to *what Moses demonstrated*. "Moreover he sprinkled with blood both the tabernacle, and all the vessels of the ministry. And almost all things are by the law purged with blood; and without shedding of blood is no remission" (9:21-22). The word *almost* is a prefix to the entire clause. Some things were not cleansed with blood; some were cleansed with water, as the writer of the epistle has but recently shown. Some sins were not cleansed at all by the Levitical ritual, for example, presumptuous sins (Num. 15:30). Study David's prayer in the light of his presumptuous sins of adultery and murder (Ps. 51:17). Some time after the public ratification of the covenant, the Tabernacle was built, and Moses sprinkled this, too, with blood. The temporary structure of the Tabernacle and the temporary agreement of the law alike had to be sprinkled with blood. Such is human sin.

Today many look with revulsion on the shedding of blood that formed such an essential feature of the Old Testament religion. They consider with equal horror the New Testament teaching concerning Christ's blood. They shudder with abhorrence at many of the gospel hymns that emphasize the efficacy of the blood of Christ. Those who thus scorn the shed blood have their eyes blinded both to God's blazing holiness and to the dreadful, radical nature of sin. Sin is a radical and terrible reality that calls for a radical and terrible cure.

So, then, the need for the death of our Benefactor is both declared and demonstrated. The Old Testament ritual, so forcibly carried out by Moses, was intended to teach the Hebrew people that their covenant was based on the shedding and applying of blood. Death was the only means to life. But these Old Testament rituals only anticipated, after all, the far greater and far more effective death of Christ.

(2) OUR INHERITANCE IS CONTROLLED FOR US BY HIS LIFE (9:23-28)

Wills are often contested in court. The benefactor's intentions are set aside, as relatives and other claimants come forward, insisting that the terms of the will be changed. Often clever lawyers can completely annul the intentions of the testator as declared in his will. To ensure that the terms of a will are carried out to the letter as intended by the testator, the ideal thing would be for the testator himself to come back and execute his will himself! Such a thing is patently impossible —except in the case of Christ. That is exactly what He has done. The remaining verses of this section show how our inheritance is now being controlled for us by our Benefactor, who, living in the power of an endless life on the resurrection side of the grave, makes quite sure that His intentions are carried out.

The section sets before us three appearings of the Lord Jesus. First there is *His present appearing* in heaven, His present appearing to deal with *sin's power*. "It was therefore necessary," the writer reminds his Hebrew readers, "that the patterns of things in the heavens should be purified with these; but the heavenly things themselves with better sacrifices than these. For Christ is not entered into the holy places made with hands, which are the figures of the true; but into heaven itself, now to appear in the presence of God for us" (9:23-24).

The Old Testament Tabernacle was a type, a model, that was cleansed ceremonially with blood. On the Day of Atonement every year, the high priest went into the Holy of Holies with a basin of blood to sprinkle afresh the mercy seat. The Lord Jesus has now entered into the reality of which the Tabernacle was but a shadow. He has gone into the real Holy of Holies in heaven, into the very presence of God. He has taken with Him better sacrifices. All the Old Testament sacrifices and offerings converge on Him, therefore His sacrifice is here stated in the plural. He has gone into God's presence on behalf of His people just as did the Hebrew high priest of old. That is the Lord's present appearing. The high priest of Israel could not stay in the Holy of Holies. Soon he had to leave, and the veil fell behind him again, shutting him out for another year. Not so Christ! He appears in God's presence to stay there in order to minister for us as our great High Priest and to deal effectively with the power of sin in our lives.

But Christ's present appearing in heaven for us results from *His past appearing*, His appearing on earth to deal with *sin's penalty*. Again the writer underlines with dogged persistency the same truth. He comes back to it from every possible angle (9:25-28a). The Hebrew Christians must grasp this basic fact: that the Levitical ritual was unremitting. He mentions the interminable foreshadowing of the truth. Year by year the sacrifices and offerings demanded by the law went on and on. The writer still has the Day of Atonement in view, but the offerings of that day were but a few of the countless offerings demanded and given under the law. There were five basic offerings besides a number of subsidiary offerings. Millions of people were obligated to make those offerings. The age of the law continued for 1,500 years. Seas of blood were shed.

The writer mentions not only the interminable foreshadowing of the truth but also the intended failure of the types. The Old Testament sacrifices were offered continually, but, in this very thing, they failed to depict the most important aspect of Christ's death. He was not to be offered again and again. "Nor yet that he should offer himself often . . . for then must he often have suffered since the foundation of the world: but now once" (vv. 25-26). What a devastating blow to the dogma of the Mass with its "unbloody sacrifice" offered daily on altars around the world! Rome says that the Holy Eucharist is a true sacrifice offered up by Jesus Christ and offered by Himself daily through the ministry of the priest whenever the priest celebrates Holy Mass. God says Christ was offered *once*.

The types themselves were wholly inadequate, even as illustrations. They were intended to fail. Obsolescence was built into them right from the start.

The unremitting sacrifices ordered by the law led directly to the unrepeated sacrifice offered by the Lord. He came once! He came at one period, for one purpose, and with one payment. "Now once in the end of the world hath he appeared to put away sin by the sacrifice of himself. And as it is appointed unto men once to die, but after this the judgment: so Christ was once offered to bear the sins of many" (9:26b-28a). Calvary was the focal point of two eternities. All the ages prior looked forward to it, and all the ages since look back to it. There, reared against the world's skyline, at the center of all the ages, is the cross of Christ with its message of eternal significance. Man dies only once and then faces the judgment; Christ can die only once and only once must He bear sin's penalty. The Hebrews had to fully appreciate this. Christendom, too, must come to grips with this truth.

To crown it all, the writer mentions *His promised appearing*, Christ's appearing to take His people away forever from even *sin's presence*. Having borne the sins of many, "unto them that look for him shall he appear the second time without sin unto salvation" (9:28b). On the Day of Atonement, the high priest, having gone into the Holy of Holies to minister on behalf of his people, always reappeared and showed himself to the people. In like manner the Lord Jesus is to appear in the air for His own.

Here, then, was what has been wrought by that better sacrifice of Christ. What folly for an enlightened Hebrew to decide to forfeit all the benefits available to him under the terms of Christ's testament! What folly, indeed, to turn away from the inheritance offered under terms of Christ's will, an inheritance already in force and administered by the risen Christ Himself to His own. Nothing but the grossest ignorance or the blindest and most stubborn unbelief could prefer the old, obsolete, ineffective covenant to the dynamic, comprehensive, glorious new testament.

B. WHAT WAS SOUGHT BY CHRIST'S SACRIFICE (10:1-18)

But the writer of Hebrews has by no means exhausted what he has to say to the Hebrew people about the scope and significance of Calvary. Indeed, his thoughts range wider and wider, higher and higher, and embrace the flickering shadows of yesterday, the solid realities available in Christ today, and the blessed outcome of it all tomorrow.

Few passages, even in an epistle that abounds in glorious truths, excel this passage for the magnificence of the truth it unfolds. It is no wonder that it is followed by one of the sternest of all the book's warnings.

1. THE SHADOWS OF THE PAST AGE (10:1-4)

In the Old Testament era, the Israelites had only shadows. The substance is in Christ. The shadow of a key cannot unlock a prison door; the shadow of a meal cannot satisfy a hungry man; the shadow of Calvary cannot take away sin.

The law was only "a shadow of good things to come, and not the very image of the things" (10:1). The endless offerings of the Levitical ritual could never "continually make the comers thereunto perfect. For then would they not have ceased to be offered? because the worshippers once purged should have had no more conscience of sins" (10:1-2). All the Levitical sacrifices did was lash the offerer's disturbed conscience.

In actual fact, on the Day of Atonement, for example, the ritual simply called back to remembrance the sins of the people. The high priest, as part of the ceremony, had to actually recite over the head of the scapegoat the accumulated misdeeds and transgressions of the entire nation! Thus was there enacted a ceremonial transfer of national sin to a trembling beast that was then led away to "a land not inhabited" (Lev. 16:22), there to expire alone, bearing symbolically the sins of the people. It was instructive, no doubt, and illustrative, but wholly ineffective.

For example, a businessman approaches his banker and requests a loan to finance a business venture. He explains why he wants the money, what profit he expects to make, how he hopes to repay the debt. A wealthy friend agrees to endorse the note and repay the debt should the venture fail. So the loan is made, the promissory note drawn up, the rate of interest agreed upon, and the date of repayment set for a year's time. The businessman signs the note, and his friend endorses it.

The year passes, but the businessman's expectations have not materialized. He goes back to the bank and asks for further credit and for an extension of time on his expired loan. On the same terms of adequate endorsement the banker agrees. He draws up a new promissory note, adding the new indebtedness to the old, staples the old note to the back of the new one, and carries forward the accumulated debt for another year.

Thus it goes on and on, the loans getting larger and larger every year, and the businessman getting deeper and deeper into debt. And each year there is a remembrance made of his former indebtedness and of his new liabilities. The only thing that keeps him afloat is the endorsement of his friend.

That is exactly what happened in the Old Testament. The animal sacrifices were so many promissory notes. By bringing them to the altar, the Hebrews acknowledged their accumulating debt of sin. Each sacrifice carried with it the endorsement of the Son of God, who guaranteed that He would fully repay all the liabilities thus acknowledged by the sinner. The time came, of course, when those notes had to be discharged, which is exactly what the Lord Jesus did when He shed *His* blood on the cross of Calvary. "For it is not possible," says the writer of Hebrews, "that the blood of bulls and of goats should take away sins" (10:4). Where sins are not removed by the blood of Christ, their guilt and liability remain as the sinner's personal responsibility. By rejecting Christ, the Hebrew repudiated the Endorser of His note, so to speak. What folly to go back to the shadows of Judaism when, in Christ, the substance that cast those shadows is to be found.

2. THE SHAPE OF THE PRESENT AGE *(10:5-12)*

Having mentioned the shadows that characterized the Old Testament era, the writer now turns to the solid realities found in the Lord Jesus. He sketches in a few bold lines the shape of things as they now are, so wonderfully different from the shadowy uncertainties of the Old Testament.

a. THE MIRACLE CONNECTED WITH THE DESCENT OF GOD'S SON (10:5-9)

The first great certainty is the coming of the Lord Jesus in the incarnation. The writer quotes from Psalm 40:6-8, draws aside the veil, and reveals the Father and the Son in conference in a past eternity. They are deciding the details of Christ's descent.

The plan was to fashion for Him *a body*. God's mighty and eternal Son would be, to use John Wesley's expressive phrase, "contracted to the span of a virgin's womb." The sacrifices and offerings of the Old Testament can now be written off. God does not want them and found no pleasure in them anyway. There is a better solution to the problem of human sin.

The Hebrews ought not to be strangers to this truth, the writer argues, because of *a Book*. In this Book *Christ's coming was foretold*. "Then said I, Lo, I come (in the volume of the book it is written of me,) to do thy will, O God" (10:7). The writer of Hebrews is still pointing to Psalm 40. The law, the psalms, and the prophets all foretold Christ's coming. His whole life was controlled by the Book. His birth, His behavior, His death, His burial, His resurrection—all were foretold. In type and shadow, in precept and principle, in prophetic vision and direct utterance, the Old Testament was full of the theme. What possible excuse could there be for a person familiar with the Book to turn his back upon the reality in Christ? This is equally true today for a person living in a land where there is an open Bible. We, too, have the Book.

Not only was His coming foretold; *Christ's cross was foretold* as well. David understood full well the total inadequacy of the Levitical system (Ps. 40:6). If David understood it a thousand years before the coming of Christ, how much more the Hebrews, living in the momentous days of Calvary, should understand it. How much more should we, with nearly two thousand years of accumulated Christian testimony upon which to draw, understand the significance of the cross!

Then, too, *Christ's competence was foretold*. Again Psalm 40 is appealed to as proof that the promised Messiah would fulfill the divine counsels. His very acts of submission, dependence, and humiliation were acts of omnipotence. The descent of God's Son from heaven to assume a human body and, in that body, to fulfill God's will was a miracle, a miracle that was foretold, foreshadowed, and foreknown.

b. THE MIRACLE CONNECTED WITH THE DECEASE OF GOD'S SON (10:10-12)

There was to be *a cross*, a sacrifice and an offering whereby we could be sanctified. The will of God took the Lord Jesus to Gethsemane where, in tears and bloodlike sweat, He yielded afresh to God's will. That will took Him to Gabbatha where His visage was "so marred" and on to Pilate's judgment hall where His back was plowed with a Roman scourge and where men heaped upon Him their ridicule and scorn. That same sovereign will took Him to Golgotha and to the grave. "By the which will we are sanctified through the offering of the body of Jesus Christ once for all" (Heb. 10:10). Once for all sin, once for all time! The result of the Lord's obedience was the procuring for us of a once-for-all sanctification, a positional sanctification that nothing can assail.

There was to be not only a cross but *a crown*. If the cross assures us of our sanctification, the crown assures us of our security. "And every priest standeth daily ministering and offering oftentimes the same sacrifices, which can never take away sins: but this man, after he had offered one sacrifice for sins for ever, sat down on the right hand of God" (10:11-12). What volumes that one statement had to say to the Hebrew! Every priest standeth; this Man sat down.

The Old Testament priest's work was never done; there was no rest for him. In all the Old Testament we read of only one priest sitting down—the man Eli,

whose whole personal life, parental life, and priestly life were one long, sad failure. The Old Testament priest had to stand, for his, symbolically, was a work that
could never be finished. Christ has sat down! We rest secure in a finished work.
This is the solid fact that the writer of Hebrews places over against all the dim
shadows of the age gone by.

3. THE SHORES OF THE PROMISED AGE (10:13-18)

Since the Lord Jesus is seated at God's right hand, the future is assured both
for Him and for us.

a. THE EXPECTATION OF A PERFECT REIGN FOR THE CHRIST (10:13)

There is, of course, the expectation of a perfect reign for Him. He is from
"henceforth expecting till his enemies be made his footstool" (10:13). What "great
expectations" there are in the heart of God's beloved Son as He sits upon His
throne! Those mysterious "times or the seasons, which the Father hath put in his
own power" (Acts 1:7) are still being worked out on earth. The Bride is being
made ready; the world is ripening fast for judgment; and the Lord Jesus is waiting, eagerly anticipating the day when He can call home His Bride and turn His
attention to those who for so long have scorned Him and mismanaged His world.
The day is surely coming when He will deal with his enemies, no matter who or
where they are, and usher in that glorious kingdom so long heralded by the
prophets of old.

b. THE EXPERIENCE OF A PERFECT REDEMPTION FOR THE CHRIS-
TIAN (10:14-18)

Along with those great expectations that fill the heart of the ascended Lord
today, there is something for His waiting people on earth: the experience of a
perfect redemption. For, in a spiritual sense, His kingdom has already come.

A new condition is first described: "For by one offering he hath perfected for
ever them that are sanctified" (10:14). The writer of Hebrews is often misunderstood. His warning passages are so dreadful, prolonged, and uncompromising
that many believe they assail the believer's security. Not for a moment! We are
"perfected for ever." What could be plainer than that? This is a positional sanctification, the birthright of every true believer in Christ. One day we will come into
the full realization of what that means, when, all our foes having been subdued,
we enter into perfect, practical sanctification as well. Already, in God's mind, we
are as perfect as His Son. The day will come when that perfection will be fully
seen in our lives—forever.

There is, also, *a new confidence*. "Whereof the Holy Ghost also is a witness to us" (10:15). This is one of the three witnesses of the Holy Spirit mentioned in the New Testament. He witnesses *to* us (Heb. 10:15), *in* us (1 John 5:10), and *with* us (Rom. 8:16). The first has to do with fact, the second with faith, and the third with feeling. Here, of course, it is fact, for the Holy Spirit witnesses to us of the truth of our security in Christ and of our perfect sanctification.

The writer of Hebrews has already discussed a *new covenant* into which the believer is brought. He mentions it again, going back once more to Jeremiah 31. His purpose is to assure believers in the Lord Jesus that they have, indeed, a perfect redemption.

In the quotation here, the Holy Spirit is expressly declared to be the author of Jeremiah's words. As the divine Author of the original statement, the Spirit of God exercises the right of any author to edit and revise and enlarge upon a previous statement. In Jeremiah 31, the covenant was clearly with the house of Israel. Here, in Hebrews, the blessings are deliberately expanded to include a more general and universal group. "This is the covenant that I will make with *them*" (Heb. 10:16, italics added). The "them" originally referred to the house of Israel, and, of course, it still does. Israel is yet to come into the good of the New Covenant as a nation. But here the "them" refers to those previously mentioned in verse 14: "For by one offering he hath perfected for ever *them that are sanctified*" (italics added). By interpretation, the Jeremiah passage belongs to the nation of Israel; by application, it belongs to the Christian.

The successive "I wills" of the covenant make its clauses sure. God's Word is to be permanently and indelibly impressed on our hearts and minds. No longer will we be forgetful or faithless in regard to the Word. The whole sin question is forever settled. We are going to *remember* intuitively all that is of God; He is going to *forget* infinitely all our guilt and shame. "Their sins and iniquities will I remember no more" (10:17).

Then comes the writer's punch line. "Now where remission of these is, there is no more offering for sin" (10:18). He says it again! The Levitical offerings are now completely meaningless. If there is no more remembrance of sins because of Calvary, why continue the offerings? The Christian believer has already entered into the spiritual side of the New Covenant.

C. WHAT WAS TAUGHT BY CHRIST'S SACRIFICE (10:19-39)

If something has been *wrought* by Christ's sacrifice (the complete banishment of sin and the probating of a new will, to be executed by the Lord Himself), and if something has been *sought* by Christ's sacrifice (the replacing of the age of shadows with the reality of the substance), then something is *taught* by Christ's sacrifice as well.

1. A TREMENDOUS WORD OF WELCOME (10:19-25)

Three great themes occupy this closing section of the great argument based on the superior provisions of Calvary. There is a tremendous word of welcome, there is a terrible word of warning, and there is a timely word of wisdom. The believer today has an access to God far greater than anything allowed by the Levitical ritual, and he therefore needs to avail himself of it. The seeker who has come this far must beware of the terrible dangers of drifting back into a dead Judaism (or, today, into a dead, Christ-rejecting religion). The believer needs to press on, for the Lord Jesus is coming again.

a. THE GREAT REALITY (10:19-21)

First the believer is given, by God, a tremendous welcome. Mention is made of *the place of access*. The believer is invited to do something only the high priest of Israel could do: have "boldness to enter into the holiest by the blood of Jesus" (10:19). We are invited into the Holy of Holies itself.

To picture what this means, imagine a Moabite of old gazing down upon the tents and Tabernacle of Israel from some lofty mountain height. Attracted by what he sees, he descends to the plain and makes his way toward the sacred enclosure surrounding the Tabernacle. It is a high wall of dazzling linen, which reaches over his head. He walks around it until he comes to the gate, where he sees a man.

"May I go in there?" he asks, pointing through the gate to where the bustle of activity in the Tabernacle's outer court can be seen.

"Who are you?" demands the man suspiciously. Any Israelite would know he could go in there.

"I am a man from Moab," the stranger replies.

"Well," says the man at the gate, "I'm very sorry, but you cannot go in there. It's not for you. The law of Moses has barred the Moabite from any part in the worship of Israel until his tenth generation."

The Moabite looks sad. "What would I have to do to go in there?" he insists.

"You would have to be born again," replies the gatekeeper. "You would have to be born an Israelite. You would need to be born of the tribe of Judah, perhaps, or of the tribe of Benjamin or Dan."

"I wish I had been born an Israelite of one of the tribes of Israel," the Moabite says. As he looks more closely, he sees one of the priests, having offered a sacrifice at the brazen altar and cleansed himself at the brazen laver, go on into the Tabernacle's interior.

"What's in there?" asks the Moabite. "Inside the main building, I mean."

"Oh," says the gatekeeper, "that's the Tabernacle itself. Inside there is a room containing a lampstand, a table, and an altar of gold. The man you saw is a priest. He will trim the lamp, eat of the bread upon the table, and burn incense to the living God upon the golden altar."

"Ah," sighs the man of Moab. "I wish I were an Israelite so that I could do that. I should love to worship God in that holy place and help to trim the lamp, to offer Him some incense, and to eat at that table."

"Oh, no," says the man at the gate, "even I could not do that. To worship in the holy place one must not only be born an Israelite, one must be born of the tribe of Levi and of the family of Aaron."

The man from Moab sighs again. "I wish," he says, "that I had been born of Israel of the tribe of Levi of the family of Aaron." Gazing wistfully at the closed Tabernacle door, he says, "What else is in there?"

"There is a veil," replies his informant. "It is a beautiful veil, I'm told, which divides the Tabernacle in two. Beyond the veil is what we call 'the Most Holy Place,' 'the Holy of Holies.' "

The Moabite is more interested than ever. "What's in the Holy of Holies?" he asks.

"There's a sacred chest in there called the Ark of the Covenant," answers the gatekeeper. "It contains certain holy memorials of our past. Its top is made of gold, and we call that the mercy seat because God sits there between the golden cherubim. You see that pillar of cloud hovering over the Tabernacle? That's the Shekinah glory cloud. It comes to rest on the mercy seat."

Again a look of longing shadows the face of the man from Moab. "Oh," he says, "if only I were a priest! I should love to go into the Holy of Holies and there gaze upon God and worship Him there in the beauty of holiness."

"Oh, no!" says the man at the gate. "You couldn't do that even if you were a priest! To enter into the Most Holy Place you would have to be the *high* priest of Israel. Only he can go in there, nobody else, only he."

The Moabite's heart yearns once more. "Oh," he cries, "if only I had been born an Israelite, of the tribe of Levi of the family of Aaron. If only I had been born the high priest! I would go in there, into the Holy of Holies. I would go in there every day. I would go in three times a day. I would worship continually in the Holy of Holies."

The gate keeper looks at him again and once more shakes his head. "Oh, no!" he says, "You couldn't do that. Even the high priest of Israel can go in there only once a year, and then only after the most elaborate of preparations, and even then only for a little while."

Sadly the Moabite turns away. He has no hope in all the world of ever entering there.

"Having therefore, brethren, boldness to enter into the holiest by the blood of Jesus" (10:19), says the writer of Hebrews. It is a revolutionary truth. It is understandable that the Lord Jesus should enter the Holy of Holies in heaven. But here it is, a tremendous word of welcome, extended to Jew and Gentile alike, to come on in and worship, not in the holiest place of the human Tabernacle, but into the Holy of Holies in heaven itself.

Think, however, of *the price of access* to that glorious place. We enter there "by the blood of Jesus, by a new and living way, which he hath consecrated for us, through the vail [veil], that is to say, his flesh" (10:19*b*-20). That's the price of access. We are taken at once back to Calvary.

The veil, a most instructive feature of the Temple, was blue, scarlet, and purple and spoke of Christ in His incarnation. The blue is the color of heaven, and it suggests to us, surely, that Jesus was the Son of God, the One who came from heaven itself. The scarlet reminds us that He was the Son of Man, the last Adam, for the very name *Adam* simply means "red." But what about the purple? If we take a measure of the blue dye and an equal measure of the red, then pour the one into the other and mix the two so that it is impossible to tell where the one ends and other begins, that's the purple. In the person of the Lord Jesus, deity is perfectly blended with humanity, and humanity is perfectly blended with deity so that it is impossible to tell where the one ends and the other begins.

Take, for instance, the Lord's meeting with the woman at the well. "Give me to drink" (John 4:7), He said. That was His humanity. He was thirsty. But a moment later He was confronting her with details about her life that as a mere man He could not possible know. That was His deity. Where does the one end and the other begin? We can never say.

Think, too, of when He slept in Simon Peter's boat. That was a demonstration of His humanity: the Lord Jesus asleep. A storm came, and the boat was filled with water so that the frightened disciples awoke Him in direst alarm. He arose and spoke to the heaving waves and howling winds. "Be still!" (Mark 4:39), He said, and at once there was a great calm. That was His deity. Where does the humanity end and the deity begin? It is impossible to say. The two are perfectly blended into one.

The veil, then, spoke of the incarnate Christ. But that veil separated men —even good, consecrated men—from God. It was a barrier to shut men out from the Holy of Holies. And is not that exactly what the life of Jesus does? His life is so perfect, so spotless, so free from taint and sin that it forms an impassable barrier. We run into it the moment we seek to approach God on our own. God says, "I demand absolute perfection. I demand a life just like the one lived by the Lord Jesus Christ." But that is more than we can ever produce, so His life, as lived on earth, is an impossible bar to God's presence.

Except for one thing. The veil was rent. When, as the Lord Jesus hung upon the cross of Calvary, the soldier took the spear and rent His side, God reached down from heaven and with His own hand rent the Temple veil. The veil has not been removed; it has been rent. We can approach God, not because of Christ's life, important and needful as that peerless life was, but because of Christ's death.

And *the proof of access?* We have "an high priest over the house of God" (Heb. 10:21). He has entered into the Holy of Holies, and because He is there we can be there. He does what no priest of Israel ever dared to do. He takes others with Him into the Holy of Holies.

That is the great reality of the Christian faith. It is a reality of which Judaism, at its brightest and its best, never dreamed. This is the wonderful word of welcome extended to us: "Come into the Holy of Holies."

b. THE GREAT RESPONSIBILITY (10:22-25)

The great reality, however, is matched by an equally great responsibility. First, there is our responsibility *as believers*. Three times the writer of Hebrews says, "Let us."

The first time he points to our Godward responsibility; he emphasizes the purity of worship demanded in the Holy of Holies. "Let us draw near with a true heart in full assurance of faith, having our hearts sprinkled from an evil conscience, and our bodies washed with pure water" (10:22). We must be *conscientious* when we come; it must be with a true heart, not with an empty profession of faith. We must be *confident* when we come; there must be no natural hesitation about approaching God. He has told us to come. We must be *cleansed* when we come; our hearts must be sprinkled from an evil conscience. The reference to bodies washed with pure water speaks of the same truth. The idea is not so much that of mere physical cleanliness (although the constant ablutions demanded under the law all urged the importance of personal hygiene); the idea is one of spiritual cleanliness. God is still a holy God.

If we have a Godward responsibility, we have a responsibility selfward, too; the writer emphasizes the possibility of wavering. "Let us hold fast the profession of our faith without wavering; (for he is faithful that promised;)" (10:23). "Faith" here is a forward-looking word. The Hebrews were in constant danger of going back because of all the pressures brought to bear upon them by religion, society, and government. In view of the dazzling heights now open to the one who is truly saved, there can be no question of going back. There can be no wavering.

Moreover, we have a responsibility manward. "Let us consider one another to provoke unto love and to good works" (10:24). One believer will encourage, help, and stimulate another believer to evidence the fruit of a saved life. It is no part of the Christian life to willfully "go it alone." Christians need the help to be derived from each other's fellowship.

This leads the writer to a final word on our great responsibility. He has been emphasizing our responsibilities as believers; he turns naturally to our responsibilities *as brethren*. "Not forsaking the assembling of ourselves together, as the manner of some is; but exhorting one another: and so much the more, as ye see the day approaching" (10:25).

I was brought up in Britain where most of the houses were not centrally heated; instead, each room had its own small fireplace. I well remember the good fire that was always kept burning in the fireplace of the living room whenever the weather was inclement and cold. The coals would be heaped up, and the flames would roar up the chimney. Occasionally we would take an iron poker and stir up the coals so that the air could circulate and the fire stay alive and hot. Once in a while a coal would fall down and roll off to one side. When it first fell it would be bright red and glowing with the fire. But after a short while—a very short while —the isolated coal would lose some of its luster. The glow would fade, and it would look dull and listless. Soon it became black with just a wisp or two of smoke ascending from it as evidence of its former heat, until presently it was cold enough to be picked up by hand.

That is the picture the writer has in mind. We are to exhort one another, stir one another up, keep the fires of the Spirit burning brightly. We need to be kept close together so that Christian warmth can be communicated back and forth from one member of the fellowship to another. And what a tragedy it is when we begin to stop attending the gatherings of those of like precious faith. We soon begin to lose our fervor. We grow, imperceptibly but surely, colder toward the things of God until, at last, for all the evidence there is of life, we are no different from the worldly, unsaved people around us.

We must note the great *imperative*, "not forsaking the assembling of ourselves together." The word is *episunagōge* ("gathering together") and is used only here and in 2 Thessalonians 2:1. Here it refers to the gathering together of believers on earth; there it refers to the gathering together of believers in the air. That gathering is no more important, no more momentous, no more thrilling than the gathering together of believers for fellowship and exhortation on earth. Both are of equal, vital importance in God's plans for His people in a cold, hostile world.

We must note, too, the great *incentive*, "and so much the more, as ye see the day approaching." "The day" here is a reference to the rapture. The expression "the day" or "that day" is usually reserved in the New Testament for "the day of Christ" (Philippians 1:6, 10; 2:16), or "the day of our Lord Jesus Christ" (1 Corinthians 1:8; 5:5; 2 Corinthians 1:14), except in 1 Thessalonians 5:4, where the context plainly indicates a reference to the day of wrath. The day of Christ stands in contrast to "the day of the Lord," a subject of much Old Testament prophecy, beginning with Isaiah 2:12 (and including the important 2 Thessalonians 2:12 where the true reading is "day of the Lord"). The day of Christ has to do with the rapture of the church to heaven; the day of the Lord has to do with the return of the Lord to earth. The day of Christ heralds joy for the church, "joy unspeakable and full of glory"; the day of the Lord heralds *judgment* for the world. The author of Hebrews is here exhorting God's suffering people to keep in mind the rapture, the coming of the Lord in the air (1 Thessalonians 4:14-17) to catch away His Bride before the day of wrath begins. *That* is the "blessed hope" of the church. It is hard to see how anyone can regard the coming great day of wrath as a "blessed hope."

As the darkness deepens all around—and what abundant evidences there are everywhere today that the Lord's coming is near—believers especially need each other's fellowship. We are to cling together and resist every pressure that would draw us away from the assembly of God's people. Business pressures, family pressures, social pressures, economic pressures, entertainment pressures, and physical pressures all militate against our being present at the gatherings of God's people. Let us face our great responsibility. Having been invited to come into God's immediate presence, we must resist anything that would draw us away.

2. *A TERRIBLE WORD OF WARNING (10:26-31)*

In the light of all that has been said, the writer now turns his attention once more to those who have made all the initial responses to the gospel but who are still about to turn away. In spite of everything, they are still looking back to a dead religion. The warning now placed before them is the strongest in the epistle. It has to do with despising the Spirit of God, and the consequences are clearly judicial.

a. THE WARNING EXPRESSED (10:26-27)

First the warning is expressed; then it is explained in fuller detail.

Note *the characteristics* of this sin. It is *a deliberate sin*. The writer warns against sinning "wilfully after that we have received the knowledge of the truth" (10:26a). It is something done, not by a sudden impulse of the will, but with settled intention. The only other use of the word *ekousiōs* is in 1 Peter 5:2, where elders are exhorted to undertake their work willingly and not by constraint. The willful sin envisioned by the writer of Hebrews is that of apostasy. The truth has been received, but not Christ. The warning is against turning from Christ in favor of an obsolete religion, a Christ-rejecting religion as, indeed, Judaism had become.

This sin is not only a deliberate sin; it is *a damning sin*. The writer warns that "there remaineth no more sacrifice for sins" (10:26b). To renounce the sacrifice of Christ is to be left without any sacrifice. There is no other place to go for salvation.

The consequences of such a sin are sobering. Such a person can anticipate nothing but "a certain fearful looking for of judgment and fiery indignation, which shall devour the adversaries" (10:27). To become an apostle is to become an adversary. This is not a case of backsliding or failure in the life of a child of God. This is a deliberate repudiation of the gospel. Vine says, "The word *krisis* here signifies the punishment following upon judicial condemnation; this is confirmed by the word 'punishment' in verse 29."[1] God's righteous wrath will descend upon a person guilty of this sin.

The history of the Christian church is littered with the debris of the lives of men who have made such shipwreck concerning the faith. One more recent example, surely, has to be that of Bishop James Pike, the one-time controversial bishop of the Episcopal diocese of California. He started out as a brilliant lawyer and became a high-placed cleric. He ended up embroiled in the snare of spiritism and was lured to his death in the burning desert on the Israel side of the Dead Sea in his attempt to make contact with his dead son.

This unhappy man's first encounter with the occult began three years after his son had committed suicide. The young man had frequently used psychedelic drugs. His sudden death shocked the bishop. The boy's body was cremated, and his ashes were scattered on the Pacific Ocean.

Then the heartbroken father took a sabbatical from his church and made a pilgrimage to his son's apartment in Cambridge, England.

There the haunting began. The bishop had long since abandoned whatever Bible faith he once had had, his only insurance against the terrible deception that now took over in his life.

From the weird phenomena he encountered in that Cambridge apartment, the bishop was lured into having sessions with one of England's best-known spiritist mediums. He was possessed by his desire to communicate with the spirit of his son. It was not long before he did indeed establish contact with a spirit that purported to be that of his son. Had he believed his Bible, the bishop would have known that all spiritism is forbidden by God and that, far from contacting his son, he was really in touch with an impersonating demon.

Even more startling to the bishop, however, was his contact with another spirit who claimed to be the ghost of the deceased German-American theologian and philosopher Paul Tillich, who had died the previous winter and who had been one of the bishop's close friends. Both had abandoned traditional Christianity in favor of soul-destroying liberal theologies. The supposed spirit of Tillich urged the bishop to keep up his campaign against historic Christian doctrines. This was timely encouragement for the bishop, who was soon to return to the United States to answer to charges of heresy before Episcopal officials.

---

1. W. E. Vine, *The Epistle to the Hebrews* (Grand Rapids: Zondervan, 1952), p. 119.

Once back in the United States, the bishop made contact with American spiritist mediums, particularly with Arthur Ford, a Disciples of Christ clergyman and an established medium, and also with George Daisley of Santa Barbara, known as a healer and a medium.

Before long the bishop became a firm believer in spiritism and an eloquent apologist for the cause. Having rejected the Christian doctrine of the bodily resurrection of Christ as the believer's ground of assurance of life after death, the bishop succumbed to the spiritist lie that there is no death. Having denied Christ's bodily resurrection and all that it promises to the believer, the rationalist bishop was robbed of all hope for life after death until his rationalism was swept away by supernatural, demonic phenomena. Step by step the bishop was lured away from the Scriptures, enmeshed in psychic manifestations, deluded into the belief that he had found the real thing, that he had found his son and his comrade in apostasy, and then lured by demons to his lonely and tragic death, overcome by heat and weakness in the Judean wilderness.

b. THE WARNING EXPLAINED (10:28-31)

Having given expression to his warning, the writer now explains in fuller detail what is involved in this warning to them. He first gives an *Old Testament* example of sin *against God's government*. "He that despised Moses' law died without mercy under two or three witnesses" (10:28). A case in point would be that recorded in Deuteronomy 17:2-7, where apostasy is in view. A person guilty of idolatry was to be stoned to death. The law of Moses revealed God's holiness and His abhorrence of false religions. No compassion was to be shown those who deliberately chose other gods. In fact, the two terrible deportations that loom so large on the pages of Old Testament history—the deportation of the Northern Kingdom of Israel by the Assyrians and the later deportations of Judah by the Babylonians—were both expressions of God's anger against the Hebrew people for their persistent idolatry and for their failure to execute His will upon the guilty.

We would do well to appreciate the seriousness of false teaching. Consider the story of a young woman with her baby traveling by train across the Canadian prairies. It was a cold, winter night, with the temperature far below freezing. Obviously anxious, the woman asked the porter several times to be sure to put her off at the right stop. Outside the wind blustered, and snowflakes burst against the window. It was dark as pitch.

A helpful salesman sitting across the aisle said, "Lady, I've traveled this line for years and know every train stop. If the porter forgets to tell you, I'll be sure to let you know when we arrive at your stop."

Presently the train stopped, and the passengers could hear the usual commotion outside, but it was too dark to see. Anxiously the woman looked around.

"This isn't your stop," said the salesman. "Yours is the next one."

Again the train pulled off into the night, and the salesman helped the woman gather her bags. Presently the train stopped, and the man carried her bags to the door while she bundled up her child. He handed her down the steps into the cold, dark blustering night. Nothing could be seen, but it was dark and the woman was sure she would be met. Anyway, she couldn't stay on the train. She thanked her helper and watched the train pull off into the night.

Shortly afterward the porter came down the coach and stopped at the empty seat. "Where's the lady who was sitting here?" he asked.

"Oh," said the salesman, "she got off at the last stop a few minutes ago. That was her stop; I've been keeping check. You forgot to tell her to get off."

The porter said in alarm, "That wasn't a station! It was a temporary signal stop. We'll have to back up the train."

The train was reversed to the emergency stop, and volunteers poured off to look for the mother and child. They found her—frozen to death with her baby—a victim of wrong information.

Religious error is even more deadly. It not only kills; it damns. God warns repeatedly against wrong information in matters involved with eternity. Under the law, a sin against God's government was met with the death penalty. In the New Testament, the sin is *against God's grace*. The writer underlines *the seriousness of the crime*. "Of how much sorer punishment, suppose ye, shall he be thought worthy, who hath trodden under foot the Son of God?" (10:29).

To set aside the law of Moses called for death; to set aside the Son of God calls for damnation. To tread under foot the Son of God! This is a total, willful rejection of the Lord Jesus Christ. This is not merely thoughtless unbelief; this is willful unbelief, the deliberate rejection of Christ by one "almost persuaded."

The seriousness of the offense goes deeper still. It involves not only rejecting the Son of God but refusing the salvation of God. Such a person has "counted the blood of the covenant, wherewith he was sanctified, an unholy thing" (10:29*b*). The person envisioned here is one who professed faith in Christ and came, as it were, under the shadow of the cross and was outwardly identified with the Christian community. He was associated in the public eye with those set apart by Christ. He was identified with "the blood of the covenant." He professed to be sanctified. But it was not real. He has turned his back on all that now. One step more and he would have truly been covered by the blood and saved forevermore, but now he has willfully refused God's salvation.

More serious still, he has repudiated the Spirit of God. He has "done despite unto the Spirit of grace" (10:29*c*). He has treated with disdain and insult the One by whom alone all grace is ministered to the soul. He has revealed himself an apostate, has gone back to Judaism (or some other dead religion), and has sinned beyond recall.

The seriousness of such a crime against God's grace is matched only by *the solemnity of the consequences* of the crime. First, mention is made of *a formal judgment*. "For we know him that hath said, Vengeance belongeth unto me, I will recompense, saith the Lord. And again, the Lord shall judge his people" (10:30). The reference is to Deuteronomy 32:35-36. The vengeance that will overtake the apostate results not from personal passion but from outraged law. We are dealing with serious issues when dealing with God's Son, God's salvation, and God's Spirit. They are not to be trifled with, ignored, or despised. And they are certainly not to be rejected with impunity.

Mention is made of *a fearful judgment*. "It is a fearful thing to fall into the hands of the living God" (v. 31). God always triumphs in the end. All hell is witness to that.

Julian the Apostate was a nephew of the Roman emperor Constantine, the man who established Christianity as the state religion of the Empire. Julian was raised in the teachings of the church. His main teacher was the celebrated Bishop Eusebius of Nicomedia.

Julian, however, secretly revolted against the Christian faith when still in his early teens, and he became the champion of heathenism. However, so long as he had no power, he played the hypocrite. But once he became the emperor he threw off all his pretense and declared himself for what he was, what he has been called for centuries—an apostate.

Julian reigned only for eighteen months. But in that short space of time he did all a human being could do, backed by almost limitless imperial power and moved by fanatical zeal, to restore to paganism the control and destiny of the world. He even went so far as to openly defy God by attempting to rebuild the Jewish Temple in Jerusalem in the mistaken notion that Christ had not only predicted the destruction of that Temple but had declared it would never be rebuilt.

Julian threw himself body and soul into pagan religion. He sacrificed every morning to the rising sun and every evening to the setting sun. He pointed his dagger to the sky, defying the Son of God, whom he contemptuously called "the pale Galilean."

Julian's short reign came to an ignominious and sudden end. He was slain in a skirmish on the Persian front. When he saw that he was wounded to death and that it was all over, he took handfuls of his own blood and threw them into the air crying: "Thou hast conquered, O Thou Galilean!" He was buried, of all places, at Tarsus, the birthplace of the apostle Paul, a man he had hated second only to Jesus Himself.

"Thou hast conquered, O Thou Galilean!" Julian the Apostate is crying it still in the desolation of a lost eternity. He sees Him now, high and lifted up, sur-

rounded by angelic throngs, mightier than all the Caesars of time. No "pale Galilean" He, but King of kings and Lord of lords, God over all, blessed for evermore.
And there he lies, the apostate, waiting his summons to the great white throne
and knowing now that it is "a fearful thing to fall into the hands of the living
God" (10:31).

The apostate's fate will be terrible beyond words. Thus the writer balances
his tremendous word of welcome with his terrible word of warning. He has one
more word to add before turning his attention to a whole new line of argument.
He adds a timely word of wisdom in which he urges his readers to take stock and
press on.

3. *A TIMELY WORD OF WISDOM (10:32-39)*

a. THE BELIEVERS SHOULD THINK ABOUT THE PAST (10:32-34)

The writer urges his readers to think about some past events. He reminds
them of *the persecution that once assailed them*. They have already endured
some fearful persecutions because of their profession of faith in Christ. "Call to
remembrance the former days, in which, after ye were illuminated, ye endured a
great fight of afflictions" (10:32). Darkness hates the light. The early church in
Jerusalem ran into persecution almost from the beginning. The sufferings of the
believers, to whom the writer addresses himself, had been severe. He calls it "a
great fight of afflictions" (10:32).

Judaism arose, virile with hate against the infant church. The spirit that led
the Jews to reject the Lord Jesus as their Messiah led them to reject Him as Savior. Peter and John were arrested for healing a lame man in the name of Jesus,
the apostles were thrashed for preaching the gospel of Christ, Stephen was mar-
tyred, James was beheaded, Peter was imprisoned, and then the militant Sanhedrin commissioned Saul of Tarsus to uproot the church at home and abroad. In
only two instances in the book of Acts did persecution initiate with the Gentiles.
The writer of Hebrews reminds his readers of the sufferings they had borne because of their enlightenment.

They had *shown the faith of Christ to sinners*. They had been made a "gaz-
ingstock" (10:33*a*). The word is "theatrize," from which comes our English word
theater. They had been put on the stage, as it were, and exposed to ridicule and
shame and contempt. In the arena of testimony, with catcalls and missiles being
hurled at them by an infuriated audience, they had endured. They had shown
their faith in Christ to sinners.

In the persecution that had assailed them, they had *shared the faith of
Christ with saints* in a most practical way, by becoming "companions of them
that were so used" (10:33*b*). They had taken compassion on those who had been

imprisoned for the confession of their faith, an act of singular courage, since it meant that the attention of the persecutors would be directed next against them.

In the midst of all these things, they had been buoyed up by their persuasion that the gospel was true, that Jesus was indeed the Messiah, the Savior, and the Son of God, and that they had found the substance behind all the shadows of their former faith. They had carefully balanced in their minds earthly loss against eternal gain.

Indeed, they had taken the spoiling of their possessions joyfully, knowing they had a better possession, an abiding one, in Christ. Yes! These Hebrew believers should think about the past. They already had taken such giant strides.

b. THE BELIEVERS SHOULD THINK ABOUT THE PRESENT (10:35-36)

But they should also think about their present condition. "Cast not away therefore your confidence, which hath great recompence of reward. For ye have need of patience, that, after ye have done the will of God, ye might receive the promise" (10:35-36). Boldness in the face of opposition is the real need.

Geoffrey Bull, who for a number of years was the prisoner of the Chinese Communists and who was subjected to long, dark months of loneliness accompanied by constant brainwashing, learned by bitter experience that no form of compromise, no matter how slight, pays off under circumstances like that.

One of Satan's favorite tactics is to "wear out the saints of the Most High." The antidote to this is patience. Think of John Bunyan's long years in Bedford Jail. How productive they became! He might have spent the time pacing the floor, gazing stolidly into space, working himself into passions of rage or fits of despair. Instead, he took his pen and began to write:

> As I walked through the wilderness of this world, I lighted on a certain place, where was a Den; and I laid me down in that place to sleep: and as I slept I dreamed a Dream. I dreamed, and behold I saw a man clothed with rags, standing in a certain place, with his face from his own house, a Book in his hand, and a great burden upon his back.

Thus his cell became "a den" from which he wrote one of the greatest classics of all times, *The Pilgrim's Progress*, a book which, in former years, was a best seller second only to the Bible itself.

"That . . . ye might receive the promise," says the writer of Hebrews. He is about to launch into a major exposition of that, summoning up a host of Old Testament saints who dared to believe God in spite of circumstances and who triumphed gloriously.

c. THE BELIEVERS SHOULD THINK ABOUT THE PROSPECT (10:37-39)

So the writer urges his readers to think about the prospect, too. "For yet a little while, and he that shall come will come, and will not tarry" (10:37). He tells them to think of the Lord's *coming return*. A little while! It seems so long to us. The centuries have come and gone, and it seems such a long, long time since the promise was given. But the Spirit says it is just a little while. In the light of eternity, what is a couple of thousand years? And, if it was viewed as "a little while" in the first century of the Christian era, what must it be today when, on every hand, the portents of His coming loom large?[2] The clue to boldness and patience in the face of opposition is to look for Christ's soon return.

In the meantime, our lives need to be kept under *constant review*. The writer closes this section in his epistle by drawing a contrast and by stating a confidence. The twofold use of the word *but* underlines his summary. "Now," he says, "the just shall live by faith: but if any man draw back, my soul shall have no pleasure in him" (10:38). It is faith that keeps a man from apostasy. He quotes from a familiar passage from Habakkuk, a verse picked up by the Holy Spirit and dropped into the New Testament three times. Each time the verse is cited the emphasis is on a different clause. "The *just* [Rom. 1:17] shall *live* [Gal. 3:11] by *faith*" (Heb. 10:38, italics added). It is faith that draws the line of demarcation between the apostate and the true believer. The apostate has neither the faith nor the faithfulness to continue, so he draws back; and in so doing, he incurs God's active displeasure. The true believer takes a fresh look at the Lord Jesus and reaffirms his faith. The emphasis on faith as the vital ingredient prepares the writer's way for the next major section of his letter in which he gives the best definition and the finest illustrations of faith anywhere in the Word of God.

Having warned again about the danger of apostasy, the writer states his absolute confidence in his Hebrew brothers in the faith. "But," he says, "we are not of them who draw back unto perdition; but of them that believe to the saving of the soul" (10:39). The "we" is emphatic and differentiates between true believers and empty professors. Perdition is not for the child of God.

Thus the writer concludes the second major section of his letter. He has demonstrated great truths concerning the superior person of Christ. He has discussed at great length Calvary's superior provisions by showing that, both in His preeminence and in His priesthood, the Lord Jesus is a better Savior. He has shown that, because of Calvary, we have not only a better Savior but a better security, a better sanctuary, and a better sacrifice—better, indeed, than anything to be found in the Hebrew religion. He has introduced three warning passages, two of them of major importance, to prove that the seeker after truth has every-

2. See John Phillips, *Exploring the Future* (Nashville: Thomas Nelson, 1983) and *Exploring Revelation,* rev. ed. (Chicago: Moody, 1987).

thing to gain by going on and everything to lose by drawing back. The substance in Christ cannot be traded away with impunity for the mere shadows of Judaism.

He is now prepared to discuss the superior principles of Christianity, and he begins by showing how, even in Old Testament times, men and women walked by faith and not by sight.

Part Three
The Superior Principles of Christianity
(11:1–13:25)

VII

The Walk of Faith (11:1-40)

A. Faith Defined (11:1-2)
  1. By Explanation (11:1)
  2. By Example (11:2)
B. Faith Demonstrated (11:3-38)
  1. By Glorious Illustration (11:3-31)
    a. The Present Age (11:3)
      (1) The Origin of the Universe (11:3a)
      (2) The Order of the Universe (11:3b)
    b. The Primeval Age (11:4-7)
      (1) Abel: Faith Worshiping Aright (11:4)
        (a) The Worth of Abel's Sacrifice (11:4a)
        (b) The Witness of Abel's Sacrifice (11:4b-c)
          i. Its Practical Witness (11:4b)
          ii. Its Perpetual Witness (11:4c)
      (2) Enoch: Faith Walking Aright (11:5-6)
        (a) The Fruit of His Faith (11:5a)
        (b) The Force of His Faith (11:5b)
          i. He Was Missed by His Fellows
          ii. He Was Marked by His Fellows
        (c) The Fundamentals of His Faith (11:6)
          i. The Great Impossibility (11:6a)
          ii. The Great Imperative (11:6b)
            a. Belief in God's Being
            b. Belief in God's Beneficence
      (3) Noah: Faith Witnessing Aright (11:7)
        (a) Mindful of the Word of God (11:7a)
        (b) Moved by the Fear of God (11:7b)
        (c) Mighty in the Service of God (11:7c)
        (d) Marked as a Child of God (11:7d)

    c. The Patriarchal Age (11:8-22)
      (1) Faith Counting on the Promises of God (11:8-19)
        (a) Abraham: Faith Having to Do with an Impossible Call (11:8-10)
          i. What God Told Him (11:8)
            a. The Immediate Exercise of His Faith (11:8*a*)
            b. The Immense Extent of His Faith (11:8*b*)
          ii. What God Taught Him (11:9-10)
            a. How to Live by Faith (11:9)
              1. As a Pilgrim in God's Purpose (11:9*a*)
              2. As a Partner with God's People (11:9*b*)
              3. As a Partaker of God's Promise (11:9*c*)
            b. Where to Look by Faith (11:10)
        (b) Abraham: Faith Having to Do with an Impossible Condition (11:11-16)
          i. As It Related to the Patriarch Personally (11:11-12)
            a. The Condition of Abraham's Own Wife (11:11)
            b. The Condition in Abraham's Own Life (11:12)
              1. The Poverty of the Soil (11:12*a*)
              2. The Prodigality of the Seed (11:12*b*)
          ii. As It Related to the Patriarchs Positionally (11:13-16)
            a. The Seeming Failure of the Promise (11:13*a*)
            b. The Sure Fulfillment of the Promise (11:13*b*-16)
              1. Their Bold Assurance (11:13*b*)
              2. Their Believing Attitude (11:13*c*-16*a*)
                (a) No Room for Complaint (11:13*c*-14)
                (b) No Room for Compromise (11:15)
                (c) No Room for Comparison (11:16*a*)
              3. Their Blessed Achievement (11:16*b*-*c*)
                (a) God Has Recognized These Men (11:16*b*)
                (b) God Has Rewarded These Men (11:16*c*)
        (c) Abraham: Faith Having to Do with an Impossible Command (11:17-19)
          i. The Magnitude of His Trial (11:17-18)
            a. God Understood That (11:17)
            b. God Underlies That (11:18)
           ii. The Magnificence of His Trust (11:19)
      (2) Faith Counting on the Purposes of God (11:20-22)
        (a) Isaac: Foreseeing the Future on the Individual Level (11:20)
          i. The Twin Boys (11:20*a*)
          ii. The Two Blessings (11:20*b*)

      (b) Jacob: Foreseeing the Future on the Tribal Level (11:21)
           i. When Jacob Blessed (11:21*a*)
          ii. Who Jacob Blessed (11:21*b*)
         iii. Why Jacob Blessed (11:21*c*)
      (c) Joseph: Foreseeing the Future on the National Level (11:22)
           i. His Challenge: A Promised Exodus (11:22*a*)
          ii. His Charge: A Personal Exercise (11:22*b*)

  d. The Patriotic Age (11:23-31)
    (1) The Faith of Moses' Parents: Triumph over This World's Dangers (11:23)
      (a) Faith's Practical Conclusions (11:23*a*)
      (b) Faith's Powerful Conviction (11:23*b*)
      (c) Faith's Personal Courage (11:23*c*)
    (2) The Faith of Moses Personally: Triumph over This World's Delights (11:24-28)
      (a) Faith's Sanctifying Virtue (11:24-26)
           i. Over Social Position (11:24)
          ii. Over Sinful Pleasures (11:25)
         iii. Over Staggering Prosperity (11:26)
      (b) Faith's Solid Victory (11:27)
           i. Over the Lure of the World (11:27*a*)
          ii. Over the Lust of the Flesh (11:27*b*)
         iii. Over the Lies of the Devil (11:27*c*)
      (c) Faith's Spiritual Vision (11:28)
           i. The Requirement of the Passover (11:28*a*)
          ii. The Reason for the Passover (11:28*b*)
    (3) The Faith of Moses' People: Triumph over This World's Difficulties (11:29-31)
      (a) Crossing the Red Sea (11:29)
           i. The Boldness of the Saints (11:29*a*)
          ii. The Brazenness of the Sinners (11:29*b*)
      (b) Conquering Jericho (11:30)
           i. Where Faith Triumphs (11:30*a*)
          ii. When Faith Triumphs (11:30*b*)
      (c) Convincing Rahab (11:31)
           i. The Product of Her Faith (11:31*a*)
          ii. The Proof of Her Faith (11:31*b*)

2. By General Allusion (11:32-38)
   a. Reference to People by Name (11:32)
      (1) An Age of Darkest Apostasy (11:32*a*)
          (a) Gideon Was Noted for His Visions
          (b) Barak Was Noted for His Victory
          (c) Samson Was Noted for His Valor
          (d) Jephthah Was Noted for His Vow
      (2) An Age of Divine Approval (11:32*b*)
      (3) An Age of Direct Appeal (11:32*c*)
          (a) Samuel
          (b) The Prophets
   b. Reference to People by Fame (11:33-38)
      (1) Those Delivered from Their Foes (11:33-35*a*)
      (2) Those Delivered to Their Foes (11:35*b*-38)
C. Faith Decreed (11:39-40)
   1. The Appeal (11:39)
   2. The Application (11:40)

Part Three
The Superior Principles of Christianity
(11:1–13:25)

VII
The Walk of Faith (11:1-40)

Faith is a common denominator of life. Everyone has faith and exercises faith almost every moment of every day. You walk into a building and immediately exercise faith in a score of ways—faith in the architect who designed the building, faith in the contractor and the workmen who constructed the building, faith in the quality and durability of the materials that make up the building—and you never give it a thought. When you mail a letter, make a bank deposit, or read a page of the newspaper, you exercise faith in the post office, the bank, and the reporter. You feel sick and go to a doctor who prescribes some medicine. You take the totally illegible prescription to the drugstore and watch the druggist pour an assortment of pills into a small container. "Take one of each three times a day," he says, and you do. You exercise faith in the doctor, in the drugstore, and in the mysterious capsules, the content of which you know nothing about.

Faith is a common denominator of life. No one can live a single day without exercising faith—faith in men. Salvation is on the same principle. God has thus made it available to all men everywhere, without regard to education, physical ability, social status, national origin, or native talent. For everyone has faith. The basic difference between the faith exercised by the individual in the daily round of life and the faith exercised by that same individual to the saving of his soul is the *object* of his faith.

The Muslim puts his faith in the Koran and in Muhammad; the idolater puts his faith in his graven images; the humanist puts his faith in himself; the philosopher puts his faith in his own ideas; the materialist puts his faith in his money; and the religionist puts his faith in his own good works. None of these can save, because the object of faith, in each case, is wrong. Saving faith is faith that rests upon Christ. The Holy Spirit, having brought enlightenment to the soul, insists that we personally put our faith and trust in the Lord Jesus. He and He alone can save. As Peter bluntly told the members of the Sanhedrin, "Neither is there salvation is any other: for there is none other name under heaven given among men, whereby we must be saved" (Acts 4:12).

The Hebrew believers had seen this truth. But some of these Spirit-enlightened Hebrews were still looking back at the things with which they had been familiar since childhood: at the Temple and its rituals, at the sacrifices and offerings, at the Levitical priesthood, at the Old Testament. All such shadowy objects of faith were now obsolete since the reality had been revealed in Christ. All these were now wrong objects of faith and, in any case, even at best had value only inasmuch as they pointed forward to Christ. Even in the Old Testament, true faith came to rest ultimately in Him. Today we look back to Calvary by faith. In Old Testament times, people looked forward to Calvary. Christ is the ultimate object of faith in both cases. To insist on the shadows when the substance has been revealed is not only nonsense; it is sin and unbelief of the very worst kind.

The writer of Hebrews thus turns his attention to the whole question of faith and presents his readers with a significant sampling of Old Testament people who believed God when faced with something entirely new. Enoch had never seen anyone translated, Noah had never known of a universal flood, Abraham had never seen the Promised Land. Each believer exercised personal faith in God. Many of them "died in faith, not having received the promises, but having seen them afar off" (Heb. 11:13). Throughout the Old Testament period this was the case, for Christ and His cross were still in the future. But now these daring Old Testament saints form a "great . . . cloud of witnesses" (12:1) standing astride the path of the Hebrew people to bar the way back to Judaism. They triumphed by looking away to the living God and by believing His Word, so that unseen things were seen and spiritual things became real. They traded earthly things for heavenly things, and God honored them. The Hebrew believers must do the same. The earthly Temple and its related system of religion were now to be traded for the ultimate realities in heaven. The marshaled examples of these Old Testament believers close ranks to witness to this truth.

A. FAITH DEFINED (11:1-2)

1. BY EXPLANATION (11:1)

The writer begins by giving an explanation of what faith is (11:1). "Faith is the substance of things hoped for, the evidence [the proving] of things not seen" (11:1). Faith gives substance to the unseen realities. The believer hopes in these things and proves their reality in his personal experience by faith. Faith is a kind of spiritual "sixth sense" that enables the believer to take a firm hold upon the unseen world and bring it into the realm of experience. All our senses do this. The eye takes hold upon the light waves that pulsate through space and make real to a person the things he sees. The ear picks up the sound waves and translates them into hearing.

But there is a whole spectrum of waves beyond the range of the senses. We cannot see them or hear them or taste them or smell them or feel them. But they are real, nevertheless, and, with the aid of modern instruments, we can pick them up and translate them into phenomena that our senses can handle. Faith reaches out into the *spiritual* dimension and gives form and substance to heavenly and spiritual realities in such a way that the soul can appreciate them and grasp them and live in the enjoyment of them.

2. BY EXAMPLE (11:2)

The explanation is followed by an example. The "elders," the great heroes of the Old Testament, were men of faith who "obtained a good report" (11:2). The heroes, from the ranks of which the writer makes his selection of illustrations, all put their faith to the test, reached out, grasped the unseen world, and found it real. Many people believe faith is vague and unreal—a kind of make-believe—trying to convince themselves that fairy stories are actually true. Nothing could be further from the truth. Faith is a reality, and it reaches out to facts that are more solid, more real, more substantial, and more eternal than anything registered by our physical senses. These Old Testament worthies all proved it true. We must prove it true as well. For the object of our faith is the most glorious, wonderful, magnificent Person in the universe.

B. FAITH DEMONSTRATED (11:3-38)

It is of interest, surely, that "we" head the list—"through faith we understand that the worlds were framed by the word of God" (11:3a).

1. BY GLORIOUS ILLUSTRATION (11:3-31)

The word for "worlds" is *aiōnes*. The thought behind the word here has been warmly debated. There are some who render the word as "ages." The word for "framed" is *katartizō*, "to arrange or set in order," or "to adjust." It occurs thirteen times in the New Testament and is translated in a variety of ways.

One view of the passage is that God is said to have arranged or set in order the various ages of time, of indefinite, concealed or unknown duration, such as the Edenic age, the patriarchal age, the church age, and so on. The point is made that Scripture sharply distinguishes between "this age" (Matt. 13:24-30, 36-43; Mark 4:19; 10:30; Rom. 12:2; 1 Cor. 2:8; 2 Cor. 4:4; Gal. 1:4; Eph. 2:2; 2 Tim. 4:10; Titus 2:12) and the "coming age" (Matt. 13:39-40, 49; 24:3; 28:20; Mark 10:30; Luke 18:30; 20:35; 1 Cor. 15:23; Titus 2:13).

Sir Robert Anderson dissents from this view. He says, "Both here and in chapter 1:2 the unlearned need to be warned that the [*Revised Version*] marginal note is misleading! 'Ages' is an *English* word, not Greek. In these passages, as occasionally in Alexandrian and Rabbinical Greek, the word which is usually translated 'ages' means the material universe."[1]

W. E. Vine concurs. He says, "Not merely . . . the ages, or various period in succession; the physical creation is referred to, but the time factor is included."[2]

a. THE PRESENT AGE (11:3)

(1) THE ORIGIN OF THE UNIVERSE (11:3*a*)

We must not lose sight of the author's immediate audience, but what a tremendously relevant statement this is for us today. On every hand the creationist view of the origin of the universe is simply laughed out of court. For a person in a secular university today, to challenge the evolutionary, mechanistic view is to court ridicule if not outright persecution.

We recall the experience of Edward Prendick on *The Island of Dr. Moreau* in H. G. Wells's fantasy. Dr. Moreau was an outlawed vivisectionist who had retired to a remote island to practice his cruel craft of manufacturing semi-human creatures out of various animals. One of these creatures was the Ape Man. Prendick tells his own tale and recounts how the Ape Man finally got on his nerves:

> He assumed, on the strength of his five digits, that he was almost my equal, and was forever jabbering at me, jabbering the most arrant nonsense. One thing about him entertained me a little: he had a fantastic trick of coining new words. He had an idea, I believe, that to gabble about names that meant nothing was the proper use of speech. He called it "big thinks," to distinguish it from "little thinks"—the sane everyday interests of life. . . . He thought nothing of what was plain and comprehensible. I invented some very curious "big thinks" for his especial use. I think now he was the silliest creature I ever met.

Later in the story, H. G. Wells takes his customary jab at Christianity. When Prendick was finally rescued from the nightmare island of Dr. Moreau, he had trouble readjusting to normal society. "Then," he said, "I would turn aside into some chapel, and even there, such was my disturbance, it seemed that the preacher gibbered Big Thinks even as the Ape Man had done."

The entire theory of evolution, so popularized by the educational system of today, boils down to sophisticated "big thinks" of a particularly dangerous kind. There is no room for God, no toleration for creationism, no room for design in the universe. All is the end product of the random working of the blind forces of chance over billions of years. The evolutionist, like the Ape Man, thinks nothing

---

1. Sir Robert Anderson, *The Hebrew Epistle in Light of the Types* (London: James Nisbet, 1911), p. 94.
2. W. E. Vine, *The Epistle to the Hebrews* (Grand Rapids: Zondervan, 1952), p. 128.

of what is plain and comprehensible. It should surely be obvious to the plainest-thinking person that the fantastic complexity of one human brain, not to mention an entire human body or the entire sweep and scope of all existing entities, calls for design. To assert that it all happened by chance is like saying that *Webster's Unabridged Dictionary* resulted from an explosion in a printing plant. There is evidence of design and omniscient genius everywhere in the universe. But design demands a Designer—and the evolutionist will not have that at any price. He has invented some curious "big thinks" for his own special use.

We take our stand on the Word of God so far as the origin of the universe is concerned. And, happily, it is not such a shaky stand as our adversaries would maintain. For, when it comes to *origins*, science is confessedly and permanently ignorant.

When a scientist or university professor presumes to speak on the subject of the ultimate origin of the universe, he is no longer speaking as a scientist but as a philosopher. He is not saying, "This is something I can prove"; he is saying, "This is what I believe." Moreover, what he believes today is almost certainly not identical to what he believed ten years ago, nor is it likely to be what he will be believing ten years from today. The whole realm of scientific discovery is expanding so rapidly that no one can afford to be dogmatic in any scientific field. We are reminded of the young fellow seen hurrying at breakneck speed across the campus. When asked, "Where are you going in such a hurry?" he said, "I have just bought the latest book on physics and want to get to class before it's out of date!"

No matter what we elect to believe as to the ultimate origin of the material universe, we are going to have to accept it by faith. We are either going to believe the word of a man, who knows nothing of origins and can never know anything of origins and whose theories are in a constant state of flux, or else we are going to believe the Word of God. "Through faith we understand that the worlds were framed by the word of God." The Christian believer takes his stand with the apostle Paul who, when standing on the deck of that heaving, storm-tossed ship in the midst of the Mediterranean, declared, "I believe God!"

(2) THE ORDER OF THE UNIVERSE (11:3b)

We believe God not only as to the origin of the material universe but also as to its order. For "that things which are seen were not made of things which do appear" (11:3b). This is a profoundly true statement of fact, a statement so true, indeed, that only in modern times could its full significance be grasped. We now know that all matter is simply energy passing into motion and motion passing into phenomena. When we arrive at the core of all material things, we find nothing but sheer energy—God's boundless, inexhaustible, resistless energy! Thus the whole basis for materialism collapses, for even "material" things are made up of something akin to the spiritual.

b. THE PRIMEVAL AGE (11:4-7)

The writer now turns his attention to what we can call "the primeval age." The three witnesses he introduces from this age are Abel, Enoch, and Noah. Abel shows us faith worshiping; Enoch demonstrates faith walking; and Noah illustrates faith witnessing. The reader might want to study the Genesis characters in this list more fully by consulting *Exploring Genesis* (Moody Press).

(1) ABEL: FAITH WORSHIPING ARIGHT (11:4)

He begins with Abel and points out *the worth of Abel's sacrifice*. "By faith Abel offered unto God a more excellent sacrifice than Cain" (11:4). Cain was the founder of the world's first false religion, a religion that has been at the heart of all false religions ever since. Essentially, Cain's religion was one of good works and human merit. According to him, salvation must be earned; he must pay the price. He offered to God the fruit of the earth, the product of his labors, the sweat of his brow, his toil and self-effort. His religion is summed up in Scripture as "the way of Cain" (Jude 11) and is rejected, root and branch, by God. It ignored Calvary and the shedding of blood. Abel, on the other hand, brought a lamb, took his stand as a hopeless sinner needing a Savior and a Substitute, and slew his lamb, shedding its blood to show his willingness to approach God in His way. His offering was accepted as "excellent" (11:4*a*) because it portrayed Calvary. Cain tried to approach God on the basis of his own works; Abel approached God on the basis of faith.

Note also *the witness of Abel's sacrifice*. Cain was rejected, but Abel received witness to both the practical and permanent value of his faith. He was pronounced righteous by God, not because he believed God and approached God in accordance with God's Word. "He obtained witness that he was righteous, God testifying of his gifts" (11:4*b*). God respects the offering of Calvary, and Abel came into the good of that by faith. Cain was infuriated and slew his brother. His religion, too refined to slay a lamb, was not too refined to murder Abel. Thus, the world's first false religion soon manifested its true character in the persecution of the true faith. But from that day to this, Abel's witness remains, for "he being dead yet speaketh" (11:4*c*). He speaks on in the Scriptures from age to age.

(2) ENOCH: FAITH WALKING ARIGHT (11:5-6)

Enoch stood midway between the Fall and the Flood. He was the seventh from Adam in the line of Seth, just as Lamech was seventh from Adam in the line of Cain. As godlessness climaxed in Lamech, so godliness climaxed in Enoch.

He was the first man to escape death, a fact rendered all the more significant by the ominous "tolling of the bell" in Genesis 5, where, of all the others, it is recorded, "And he died." "By faith Enoch was translated that he should not see death" (11:5a). That was *the fruit of his faith*.

Enoch was missed by his fellows. In Genesis it says of Enoch that "he was not" (5:24); here it says that "he was not found" (11:5b). *The force of his faith* is seen in the impact he made upon his generation. The capital value of a saint of God is rarely appreciated by his contemporaries; it is not until he is gone that they realize what a veritable giant he was among them and what his influence meant. The world frequently despises and maligns the dynamic believer during his lifetime. Even other believers do not always properly value the saint in their midst. His standards are too rigid, his beliefs too old-fashioned, his example too cutting. But once he was gone, *he was missed* by sinner and saint alike. Enoch was missed so much that they tried to find him, but in vain, because God had honored his faith in a signal way and had taken him alive to glory.

He was marked by his fellows. Even before his translation he "had this testimony, that he pleased God" (11:5c). During his lifetime, men marked him out as a man whose life and testimony were godly. That was the force of his faith; he had an impact upon other people.

David Livingstone was such a man. He gave his life to the pursuit of three major objectives: exploring, evangelizing, and emancipating. He opened Africa to the gospel and struck a blow against the devilish slave trade, but, above all, he won people to Christ. During his lifetime, he was often criticized because of his unswerving devotion to these goals. He was bitterly denounced for leaving his wife and children behind as his path took him into dangerous places. But his worth was well known by others, and honors were heaped upon him for his discoveries. He made a mark upon his time. Then, upon his death, his body was brought home to England to be buried in Westminster Abbey, England's national shrine for the greatest of her dead. On the day of his funeral, one of England's best-read papers blazed forth these banner headlines: "Granite May Crumble, But This Is *Living Stone!*"

The writer of Hebrews hurries to underline *the fundamentals of Enoch's faith*. It demonstrated clearly two important things. First, it demonstrated *the great impossibility*: "Without faith it is impossible to please him" (11:6a). The use of the aorist tense marks the absolute impossibility of a person's pleasing God in any other way. "Whatsoever is not of faith is sin" (Rom. 14:23). That is why all religious systems that emphasize works as essential to salvation are displeasing to God. In a day and age when belief in God was rarely seen, Enoch exercised faith, lived by faith, and was taken home to heaven by faith.

Moreover, Enoch's faith demonstrated *the great imperative*: "He that cometh to God must believe that he is, and that he is a rewarder of them that diligently seek him" (11:6*b*). Faith begins by grasping this one great, basic, essential fact: there is a true and living God. The Bible does not begin by seeking to prove that God *is* but simply states it as an incontrovertible fact: "In the beginning God" (Gen. 1:1).

Having grasped this fundamental fact, faith goes on to believe that God is a beneficient, gracious, loving, rewarding God, who reaches out eagerly to encourage, help, and reward those who seek Him.

The writer's Hebrew readers had been thus reaching after God. Tremendous new and vital revelations had been given to them in Christ. It was now or never for them. They had to capitalize on their faith and please God by seeking after Him in the full light of the truth as it is in Christ Jesus.

(3) NOAH: FAITH WITNESSING ARIGHT (11:7)

When God first spoke to Noah about the building of the ark more than a hundred years before the Flood, there was no sign that such a catastrophe would take place. For a full century things on earth would continue as they were, with evil men and seducers waxing worse and worse. If, as some believe, it had never rained before the Flood, then the Lord's pronouncement must have seemed all the more unlikely of fulfillment.

But Noah was *mindful of the word of God*. God had spoken, and that was enough. He was "warned of God of things not seen as yet" (11:7*a*).

He was also *moved by the fear of God*. He was "moved with fear" and therefore "prepared an ark to the saving of his house" (11:7*b*). We are told of the Lord Jesus that in Gethsemane He was moved by both devotion and dread—devotion to the Father and dread of what lay ahead when He must face God's wrath. Similarly, Noah was moved to build the ark.

Noah was *mighty in the service of God*. Through the building of his ark he "condemned the world" (11:7*c*). The majority of people simply refused to believe his witness concerning the coming Flood. Yet, in bold faith, he went on working and witnessing, building the ark and warning of judgment to come. Then, as a final act of faith, Noah stepped into the ark and those who believed stepped in with him. His witness, which might have been "unto life," proved to be "unto death." He had demonstrated saving faith to an unbelieving generation, thus leaving that generation without excuse. Not only had salvation been provided and proclaimed, but saving faith had been demonstrated. Those who persisted in unbelief were thus justly condemned. What a warning to the Hebrews who were drawing back from a total commitment to Christ!

In addition, Noah was *marked as a child of God*, for he "became heir of the righteousness which is by faith" (11:7*d*). This was the identical kind of righteousness that was being offered to the Hebrews. The writer now moves on to consider saints from the patriarchal age.

c. THE PATRIARCHAL AGE (11:8-22)

The greatest star in the Hebrew firmament was Abraham, the founding father of the Hebrew race. No wonder the writer of Hebrews devotes so much space to this magnificent believer, a man actually called "the father of all them that believe" (Rom. 4:11).

(1) FAITH COUNTING ON THE PROMISES OF GOD (11:8-19)

He discusses Abraham at length, goes on to talk about Sarah, and then comes back to Abraham again. He wishes to demonstrate in detail, from Abraham's story, how faith counts both on the promises and on the purposes of God.

(a) ABRAHAM: FAITH HAVING TO DO WITH AN IMPOSSIBLE CALL (11:8-10)

First, then, Abraham's faith is appealed to. The writer reminds his readers of *what God told Abraham*. "By faith Abraham, when he was called to go out into a place which he should after receive for an inheritance" (11:8*a*).

It was *an immediate step of faith*. One moment Abraham was a pagan moon worshiper, no different from his fellow citizens of Ur. The next moment he was a believing man with his back toward his old way of life and his face toward the Promised Land. There was no vacillating, no seesawing back and forth. What a lesson for the hesitant Hebrews, drawn to Christ yet hankering after the dead forms of the law!

It was not only an immediate step of faith but also *an immense step of faith*, for "he went out, not knowing whither he went" (11:8*b*). God did not pull out a map of the Fertile Crescent, spread it out before Abrahm, and show him the whole journey. He told Abraham to take the first step; the rest of the steps were revealed as time went on. The Hebrews, reading these words, might well have been challenged. They had far more light than Abraham had. They were dwelling in the full blaze of that light that floods the world through Christ. Surely they could take that first step and make a full commitment to Christ and trust Him to lead on from there each step of the way!

The writer presses on with his example. His readers must observe *what God taught Abraham:* how to live by faith.

First God taught him *how to live by faith*. He lived *as a pilgrim in the purposes of God*, for "by faith he sojourned in the land of promise, as in a strange country" (11:9*a*). When Abraham finally entered Canaan he discovered the country had already been occupied by a foul and degraded race. He made no attempt to acquire territorial holdings in the land either by marriage with a chieftain's daughter or by means of his wealth. He lived by faith as a pilgrim, daring to believe that, in His own good time, God would make good His promise.

He lived by faith in Canaan *as a partner with the people of God*, "dwelling in tabernacles with Isaac and Jacob" (11:9b). God's purposes did not end with Abraham, for the promise was to his seed as well. God did not make good the promise in Abraham's life, nor in the life of his son, nor even in the life of his grandson. But Abraham could afford to wait, and wait he did, enjoying the fellowship of fellow believers, his own sons both by nature and through grace.

He lived by faith *as a partaker of the promises of God*, for Isaac and Jacob were "heirs with him of the same promise" (11:9c). They believed God would make good His promises in due course. Since faith is ever dependent on the Word of God (Rom. 10:17), Abraham and his fellow believers were not without a word from God to cover the period of waiting. God had already told Abraham he would die before the land grant of Canaan was made good to his seed. He had told Abraham that his descendants would leave the Promised Land, in the will of God, and would return again in the fourth generation to receive full implementation of the promise (Gen. 15:13-16). And so it came to pass. The grandson of Abraham, Jacob, went down to Egypt. The fourth generation from him brings us to Moses (Levi, Kohath, Amram, Moses); thus God kept His word to the very letter, all of which Abraham and the patriarchs expected Him to do.

But if Abraham learned how to live by faith, he also learned *where to look by faith*. "He looked for a city which hath foundations, whose builder and maker is God" (11:10). The word for "looked" means that he "expected eagerly." Abraham's horizons were not dominated by the land of Canaan or by earthly things. He thoroughly understood that God was calling him to a heavenly country and to the coming age when the material promises would all have their ultimate fulfillment in heaven's spiritual realities. What a challenge to the Hebrew readers of this letter who were being urged to see beyond the earthly Temple and the Levitical priesthood, so dominated by the sights and sounds of a visible ritual, to the eternal, heavenly realities in Christ!

(b) ABRAHAM: FAITH HAVING TO DO WITH AN IMPOSSIBLE CONDITION (11:11-16)

The writer begins by showing how this related to *the patriarch personally* (11:11-12). He turns his attention to Abraham's wife and the impossible conditions against which she and Abraham dared to believe.

There was, first of all, *the condition of Abraham's own wife*. "Through faith also Sara herself received strength to conceive seed, and was delivered of a child when she was past age, because she judged him faithful who had promised" (11:11). God had promised Abraham a seed and had made it plain that the seed was to come through Sarah. But how? Sarah was ninety years old and long past the time when she could have children. The solution was not in some kind of compromise. Abraham had tried that with Hagar—with disastrous results. For thirteen long years Abraham received no fresh word from God (Gen. 16:16; 17:1). The solution was to believe God, something both Abraham and Sarah did, with the eventual result that the impossible happened. For what is impossible with men is not impossible with God.

Linked with the condition of Abraham's wife was *the condition in Abraham's own life*. He was "as good as dead" (11:12). Thus the Holy Spirit describes the poverty of the soil with which he had to work. Abraham was a hundred years old; he, too, had passed the age of fertility.

But the poverty of the soil only brings additional glory to God when compared with the prodigality of the seed. "Therefore sprang there even of one, and him as good as dead, so many as the stars of the sky in multitude, and as the sand which is by the sea shore innumerable" (11:12). What a God we have! What faith can do when it links dead, barren humanity to Him! It is like the hidden wire that runs through the wall of a house linking the outlet to the powerhouse. Faith reaches up to God and conveys all the immense resources of Deity to the source of need in human lives.

The impossible condition applied not only to Abraham personally; it applied equally to *the patriarchs positionally* (11:13-16)—that is, to Abraham, Isaac, and Jacob. All three generations had to face *the seeming failure of the promise*. True, the seed was there, a single son born to Abraham, a single son born to Isaac (for other sons born to them were outside the line of promise). But what about the Promised Land? "These all died in faith, not having received the promises" (11:13*a*).

But the promises cannot fail, no matter what circumstances say. Thus the patriarchs staked everything on *the sure fulfillment of the promise*. We note their *bold assurance*. They were bold enough to believe they had what God had promised, even though the actual fulfillment of the promise was yet future. They saw and greeted the promises from afar. When Abraham died, a tomb in Canaan was all the actual real estate he seemingly owned. Isaac died with not a scrap more. Jacob died in Egypt, coveting a burying place in Canaan.

But how bold was their assurance! "Hello there, promise!" they cried. "We see you! You're ours! We welcome you!" The land was as safe and as sure as though they had already conquered and colonized it, because God had promised it. God's promissory notes are drawn by His own hand and cannot fail. A promise from God is a surer thing than a post-dated check from a billionaire.

With this bold assurance that the promises of God could never fail, the patriarchs of old developed a *believing attitude*. There was *no room for complaint*. They "confessed that they were strangers and pilgrims on the earth. For they that say such things declare plainly that they seek a country" (11:13c-14). Above and beyond the earthly promise was the heavenly promise. The earthly Canaan was but a shadow of the heavenly Canaan! This vision made them hold lightly the earthly side of things. Ultimately, they were sure, God would give them the earthly Canaan. In the meantime, there was heaven!

The patriarchs were characterized by two objects: a tent and an altar. With the tent they confessed their attitude toward this world; they would not let its attractions blind them to spiritual realities. With the altar they confessed their relationship to the world to come; they were believers! Thus they adopted the attitude that, as far as this world was concerned, they were strangers (away from home) and pilgrims (going home). God had truly weaned their hearts away from the earthly to the heavenly. This, of course, was the very thing the Spirit of God was seeking to accomplish in the lives of the Hebrews to whom the letter was addressed, so the relevancy of the whole passage is evident.

In the believing attitude, adopted by the patriarchs, there was no room for complaint, and there was *no room for compromise* either. "And truly, if they had been mindful of that country from whence they came out, they might have had opportunity to have returned" (11:15). There was no going back to Mesopotamia. Abraham had forsaken all that kind of thing once and for all. When his servant suggested that perhaps Isaac could go to Mesopotamia to seek a bride, he was strictly forbidden by Abraham to permit anything of the kind (Gen. 24:5-6). To go back to Ur would be a disaster, a denial of everything Abraham believed. It would be apostasy. There was no physical obstacle to prevent his going back, but there was every possible spiritual obstacle. There was "a great gulf fixed" between all that Ur represented and all that Canaan represented. The Hebrew readers of the epistle were surely challenged afresh by this. They had been invited to a realm where they were to become pilgrims and strangers on the earth; they were to enter into heavenly realities. There could be no more going back to the old life. There was no room for compromise.

There was *not even room for comparison*. The writer now makes the point toward which he had been steering all along: "But now they desire a better country, that is, a heavenly" (11:16a). No doubt the earthly Canaan was "a land flowing with milk and honey" (Ex. 3:8) and a land "beautiful for situation, the joy of the whole earth" (Ps. 48:2). But even such a land could not be compared with heaven. Once a person gets a vision of heaven, the best of earthly prospects grows dim. The word for "desire" is a word that means "to stretch out the hand" or "to reach after." The picture is that of a man, with arms outstretched, yearning after his homeland. If the Hebrew readers of this epistle once got the vision of those heavenly realities being offered to them in Christ, they would long and yearn after them. What did an earthly Judaism have to offer in comparison?

The patriarchs' bold assurance and believing attitude resulted in a *blessed achievement*, noted thus: "Wherefore God is not ashamed to be called their God" (11:16*b*). Often He described Himself as "the God of Abraham, the God of Isaac, and the God of Jacob" (Ex. 3:6). What a distinction! What a blessed achievement of faith!

God has not only recognized these men, but He has also rewarded them. "He hath prepared for them a city" (11:16*b*). The word *prepared* is in the aorist tense, meaning that it has already been done. Thus faith surmounted the impossible condition. Did God promise a seed to a man and woman long past the age of childbearing? Nothing is impossible with God. Did God promise a country to Abraham and his descendants, and was that promise delayed? God had His purposes in postponing the earthly so that the heavenly could be more clearly seen. Faith seized upon these things and became, indeed, "the substance of things hoped for, the evidence of things not seen" (11:1).

(c) ABRAHAM: FAITH HAVING TO DO WITH AN IMPOSSIBLE COMMAND (11:17-19)

Abraham's magnificent faith, his daring hold on God, and his glorious optimism based on God's promises were destined to be tested to the uttermost before he was through. Consider *the magnitude of Abraham's trial*. "By faith Abraham, when he was tried, offered up Isaac: and he that had received the promises offered up his only begotten son" (11:17). "Offered up," says God, emphasizing the completeness of the act. He completed the dread deed in intent, even though God, in mercy, stayed his hand as the knife was about to fall. "Was offering up," says God, lingering as it were over the delightful trust and obedience of His friend.

And, as though that were not enough, God underlines it: "Of whom it was said, that in Isaac shall thy seed be called" (11:18). All God's promises to Abraham were "yea and amen" in Isaac. They all came to a focal point in him. Take away Isaac and nothing remained. Abraham had waited twenty-five years for God to make good his pledge and give him Isaac, and now that Isaac was about thirty-three, he was to immolate him upon an altar of sacrifice. So here it was: the impossible command.

But if the text underlines the magnitude of Abraham's trial, it also emphasizes *the magnificence of Abraham's trust*. Abraham went through with it, "accounting that God was able to raise him up, even from the dead; from whence also he received him [back] in a figure [parable]" (11:19). Up to this point in human history nobody had ever been raised from the dead. Abraham did some figuring and made up his mind that God could do even that. Accounting that God could do the impossible, Abraham did the impossible.

All this, of course, was of special relevance to the seeking Hebrews, confronted with the great central fact of Christianity: Christ's death and resurrection. It had happened! Surely, with the evidence of this fact—common knowledge in Jerusalem—they could believe. Abraham could believe without such evidence to buoy his faith. Could they not believe in the face of all the overwhelming evidence for Christ's resurrection from the dead?

(2) FAITH COUNTING ON THE PURPOSES OF GOD (11:20-22)

Having finished his lengthy passage on Abraham and the patriarchs in general, the writer now concentrated on three generations of the descendants of Abraham: Isaac, Jacob, and Joseph. Each of these acted similarly in faith. Each had an appreciation of God's ultimate purposes and consequently acted in a way that revealed faith in the chosen people's future. Isaac's faith was concerned with the future on an *individual* level; Jacob's with the future on a *tribal* level; and Joseph's with the future on a *national* level.

(a) ISAAC: FORESEEING THE FUTURE ON THE INDIVIDUAL LEVEL (11:20)

Jacob and Esau were twins, but Esau had been born ahead of his brother and was therefore officially the firstborn. God, however, had decreed that "the elder should serve the younger" (Gen. 25:23). The problem was that Esau, the older, was Isaac's favorite, so his father determined that the patriarchal blessing would go to him. Three basic elements were in the patriarchal blessing. First, there was the right to the family *progenitorship*, the right to be the one through whom the line of descent to the Messiah would run; second, he had a right to the position of *priest* in the family; and third, he had a right to a double portion of the family *property*. This last item was the only one that interested Esau.

Jacob and his mother knew of Isaac's intent and schemed to keep Esau from receiving the full blessing. They were successful, and the blessing in its fullness went to Jacob. Afterward, when Esau appeared on the scene seeking to receive the blessing, Isaac realized that his self-will had been overruled by God and that Jacob had indeed been blessed. He did give Esau a secondary blessing; nevertheless, he assured his favorite son that the full patriarchal blessing was Jacob's after all. Thus both boys were blessed, and both were blessed concerning "things to come" (Heb. 11:20). All history has proved the accuracy of Isaac's prophecy concerning his two boys. From Jacob came Christ; from Esau came Herod.

(b) JACOB: FORESEEING THE FUTURE ON THE TRIBAL LEVEL (11:21)

The writer is still dealing with familiar things when he speaks of Jacob blessing Joseph's sons. His Hebrew readers knew all these stories by heart. The future now expands from the individual to the tribe.

When Jacob was dying, he summoned Joseph to impart to him one of the most significant blessings in the Old Testament. Joseph, the son of his beloved Rachel, was his favorite. Joseph had been lost and found again, sitting in the seat of highest power in Egypt at the right hand of Pharaoh. He had taken a Gentile bride, and two sons, Ephraim and Manasseh, had been born to him.

Jacob had seated himself with the two boys before him and had deliberately given the right-hand blessing to Ephraim, the younger of the two, adopting the two boys as his own and giving Ephraim the preeminence.

It was done in a spirit of worship, done knowingly, and done with full prophetic insight. For, as history proved, Ephraim was indeed the dominant of the two tribes, so dominant, in fact, that the ten-nation kingdom of Israel was often called "Ephraim."

(c) JOSEPH: FORESEEING THE FUTURE ON THE NATIONAL LEVEL (11:22)

Again the prophetic focus is enlarged until it encompasses the entire Hebrew nation. The circumstances of Joseph's prophetic words are romantic enough. His brothers were standing before him with all the evidence of Joseph's power and semi-royalty before them. This old man, on the edge of eternity, was about to say his last words.

First he "made mention of the departing of the children of Israel" (11:22). He was looking centuries into the future. Before his enlightened understanding rolled the wretched years of slavery when there would arise a dynasty of pharaohs "which knew not Joseph" (Ex. 1:8). The descendants of Israel must be mightily oppressed, and a kinsman-redeemer must be found. But unquestionably, God would visit the oppressed people, and one day they would leave Egypt. So Joseph spoke of a promised exodus. And, along with that, he spoke of his own personal exercise. When the time came for the Hebrew people to leave Egypt, they were told to take his bones with them.

Bequeathing his bones to his brethren was a significant act, one so impressive, indeed, that, out of a remarkable life that typifies Christ in scores of ways, the Holy Spirit selects just this one incident to record in Hebrews 11. Joseph gave his brethren a memorial body. All through the long intervening years and all along the wilderness way, that body would have a message for them. It would remind them that the God who would surely visit them and bring them out of Egypt would just as surely bring them safely into Canaan.

The writer of Hebrews brings this truth forcibly home to his readers. Abraham, Isaac, and Jacob all looked to the future. Joseph looked to the future. The past had its lessons, but it was in the future that the promises would be fulfilled. The early Hebrew Christians had to learn this truth. Israel's remarkable history was all well and good, but they had to look away from that to the future. Just as Joseph foresaw sweeping changes, so these early Hebrew Christians had to move with the times. They could not cling to the past at the expense of the future. They had to go in step with God's purposes.

d. THE PATRIOTIC AGE (11:23-31)

The writer of Hebrews now turns his attention to the patriotic age. He leaps over the silent centuries of the Egyptian bondage to the days of Moses, a man who ranked almost as high as Abraham in the Hebrew hall of fame.

(1) THE FAITH OF MOSES' PARENTS: TRIUMPH OVER THIS WORLD'S DANGERS (11:23)

First, the faith of Moses' parents resulted in *practical conclusions*. They hid Moses for three months, for as long as they could. With the death sentence hovering over him by the decree of Pharaoh, Moses was sheltered because his parents took a vigorous step of faith. *How does God save a person condemned to death?* they asked themselves. Then they thought of Noah and his ark. "We will do that!" they said. "We will make a little ark. We'll put Moses in the river, as commanded by Pharaoh, but we'll put him in the ark first. We'll put the ark between him and the waters of death, and we'll trust God to do for Moses what He did for Noah."

They took note of Moses that he was "a proper child" (11:23b). The expression means that he was beautiful, and it can be applied to both physical and moral beauty. There was something so extraordinary about Moses' good looks that his parents' faith was quickened into a *powerful conviction*. This was a child of destiny. As a matter of fact, it was Moses' personal beauty that afterward melted the heart of Pharaoh's daughter and caused her to spare the child and rear him as her own.

Moses' parents acted with great *personal courage*. They were "not afraid of the king's commandment" (11:23c). It was no light thing to defy the royal decree, but Amram and Jochabed (Ex. 6:20) were made of the stuff that makes martyrs. Their faith drove out their fear; their eyes were on a greater King than Pharaoh. Thus, they triumphed over this world's dangers. What a lesson for the beleaguered Hebrew Christians who were being forced to decide whether to go with Christ in the face of mounting opposition or to deny Him. Moses' parents might have succumbed to pressure and, with personal anguish and tears, cast their little one to the crocodiles of the Nile. But they didn't; they defied danger. The Hebrew

Christians could bow to pressure and cast Christ aside, but they must not. They must dare for Christ what Moses' parents dared for their child: the wrath of men.

(2) THE FAITH OF MOSES PERSONALLY: TRIUMPH OVER THIS WORLD'S DELIGHTS (11:24-28)

If ever this world put on a fair disguise and made itself attractive, it did so for Moses. It offered him everything on earth. Moses' faith triumphed, however, over this world's delights.

(a) FAITH'S SANCTIFYING VIRTUE (11:24-26)

He refused its *social position*. As the adopted son of Pharaoh's daughter, Moses had every reason to believe that even the throne of Egypt was not beyond his grasp. "Once firmly seated on the throne," the world would whisper, "you can use your power and influence to further the cause of God and His people. God needs men like you in high places." That, however, was not God's way, as Moses realized, so "when he was come to years, [he] refused to be called the son of Pharaoh's daughter" (11:24).

He rejected the world's *sinful pleasures*. They were his for the asking, his in abundance, his with the ready approval of his peers. Every pleasure and vice this world had to offer was pressed upon him with a prodigal hand. "The lust of the flesh, and the lust of the eyes, and the pride of life" (1 John 2:16) all were there. He triumphed gloriously, "choosing rather to suffer affliction with the people of God, than to enjoy the pleasures of sin for a season" (Heb. 11:25).

He set aside the *staggering prosperity* offered him by the world. The enormous treasures unearthed from ancient Egyptian tombs give an idea of the wealth that Moses scorned. Riches beyond the dreams of avarice were proffered him. But "esteeming the reproach of Christ greater riches than the treasures of Egypt . . . he had respect unto the recompense of the reward" (11:26). Such was faith's sanctifying virtue. It kept Moses from trading heavenly things for earthly things. It was this very lesson that the writer of Hebrews was pressing upon his readers. They were standing where Moses had stood. The world was offering them all kinds of compensation if they would give up their hope in Christ. They had to do what Moses did.

(b) FAITH'S SOLID VICTORY (11:27)

Having made his "decision for Christ," Moses pressed on in solid victory. "By faith he forsook Egypt, not fearing the wrath of the king: for he endured, as seeing him who is invisible" (11:27). His victory was over the world, the flesh, and the devil. The land of Egypt represented for Moses the world in its most attractive form. Moses forsook it.

The wrath of the king must have made a powerful appeal too. "Play it safe" was the counsel of the flesh. Moses must have had fears about the form the king's wrath would take. Pharaoh could not but be enraged at the ingratitude of a foundling boy, reared and trained by his bounty, offered the highest posts in the land, yet stolidly refusing them all for "pie in the sky, bye and bye." But Moses endured "as seeing him who is invisible."

He spurned, along with all the rest, the very gods of Egypt, gods and idols that were the habitation of demons. He triumphed over Satan himself, who, in perchance offering to Moses the throne of Egypt also offered him the opportunity to become Egypt's god. For the pharaoh was the supposed incarnation of Ra, the chief Egyptian god. Again the writer of Hebrews makes his point. His readers must lay hold of the invisible world. The visible world of Judaism was as enticing to them as Egypt was to Moses, but they, too, must endure "as seeing him who is invisible." They could not have both Judaism, the obsolete, visible religious system, and Christ, the risen, ascended, invisible, soon-coming Messiah.

(c) FAITH'S SPIRITUAL VISION (11:28)

His solid victory was followed by spiritual vision. Faith sometimes sees issues that are hidden from the unregenerate man. Moses bowed to *the requirement of the Passover*. "Through faith he kept the passover, and the sprinkling of the blood" (11:28). By the time God revealed to Moses the need for instituting the Passover feast, Moses was unquestionably the greatest man in the world. He had, under God, humbled the greatest world power of his day to the dust and spoiled it from the Mediterranean Sea to its furthest reaches along the Nile. His name was known and dreaded in every Egyptian home. The fame of his actions rang around the world. He was the acknowledged hope and savior of his people. Surely, of all men, Moses, God's chosen instrument, could dispense with the Passover as a personal requirement for himself and his family. Not so! Moses bowed to its requirement. "Through faith *he* kept the passover." He was as much in need of the sheltering power of the blood as the meanest slave in the poorest Hebrew household.

He bowed to *the reason for the Passover*. The destroyer of the firstborn was to be let loose in the land, and Moses and his family needed the protection of the Lamb as much as anyone else. His eyes had been opened to spiritual truth, and with enlightenment came urgent responsibility. Surely the point must have been obvious to the early Hebrew readers of this epistle! Their eyes had been opened, too, to the realities of salvation in Christ, so clearly foreshadowed by their annual

Passover feast. They now stood where Moses stood, and their enlightenment was accompanied with equally grave responsibilities.

(3) THE FAITH OF MOSES' PEOPLE: TRIUMPH OVER THIS WORLD'S DIFFICULTIES (11:29-31)

(a) CROSSING THE RED SEA (11:29)

As the wails of the bereaved arose to heaven from every desolate home in Egypt, Israel marched out of the land, laden with spoil. On his throne, Pharaoh brooded wrathfully over his humiliation and defeat. What had he done? He had weakened and allowed some three million slaves to slip through his fingers. Now, furious, he determined to arm himself and mobilize his army and bring them back.

Soon the shouts of triumph echoing from the ranks of the Hebrew people turned to cries of despair. The rear guard had reported the appearance of the Egyptian army on the horizon. The troops were deploying all along their rear. With the Red Sea before them and the Egyptians behind them, they were trapped.

Then God stepped in and parted the waters of the Red Sea. "Speak unto the children of Israel that they go forward" (Ex. 14:15) was the encouraging word from God. So "by faith they passed through the Red sea as by dry land" (Heb. 11:29). It was a demonstration of *the saint's boldness* in the face of this world's difficulties.

It was also a demonstration of *the sinner's brazenness*, for the Egyptians, seeing the Israelites crossing over the Red Sea, decided to do the same. But unbelief cannot stand where faith stands, and the Egyptians were "drowned" (11:29).

What lesson could the early Hebrew Christians derive from this? The obvious lesson, surely, was that they, too, must "go forward," scorning the difficulties before them and the dangers behind them. But, to go forward, they must be truly saved, for each step along this way is by faith. Unbelief may try to imitate the example of the believer, but brazen confidence in the flesh, efforts to do by natural energy what can only be done by spiritual power, can only end in disaster.

(b) CONQUERING JERICHO (11:30)

Jericho barred the way into Canaan. It was a massive fortress standing squarely astride the entrance into the Promised Land and blocking any advance. It was Satan's device for keeping the children of Israel from entering into their possession. It was a formidable obstacle and would have been so to a well-equipped, highly trained, and well-seasoned army of Roman legionnaires, let alone to the Hebrews who were barely more than novices in the art of war.

To them, Jericho was insurmountable, but that is exactly *where faith triumphs*. "By faith the walls of Jericho fell" (11:30). Human wisdom would have advocated the purchase of slings and catapults and the amassing of huge stockpiles of stones for ammunition. Human wisdom would have suggested digging trenches to enable sappers to creep up to the walls and undermine them. Human wisdom would have called for starving the people of Jericho into submission. But faith had a better way. Faith does not oppose Satan's devices with human devices. "For the weapons of our warfare are not carnal, but mighty through God to the pulling down of strong holds" (2 Cor. 10:4).

Note also *when faith triumphs*. Faith triumphed after the walls of Jericho "were compassed about seven days" (11:30). Only complete obedience to the Word of God could deal with Jericho. The daily procession of the Israelites must have looked like the height of folly to the watchers on Jericho's walls. Not so! It was faith moving forward in the line of God's will. Faith is not unreasonable; it is based on a premise even more sure than that upon which the natural man rests his opinions. It is based squarely on the Word of God. The natural man bases his conclusions on that which seems rational to him. The believer rests his convictions on that which has been revealed to him. The believer goes beyond the natural to the supernatural, to God.

So, once again, the writer of Hebrews makes his point. Satan has his devices to hinder spiritual progress. They are ominous enough, but faith rests itself on God's Word and goes forward, even though the world may mock at what is being done. The towering walls of organized Judaism seemed indeed an insurmountable obstacle. But faith would simply march around those walls, and they would melt like snow before the noonday sun.

(c) CONVINCING RAHAB (11:31)

In its simplest form, the product or prize of faith is salvation, and this is what Rahab procured. Sir Robert Anderson has an interesting note here. He says,

> *Rahab the harlot*! Those who seek for proofs of the divine authorship of Scripture may find one here. Was there ever an Israelite who would have thought of preferring that woman's name to the names of David and Samuel and the prophets, and of coupling it with the name of the great apostle and prophet of the Jewish faith, "whom the Lord knew face to face," and to whom He spoke "as a man speaketh unto his friend"! And what Jew would have dared to give expression to such a thought? But God's thoughts are not our thoughts. And He who immortalized the devotion of the widow who threw her last two mites into the Temple trea-

sury has decreed that the faith of Rahab who, like Moses, took sides with the people of God, shall never be forgotten.[3]

"By faith the harlot Rahab perished not with them that believed not" (11:31). Jericho was doomed together with all who resided within its walls. It was a known fact, a fact accepted as such by Rahab and confessed by her to the spies. Rahab knew little or nothing of God's great plan of salvation, of all the exceeding great and precious promises He had made to Israel, of salvation daily demonstrated in the altar and the sacrifice. She knew only that she was deservedly doomed, and therefore she pleaded for a salvation she knew could come only from Israel's God. And God honored her faith.

The proof of her faith was demonstrated in that she "received the spies with peace" (11:31). They were her only link with the true and living God, and, through them, she reached out for the salvation that was, ultimately, in Christ Jesus. As a matter of fact, God so honored this faith of hers, that He put her in the royal line through which, eventually, Christ Himself came.

Like Rahab, the early Christians had confessed themselves hopeless sinners and had reached out to Christ. Had Rahab drawn back by refusing to bind the scarlet line in the window of her home she would have perished, for her failure to follow through would have proved her faith unreal. The Hebrews must not draw back. They must follow through with their faith just as Rahab did.

2. BY GENERAL ALLUSION (11:32-38)

Time would indeed fail to tell of the exploits and the experiences of the men now brought forward to illustrate the writer's theme.

a. REFERENCE TO PEOPLE BY NAME (11:32)

The author refers to four judges, a king, a prophet, and a whole order of prophets.

(1) AN AGE OF DARKEST APOSTASY (11:32a)

The four judges came from an age of darkest apostasy. Around the names of Gideon and Barak and Samson and Jephthah whole books could be written. Gideon was the exercised man, Barak was the exhorted man, Samson was the exceptional man, and Jephthah was the excommunicated man.

Standing somewhere in the shadows in the life of each of these men was a woman. Behind Gideon was a concubine, a woman who *endangered* him. Indeed,

3. Ibid., p. 100.

her son Abimelech was a bramble of a man, a man who massacred all but one of Gideon's sons and who proclaimed himself a king in defiance of God's law. For, like Solomon after him, Gideon loved many women, had numerous wives, and set a bad example to Israel.

Behind Barak was Deborah, a woman who *encouraged* him. Indeed, without her we might never have heard of Barak at all. It was she who kindled the fire under his faith.

Behind Samson was Delilah, a woman who *enslaved* him. She left him shorn of his locks, bereft of his power, weak as other men, a prey to his foes.

Behind Jephthah was his daughter, a woman who *ennobled* him and taught this world a lesson in filial devotion and love it should never forget.

Gideon was noted for his visions, for the way he was visited by God, given signs, and led by dreams. He became a hero of the faith because he acted according to God's revealed will.

Barak was noted for his victory, and a mighty, resounding victory it was. All was of God. The enemy's nine hundred chariots of iron were simply bogged down in the mud. God stepped in with storm and flood, and the impossible became the possible.

Samson was noted for his valor. His picturesque and colorful victories stand out boldly on the canvas of his times. Even after his dreadful fall, Samson laid hold of God for one last surge of power and for a demonstration that he could be faithful, even unto death.

Jephthah was noted for his vow, a rash vow, indeed, but one which, after all, did lay hold of God in mighty yearning and desire.

What lessons the Hebrew readers of this epistle could glean from the lives of these men whose histories were so familiar to them: lessons of faith doing what God demanded, of faith believing God for the impossible, of faith picking itself up after a disastrous fall to become true to death, of faith desiring God above all earthly ties and joys.

(2) an age of divine approval (11:32b)

Moving from an age of darkest apostasy, the days of the judges, the writer stops at the age of divine approval and tells us that "time would fail me to tell of . . . David" (11:32b). Was there ever a man subject to so many trials and temptations as David? To such constant persecutions? On some twenty-four different occasions, King Saul either sought to murder David himself or arranged to have him murdered. Yet David patiently endured, refusing to retaliate even when his enemy was in his hand. Touch the life of David at scores of points and immediately you see Christ shining through. He is one of the greatest types of Christ in the

Old Testament. The Hebrews could learn much from David's life of patience under persecution, of growing in grace and increasing in the knowledge of God, of maturing under opposition into an instrument meet for the Master's use, of becoming Christlike. The writer of the epistle does not tell them any of this. He leaves them to go back to David for themselves, to read the record of his life, to spend time with his psalms, to apply the lessons that they learn.

(3) AN AGE OF DIRECT APPEAL (11:32c)

And what of Samuel and the prophets, of an age of direct appeal? Is there a more gracious, generous, faithful man than Samuel, the last of the judges and the first of the prophets? He found Israel in chaos and left it in David's hands. Traveling from place to place, he taught the Word of God faithfully to all. He founded the prophetic order so that, long after him, God's Word might be studied and proclaimed. What volumes could be written of Samuel, the man who faithfully withstood Saul's failure and ultimate apostasy and died in peace, having seen God's salvation, as it were, in David.

The great word that sums up Samuel's life and the lives of Israel's illustrious prophets is "faithfulness." They were faithful men, standing for God in stormy weather as well as when the sun shone warm. The Hebrews would do well to learn from this.

b. REFERENCE TO PEOPLE BY FAME (11:33-38)

(1) THOSE DELIVERED FROM THEIR FOES (11:33-35a)

There were those "who through faith subdued kingdoms" (11:33a), such men as Moses and Daniel. Moses subdued Egypt by power from without, and Daniel subdued Babylon and Persia by promotion from within. Men like these were raised up by God to control the destinies of vast empires and to help move forward His plans for their age.

There were those who "wrought righteousness" (11:33b; faith behaving) and who "obtained promises" (11:33b; faith believing). We think instinctively of a man like Daniel, who in his youth took his stand upon the Word of God and refused to eat meat sacrificed to idols and who, in his old age, boldly took his stand upon the promises of God to Jeremiah and sought God's face for an end to the captivity. In keeping with this, we are reminded of Daniel again, who "stopped the mouths of lions" (11:33c).

Then there were those who "quenched the violence of fire" (11:34a), obviously a reference to Daniel's three friends who dared the burning, fiery furnace rather than apostatize and bow before the graven image of the king. Others "escaped the edge of the sword" (11:34*b*). For long years the edge of the sword was never far from David, yet God preserved him. Elisha, too, knew how to call upon God for the protection of heavenly armies and how to call down fire from heaven to consume his foes. Some "out of weakness were made strong" (11:34*c*), as the book of Judges amply illustrates. Again and again, in that day, God chose weak and foolish things to confound the things that were mighty and wise. He used a younger brother, a woman, a left-handed man, a lamp and a pitcher, an oxgoad, a nail, the jawbone of an ass. Others "waxed valiant in fight, turned to flight the armies of the aliens" (11:34*d*). What did Joshua, for example, know about war, having been reared a slave in Egypt? Yet God raised him up and used him to subdue all of Canaan.

"Women received their dead raised to life again" (11:35*a*). Only two examples of this are given in the Old Testament, one from the days of Elijah (1 Kings 17:17-24) and one from the days of Elisha (2 Kings 4:18-37).

All these examples illustrate faith's bringing people to deliverance from their foes. Example after example is given to assure the Hebrews that, no matter what they might be called upon to face for their profession of faith in Christ, God is well able to deliver if He so wills.

(2) THOSE DELIVERED TO THEIR FOES (11:35*b*-38)

But other examples are given of those, not delivered from their foes but, in the mysterious, sovereign will of God, delivered over to their foes. For "others were tortured, not accepting deliverance; that they might obtain a better resurrection" (11:35*b*). The early Christians were soon to prove, when finally their witness aroused the ire of Rome, that a pinch of salt on some pagan altar might have won them freedom from torture. But the prospect of a better resurrection (better than the two just mentioned) must spur them on to submit to torture rather than to renounce the faith, just as in old times many a Jew chose death in preference to dishonor.

Others "had trial of cruel mockings and scourgings, yea, moreover of bonds and imprisonment" (11:36). Belittled and beaten, bound and bruised, they marched triumphantly forward. They "were stoned" (11:37*a*). This was the common form of execution among the Jews. They were "sawn asunder" (11:37*b*). The tradition is that evil King Manasseh subjected the godly prophet Isaiah to this fate, putting him in the hollow trunk of a tree and then commanding that the tree be sawn down. Such is the cruelty of man! "They were tempted" (11:37*c*), as for example was Joseph, with sore temptations. "They were slain with the sword" (11:37*d*), as when, in a jealous rage, King Saul ordered the execution of the priests who had befriended David. "They wandered about in sheepskins and in goatskins; being destitute, afflicted, tormented (of whom the world was not worthy), they wandered in deserts, and in mountains, and in dens, and caves of the earth" (11:37*e*-38). Beggared and banished, counted as the filth of the earth, many a saint of God has borne the brunt of this world's hate.

What need was there for the writer to cite cases? The Scripture and the history of the Maccabees were filled with illustrations of these things, every one of them perfectly well known to the Jews. If, the writer of Hebrews argues, men and women could bear such things for the faith in the old days when they lived in the shadowlands of faith, how much more should Christian believers, dwelling in the full blaze of light brought to men by Christ, be willing to dare all for Him! So then, whether delivered from their foes or delivered to their foes, they should be willing to remain true to Christ.

C. Faith Decreed (11:39-40)

It remains only for the writer to make his point. At great length he has marshaled his witnesses and demonstrated the life of faith. But was the life of faith only for Old Testament believers? Not at all. It is for all.

1. THE APPEAL (11:39)

"And these all, having obtained a good report through faith, received not the promise" (11:39). Throughout the entire Old Testament period, believing men and women, no matter what their circumstances, looked forward by faith to a coming day in which all God's promises would be "yea and in him Amen" (see 2 Cor. 1:19-20). Thus they stand, the illustrious saints of the Hebrew faith, making a grand appeal to the believers of this age. Were these Hebrew Christians facing persecution for their faith in Christ? Let them bear it with fortitude, for they had far more light than those who, in the glimmerings of the Old Testament age, dared so much. They looked ahead. Could these Hebrew believers standing on the resurrection side of Calvary do less? Can we?

2. THE APPLICATION (11:40)

So the great appeal merges into the great application. "God having provided some better thing for us, that they without us should not be made perfect" (Heb. 11:40). The Old Testament saints had only the shadows; we have the substance. They had good things; we have better things. Their sphere and horizon was earthly; ours is heavenly. Thus the writer of Hebrews applies the lessons from all the lives he has been considering, applies them with great leverage and tremendous pressure, to the lives of the Hebrew Christians to whom he wrote. "Go on," he says. "Go on. Never go back. Go on."

VIII

The Wisdom of Hope (12:1-29)

Hope is the soul's anchor. We can, perhaps, best appreciate the importance, need, and strength of hope by looking at it from a negative point of view. We tend to think of hope as an anemic word compared with faith or love. Ask a person, "Are you saved?" and receive the reply, "I hope so!" And the response seems so vague, so uncertain, so lacking in faith, that it is all too inadequate a reply to the question. But think of what a life is *without* hope, and the value of this moral attribute immediately takes on a sharper focus. A person is lying in a hospital ward, and the doctor looks at the relatives gathered around the bed and shakes his head. "There's no hope," he says. All is lost. A prisoner stands before the judge, having exhausted his last court of appeal, and sees the look in the judge's face and hears the dread sentence of death being confirmed. His case is hopeless. All is lost.

The great theme of Hebrews 12 is hope. Hope, in the Scriptures, is not something vague, based on wishful thinking and uncertainties. Hope is vital and dynamic and real, because it is based on eternal verities. In Hebrews 12, God speaks to His children. That they are His children is evident because He chastens them. He sets before them grand and glorious future prospects, for He wants them to patiently endure present trials and testings. God is going to establish His kingdom, so amid all of earth's upheavals this "blessed hope" should be the guiding star, the pledge of complete victory both today, as we trudge on through the desert sands, and tomorrow, when all His bright purposes are fully seen.

A. To Run in the Heavenly Race (12:1-13)

If hope is to do its vital work in the believer's soul, then it must be firmly fixed on the Lord Jesus. Contemplation of Him will bring two forms of discipline into our lives: self-discipline and spiritual discipline.

B. To Rest in the Heavenly Grace (12:14-29)
  1. The Stringent Command (12:14-17)
    a. The Need for a Holy Life Declared (12:14-15)
      (1) The Delights of Following in This Path (12:14)
        (a) Living in Harmony with Man (12:14*a*)
        (b) Living in Holiness Before God (12:14*b*)
      (2) The Dangers of Falling from This Path (12:15)
        (a) The Inference of Such a Fall (12:15*a*)
        (b) The Influence of Such a Fall (12:15*b*)
    b. The Need for a Holy Life Demonstrated (12:16-17)
      (1) What Esau Did (12:16)
      (2) What Esau Desired (12:17*a*)
      (3) What Esau Discovered (12:17*b*)
  2. The Striking Contrast (12:18-24)
    a. The Old Covenant Made Distance Imperative (12:18-21)
      (1) The Mount of God (12:18-19*a*)
        (a) The Fearful Vision (12:18-19*a*)
        (b) The Fearful Voice (12:19*b*-20)
      (2) The Man of God (12:21)
    b. The New Covenant Makes Distance Impossible (12:22-24)
      (1) The Plane on Which Believers Now Live (12:22*a-b*)
        (a) Remarkable for Its Security (Mount Zion) (12:22*a*)
        (b) Remarkable for Its Society (City of the Living God) (12:22*b*)
      (2) The Presence in Which Believers Now Live (12:23*c*-24)
        (a) The Marvel of It (12:23*c-d*)
          i. I Am There as a Justified Man (12:23*c*)
          ii. I Am There with All Justified Men (12:23*d*)
        (b) The Means of It (12:24)
          i. The Continuing Work of Jesus (12:24*a*)
          ii. The Completed Work of Jesus (12:24*b*)
  3. The Stirring Conclusion (12:25-29)
    a. The Appeal (12:25-27)
      (1) By Way of Exhortation (12:25*a*)
      (2) By Way of Example (12:25)
        (a) The Danger of Insulting the Person of God (12:25*c*)
        (b) The Danger of Ignoring the Power of God (12:26-27)
          i. What God Demonstrated So Forcibly Then (12:26*a*)
          ii. What God Declares So Forcibly Now (12:26*b*-27)
    b. The Application (12:28-29)
      (1) We Are to Be Moved by a Glorious Fact (12:28*a*)
      (2) We Are to Be Moved by God's Gracious Favor (12:28*b*)
      (3) We Are to Be Moved by a Godly Fear (12:29)

VIII

The Wisdom of Hope (12:1-29)

A. To Run in the Heavenly Race (12:1-13)
  1. The Call to Self-Discipline (12:1-3)
    a. The Stand (12:1a)
    b. The Struggle (12:1b-c)
      (1) Away with All Impediments (12:1b)
      (2) Away with All Impatience (12:1c)
    c. The Strategy (12:2-3)
      (1) The Glorious Perspective (12:2)
      (2) Our Grand Persuasion (12:3)
  2. The Call to Spiritual Discipline (12:4-13)
    a. The Explanation (12:4)
    b. The Exhortation (12:5-6)
      (1) That Which Was Quite Forgotten by the Readers (12:5a)
      (2) That Which Was Quoted Forcefully by the Writer (12:5b-6)
    c. The Expectation (12:7-8)
      (1) Evidence That a Person Is a Son, Not a Sinner (12:7)
      (2) Evidence That a Person Is a Sinner, Not a Son (12:8)
    d. The Example (12:9-10)
      (1) The Lesson from Human Chastening (12:9)
      (2) The Limitation of Human Chastening (12:10)
    e. The Experience (12:11-13)
      (1) The Change to Be Considered (12:11)
        (a) The Present Experience (12:11a)
        (b) The Promised Experience (12:11b)
      (2) The Challenge to Be Considered (12:12-13)
        (a) Be Strong (12:12)
        (b) Be Straight (12:13)

1. *THE CALL TO SELF-DISCIPLINE* (12:1-3)

The picture set before us is that of a race. The names have been entered, but the course has not yet been run. This was exactly the position of many of the Hebrews to whom this letter was addressed. They had professed the faith but had not yet made any forward move. Indeed, some, seeing the formidable length of the course, the stiffness of the gradients, the hindrances strewn along the way, were about to withdraw. Their attention was therefore drawn to three things.

a. THE STADIUM (12:1a)

First, there was the stadium, the grandstand packed with spectators, each one of whom was himself an overcomer in the race. "We also are compassed about with so great a cloud of witnesses" (12:1), the writer says. What a galaxy of the great there is assembled there! Each has run the course and has triumphed. Each wears the laurels of victory. From out of the past they look at us as we stand at the starting line or press forward down the track. What an incentive to win, to persevere to the finishing line, to make it all the way! But it will not be without a struggle.

b. THE STRUGGLE (12:1b-c)

"Let us lay aside every weight, and the sin which doth so easily beset us" (12:1). In other words, *away with all impediments!* Weights are essentially harmless in themselves. Athletes in training often deliberately use weights as handicaps but only so they can fling them aside when the race itself begins and fly down the track with winged feet, suddenly free from all clogging loads. Legitimate things can become weights to hold us back—love of home and family, love of country, love of comfort and ease, contentment with job, security at work. These legitimate things can become weights to hold us back in the race. Sins are evidently harmful in themselves. Obviously we must get rid of these.

And, once begun, *away with all impatience!* This is no one-hundred-yard dash. Set before us is a long, winding way with many things to discourage and dismay. We are not trapped or beguiled into this race. It is set before us. Before we start, we are given some idea of what lies ahead. The phrase "let us" underlines the voluntary nature of the undertaking. God urges everyone to enter, but He coerces none.

c. THE STRATEGY (12:2-3)

The incentive to win is in *the glorious perspective* we have because we are "looking unto Jesus" (12:2a). The word *looking* is *aphoraō*; it occurs only here and means "looking away from all else, looking at that which fills the heart." We are going to run, not because of the prize at the end and not because so many illustrious saints have run the course in the past and have been gloriously crowned, but because the vision of Jesus thrills the soul.

We are filled with thoughts of *His person*; He is "the author and finisher of . . . faith" (12:2*b*). He, above all others, has been down this course. He knows how it should be run. The word *author* is really "leader," suggesting that He is going to remain a pace or two ahead of us all the way, to show us where the obstacles are and to direct each step.

We are filled with thoughts of *His passion*: "who for the joy that was set before him endured the cross, despising the shame" (12:2*c*). No runner in the race ever had such terrible experiences as He. Yet, He kept looking ahead and pressing on with His heart fixed on the coming joy.

We are filled with thoughts of *His position,* for He "is set down at the right hand of the throne of God" (12:2*d*). There He is, crowned! There He is, smiling down from the utmost height upon those who, for His name's sake, would enter the race and follow His lead.

Is there anything the writer of Hebrews has overlooked in pressing home to his Hebrew readers the need for going on? He seems to have thought of everything!

But it is not only the glorious perspective we have of Jesus that thrusts us into the race; it is *our grand persuasion* as well. We "consider him" (12:3*a*). The word is *analogizomai*, another word that occurs only here and means to "reckon up." We take full note of Him. He "endured such contradiction of sinners against himself" (12:3*b*). We count up all that was against Him, yet He won. The things arrayed against us are petty compared to the opposition He faced. We can win too. Therefore, we are to consider Him "lest ye be weary and faint in your minds" (12:3*c*). We must consider Him, and that will keep us from drooping, keep us from discouragement. He is the great stimulant to nerve the soul to the utmost. When tempted to give in, we need only think, "He's watching!" What a difference it makes, even in human affairs, to know that in some great contest a loved one is eagerly watching to see us win!

This section shows the need for chastening as a spiritual discipline in life, for, if the race is to be won and our hope to be realized, God has to bring pressure upon us in certain areas of our lives to help us get rid of weights and sins.

2. *THE CALL TO SPIRITUAL DISCIPLINE (12:4-13)*

a. THE EXPLANATION (12:4)

First comes the explanation. "Ye have not yet resisted unto blood, striving against sin" (12:4). No doubt two sins are in view here: the "besetting sin," things in the life that trip us, entangle us, and bring us down; and the crowning sin of throwing in the sponge, of giving up the race altogether, which is a sure mark of apostasy. This explanation sets the stage for the following discussion on the need for chastening. For, in the final analysis, it was a matter of submitting to the chastening and being proved a true child of God or of refusing the chastening and being exposed as a charlatan.

b. THE EXHORTATION (12:5-6)

It deals first with that which was quite forgotten by the readers. "And ye have forgotten the exhortation which speaketh unto you as unto children" (12:5a). The quotation is from Proverbs 3:11-12. The passage evidently meant much to the writer, who seems to have roamed the entire Old Testament in his quest for arguments to encourage the true believers and enlighten the false professors. His Hebrew readers were probably familiar enough with this quotation, but possibly they had not thought of applying it to themselves.

The Scripture forcibly quoted by the writer declares, "My son, despise not thou the chastening of the Lord, nor faint when thou art rebuked of him; for whom the Lord loveth he chasteneth, and scourgeth every son whom he receiveth" (12:5b-6). Scourging is to be taken *soberly*. It is not to be treated with carelessness. We should ask, Why is this happening to me? It is to be accepted *sensibly*. We are not to faint under the Lord's dealings, for He does not flog us in blind rage but measures the weight of each stroke.

One of the great passages in *How Green Was My Valley* tells of the flogging of Huw Morgan by the schoolmaster, Elijah-Jonas-Sessions. The boy had been fighting and was made to bend over in such a way that his back was stretched to receive the stick. The stick swished twice as the bullying schoolmaster limbered up for his task, and the sound of the stick awoke all Huw's tingling nerves in anticipation of coming hurt. Then the stick swished again, and Huw saw its shadow on the floor and felt the first sharp, shocking, burning of its work.

Again, again, and again the strokes came as the boy across whom it was stretched staggered at the weight of the blows. Without pause, as the clock works, the sound changing as the strokes fell, the stick soared upward and down again until Huw Morgan's back seemed to be in flames and his eyes blind and his head filled with thunder, and the strokes were still coming. Only now they were but a hard, dull laying on until the stick broke.

"Now then," said Mr. Jonas, in falsetto and breathless, "fight again! That was just a taste! Back to your place! No more nonsense! Teach you manners!" The brutal schoolmaster himself was exhausted by the flogging; his face twitched; his hands trembled from his spent passion. And poor Huw got his legs to bring him to his seat and saw that one of the girls had torn her handkerchief to shreds under the emotion of watching the scene.

God is not like that schoolmaster. Each stroke He administers is weighed by Him in fairness and firmness to suit our needs exactly and to bring us to our senses, not lay us senseless in the dust.

Scourging is to be taken not only soberly and sensibly, but *spiritually*, as well. The spiritually discerning believer will recognize the disciplines of life to be evidence of the Lord's love.

c. THE EXPECTATION (12:7-8)

Then comes the expectation. It is to be expected that chastening will accomplish something. It will, indeed, demonstrate one of two things.

First, it will give *evidence that a person is a son, not a sinner*. "If ye endure chastening, God dealeth with you as with sons, for what son is he whom the father chasteneth not?" (12:7). Thus God dealt with Job and Eliphaz; and although Eliphaz was wrong both in the spirit in which he spoke and in his understanding of what was really happening, he was right in what he said: "Happy is the man whom God correcteth: therefore despise not thou the chastening of the Almighty" (Job 5:17). The very fact that God chastens proves us to be sons.

But, second, it will give *evidence that a person is a sinner not a son*. "But if ye are without chastisement, whereof all are partakers, then are ye bastards, and not sons" (12:8). That is a strong statement. God does not own those whom He does not chasten. They are without true parentage. Christendom may be their mother, but God is not their father.

d. THE EXAMPLE (12:9-10)

Next he gives an example, an analogy from everyday life. There is the obvious lesson from parental chastening. Since we have had to submit to human chastening and have learned to respect our fathers because of their authority, how much more must we yield to God and hold Him in awe. Yet, how many people rebel and say, "Why is this happening to me? Why should I have to suffer? How can this be for my good?"

The obvious lesson from human chastening lies in its equally obvious limitations. With all the best intentions in the world, parents make mistakes. They underdiscipline, overdiscipline, fail to discipline at all, or discipline from wrong motives, in the wrong way, and at the wrong time. God makes no such mistakes. He always chastens for our good and to draw us closer to Himself.

D. L. Moody told of a wealthy couple whose only child died as a baby. They were brokenhearted and inconsolable, and, trying to fill up the void left in their lives, they took a trip to the Holy Land. There they saw a shepherd trying to coax some sheep across a stream, but the fast-running water frightened the sheep, and they held back. The shepherd stooped down and took a lamb and carried it across the river. The bleating ewe sheep watched her young lamb being taken away, and suddenly she lost all her fright of the stream. Looking where her treasure had gone, she followed, too, and soon the whole flock was on the other side.

The incident spoke to the bereaved parents. Suddenly they realized what God was doing in their lives. He was making heaven more real, more significant to them. They had never entertained thoughts of heaven before and had been heedless of God's gentler dealings with them. Seeing in a flash the stern lesson their chastening had been intended to accomplish, they returned home to spend their lives focused on heaven rather than on earth.

e. THE EXPERIENCE (12:11-13)

The actual experience of chastening is not pleasant, and the writer of Hebrews has more insight than to pretend that it is. However, chastening does bring about *a change*. Who ever heard of a boy relishing a whipping. "Oh, boy! I'm going to get the belt! I can't wait. I love being beaten. I hope Dad can find a switch with plenty of spring to it so that it'll hurt real bad." Nobody talks like that!

But afterward it "yieldeth [the] peaceable fruit . . . of righteousness" (12:11). The important thing is to see God's loving hand in the chastening and to cooperate so that the intended result will be realized speedily.

So, then, here's the challenge: *Be strong!* "Wherefore lift up the hands that hang down, and the feebled knees" (12:12). The word *anorthoo* means to "set aright" and is used of the restoration of ruins. As a boy, I remember frequently passing a tumbledown old castle on the edge of my hometown. Time had done its worst with the ruins, and many a fallen stone littered what had once been the castle courtyard. The whole structure looked as if it would collapse before many more years. The last time I was back, the building had been greatly restored. The fallen stones had been fitted back into the walls. The renovation had restored the castle's former appearance. It had been "set aright." That is what chastening is intended to accomplish in our lives; it will make us strong, setting things aright.

The challenge is not only to be strong but also to *be straight*. "And make straight paths for your feet, lest that which is lame be turned out of the way; but let it rather be healed" (12:13). The condition in the believer's life that calls for chastening frequently involves his relationship with others. They have stumbled, and this is a serious matter. The problem may not only be that of some crookedness in the life but also of some crankiness there; hence the injunction not only to make straight paths but also to follow peace.

B. TO REST IN THE HEAVENLY GRACE (12:14-29)

1. THE STRINGENT COMMAND (12:14-17)

Chastening leads to holy living, and this, in turn, involves living in harmony with our fellowmen.

a. THE NEED FOR A HOLY LIFE DECLARED (12:14-15)

The writer emphasizes *the delights of following in this path* (12:14). Thus, we are told to "follow peace with all men, and holiness, without which no man shall see the Lord" (12:14). To be peaceable does not mean we must surrender conviction, but it does mean that we will be courteous, considerate, and willing to comply with legitimate social customs and will refuse to quarrel.

Many Christians seem to believe that being a Christian absolves them from the ordinary obligations of social intercourse and allows them to behave in a rude and unmannerly way not only toward non-Christians but also toward each other. The Lord Jesus was a perfect Gentleman, gracious, thoughtful of other people, and tactful, even though firm and unsparing in His attitude toward sin.

True sanctity of life will involve more than harmonious living with other people; it will involve living in holiness before God. This is why mention is made of that "sanctification [holiness] without which no man shall see the Lord." The writer of this epistle has already described the believers as "holy brethren" (3:1). This is the unassailable position of every believer; he enjoys positional sanctification. Each one's calling is to be "a saint" (see 1 Cor. 1:2; Col. 1:2). But our daily conduct may not be in keeping with our divine calling, so we are to "follow after," that is, actively pursue sanctification. By deliberate choice, we are to seek cleansing from daily defilement. We are deliberately to choose those things that make for godliness. Pursuing practical sanctification is the proof that we possess positional sanctification.

Then what about *the dangers of falling from this path* of holiness (12:15)? First the writer underlines *the inference of such a fall*. "Looking diligently," he says, "lest any man fail of the grace of God" (12:15a). So a fall from grace is possible. However, a person who falls from grace, in this context, is not a person who loses his salvation but a believer who fails to avail himself of the "means of grace" made available to him by God to help him in his Christian life. Such means of grace are the ordinances of baptism and the Lord's Supper, fellowship with other believers, the Word of God, prayer, the indwelling Holy Spirit, and similar things. The believer who neglects these things falls into sin and loses, not his salvation, but his reward.

The writer, however, gives more than a statement about the inference of such a fall from grace; he underlines *the influence of such a fall*. For no man lives in a vacuum, the true believer less than anybody else. He is a member of the mystical Body of Christ, and his conduct, conversation, and character all have a direct influence upon the lives of other believers. Therefore, he is to beware "lest any root of bitterness springing up trouble you, and thereby many be defiled" (12:15*b*). The writer of Hebrews is here citing a well-known precept of the Mosaic law: "Lest there should be among you man, or woman, or family, or tribe, whose heart turneth away this day from the Lord our God, to go and serve the gods of these nations; lest there should be among you a root that beareth gall and wormwood" (Deut. 29:18). A person who lives an unsanctified life has a bad influence on others. Evil spreads, whether it be moral or doctrinal. It leads to bitterness between believers and to lives contaminated with the poison of gossip and resentment. People invariably take sides.

b. THE NEED FOR A HOLY LIFE DEMONSTRATED (12:16-17)

The need for a holy life is demonstrated by reference to Esau, Jacob's twin brother. Esau was brought up in the patriarchal family, but he was devoid of any vestige of spiritual life.

Our attention is directed first to *what Esau did*. He is called a fornicator, although his offense was not moral but spiritual. He was branded as impure and impervious to spiritual privilege and responsibility. He was "profane," that is, his life had no sacred enclosure where God could dwell. His body was not the temple of the Holy Spirit. He treated spiritual things as being of no account and proved it by selling his birthright for the immediate gratification of appetite. Esau cared nothing for his birthright—the right to be the family priest—and he cared nothing about being in the genealogical tree of Christ. As for inheriting a double portion of his father's property, he preferred something that was here and now rather than waiting until the future for that. So he sold his birthright for a "morsel of meat" (12:16)—a bowl of stew!

The Hebrews are then reminded of *what Esau desired*. Later on he wanted the blessing. Too late he realized the value of what he had lightly thrown away. For while Esau wasted no regrets over the lost right to be the family priest, and although he cared nothing for the privilege of being related to the coming Christ, he did desire the double portion of the property. He did want that part of the blessing.

Finally, notice is taken of *what Esau discovered*. "He found no place of repentance, though he sought it carefully with tears" (12:17*b*, margin). The repentance spoken of here was not repentance on Esau's part. It was repentance, a change of mind, on the part of his father, Isaac, that Esau wanted. Isaac had given the blessing to Jacob, and though Esau pleaded and entreated for Isaac to reverse his action and give the blessing to him, it was all in vain. Esau was forever the loser, because he had so lightly valued spiritual realities and thrown them away for a brief moment's physical comfort.

The principle ever holds good; the believer who throws away golden opportunities in order to indulge some carnal desire will pay for it in the end. Thus the writer again presses home his point. God has a stringent command that believers must follow holiness. They must not draw back, for if they do, if they settle for something less, if they trade spiritual things for earthly things as Esau did, they surely will live to regret it.

2. THE STRIKING CONTRAST (12:18-24)

a. THE OLD COVENANT MADE DISTANCE IMPERATIVE (12:18-21)

The epistle's readers are again taken back to when the Old Covenant was ratified at Sinai at the giving of the Mosaic law. They are reminded of the dreadful sights and sounds that heralded God's presence on the mountain. They can be thankful that they have not come to a place like that.

There was the fearful vision of burning and blackness, of tempest and trumpet. There were fearful manifestations of divine power, enough to chill the stoutest heart. Everything was designed to impress God's awesome holiness upon the people. God was not to be trifled with.

Along with the fearful vision was the equally fearful voice, "the voice of words; which voice they that heard intreated that the word should not be spoken to them any more" (12:19). It was a voice that smote terror to the soul. Such was the giving of the law. But worse, "they could not endure that which was commanded" (12:20). The law itself was terrible. If even a beast so much as troubled the mountain, it had to be stoned to death. The whole lesson was one of God's unapproachable holiness and of the defilement of sin of every man and beast.

Even Moses could not stand it. "So terrible was the sight, that Moses said, I exceedingly fear and quake" (12:21). Moses, who had met God at the burning bush and who had proved God's love and grace in a score of ways, ascended the mount with quaking limbs, his whole body shaking with fright. The Old Covenant made distance imperative.

b. THE NEW COVENANT MAKES DISTANCE IMPOSSIBLE (12:22-24)

But the New Covenant makes distance impossible. What folly to do what Esau did—trade something of inestimable value for something that, after all, could never satisfy. What folly to trade the sweet and gentle blessings of Christianity for the cold, hard, formal, fearful offerings of Judaism!

Attention is first drawn to *the plane on which believers now live*. It is a plane remarkable for its security. "But ye are come unto mount Zion" (12:22*a*). Mount Zion in Jerusalem was crowned by David's citadel. It was the strongest point in the city, much like the Tower of London was in England in medieval times. Mount Zion was a vital part of Jerusalem's defenses. It speaks of security. We have come to the heavenly Zion, to a place of absolute security.

We have come to "the city of the living God, . . . the heavenly Jerusalem" (12:22*b*). God first placed man in a garden; now He places him in a city. His city, a place where all His own are gathered in a glorious, eternal community. Three things are associated with cities—position, population, and progress. In olden days, cities were located on rivers or hills where they could command the surrounding countryside by occupying a strategic position. Cities attract all manner of men; they exist to make life richer by means of their organization and wealth.

The city of the living God is like no city on earth. As to its *position*, it is settled in heaven; as to its *people*, it is the eternal home of the redeemed; and as to its *purpose*, it exists to make life rich and glorious for the saints throughout the endless ages of eternity. It is a place where God's order is fully observed. The apostle John used a whole chapter to describe it, and what a city it is! It will be brought down from heaven during the Millennium and placed in stationary orbit over the earthly Jerusalem, to be the ultimate seat of authority during the golden age. The redeemed are so completely saved that, in spirit, they already have come to that city. Their citizenship already has been lodged there. They remain in this world as its ambassadors, representing the city's glorious King at the court of human hearts.

If the plane on which we dwell is in the heavenlies, the people with whom we dwell are no less glorious. We are associated with the *servants* of God. We are come to an "innumerable company of angels, to the general assembly" (12:22*c*-23*a*). The reference here is not to the church but to the angelic hosts. The angels were present at Sinai at the giving of the law, but what a difference there is now! Instead of the manifestations of awesome power, there is "joy in the presence of the angels of God" (Luke 15:10) because the sons of men are being redeemed. We who believe are brought into the company of the angels because they are "ministering spirits" sent into the world to wait upon us (see Heb. 1:14). Here we catch a brief glimpse of the great gathering center from which they rush forth to care for the needs of God's children.

We are associated with the *sons* of God. We are come to the "church of the firstborn which are written in heaven" (12:23*b*). No creature has ever seen that church in its entirety, but it is already complete in the counsels of God. The day is yet to come when the last person will be added to its roll and the completed Body of Christ will be caught up to meet the Lord in the air. In the meantime, we belong with this grand company. These are the persons with whom we live, the angels and the saints of God.

But then there is *the presence in which believers now live*. We live in the presence of God, for we are come "to God the Judge of all" (12:23c). God has already judged us in the cross. Because of Christ's work, we are pronounced justified. What an amazing fact! We live in God's presence, in the presence of His character, of all things, as *Judge*! We have no fear, no dismay, no apprehension, no sense of shame or loss of guilt. For not the slightest stain of sin, not even the faintest memory of guilt, remains. So perfect is our justification that we can bask in the presence of Him from whose face the heavens and the earth will one day flee away.

Years ago, in a Southern congregation, a preacher waxed eloquent in prayer over this very passage from Hebrews. "Lord," he said, "we are come to the mountain of Zion!" One of his people, a wrinkled old lady, cried out in ecstasy, "Glory to God!"

"Lord, we are come to the city of God!"

"Glory to God!" cried the old woman.

"Lord we are in the heavenly Jerusalem!"

"Glory to God!"

"And, Lord, we are with the multitude of the angels!"

"Glory to God!"

"And we are enrolled in heaven, Lord!"

"Glory to God!"

"And we are with the general assembly!"

"Glory to God!"

"And Lord," cried the preacher, lifting up his hands, "Lord, we aren't fit for such honor, Lord!"

"Glory to God!" cried the old woman. *"It's a lie!"*

And she was right. We are brought into this company as *justified* men and women.

But we are not only there as justified people; we are there *with* justified people. "Ye are come to . . . the spirits of just men made perfect" (12:22-23). Some time ago my saintly mother was taken home to heaven. It occurred to me with particular force one day when, by habit, I began to mention her name in prayer, that I could no longer pray for my mother. I felt a real sense of sorrow and thought of the many times when I could and should have prayed for her and had not done so. And now, I could pray for her no more. Then the Spirit of God whispered in my soul, "But you can give praise for her even if you cannot offer prayer for her." Later, I was sharing this with my wife, and she asked, "Yes, and you cannot only praise God *for* her; you can praise God *with* her." What a blessed thought that was!

Surely this is what the writer of Hebrews means here. We have come to the spirits of just men made perfect. We are brought into a realm where time and sense are immaterial and where together—the saints on earth and the saints in glory—we can lift our voices in harmony around one common mercy seat.

We have come to all this because of Christ's continuing work. We have come to "Jesus the mediator of the new covenant" (12:24a). There He is in heaven, His hands upraised, mediating that covenant that banishes all distance, engaged in what has been happily called "His unfinished work" at God's right hand. And we have come to "the blood of sprinkling, that speaketh better things than that of Abel" (12:24b).

We are brought near because of Christ's completed work. The blood of Abel cried out to God from the ground for vengeance. It is, of course, quite possible that "the blood of Abel" refers not to his own blood crying for vengeance but that the comparative "better" refers to the blood of Abel's *sacrifice* (11:4) as compared with the blood of Christ's sacrifice.

The blood of Jesus speaks of vengeance already past. It is the blood that slaked the fire of God's wrath. The fire on Israel's altar always cried for more, more, more. But this blood has quenched the flame, and it speaks to God and man alike of justice satisfied fully and forever.

This is the last of the five warning passages in Hebrews. In view of the marvelous position now occupied by God's people, we must beware of disobeying God's summons. Since reference to Mount Zion has special significance in view of the Millennium, it would seem that the punishment emphasis here is millennial. Much of the training through which we are going today is to fit us for millennial position and responsibility. Believers can lose out on many a position of power, responsibility, and glory during the Millennium age. True, our position in eternity cannot be affected by a careless life, for everything there rests upon Christ's perfect and finished work, but our position in the Millennium kingdom is an entirely different matter. That can be affected by the quality of life we live now during our probationary period on earth.

3. THE STIRRING CONCLUSION (12:25-29)

a. THE APPEAL (12:25-27)

In making his appeal, in view of the magnificent position and prospect of the believer, the writer begins with *an exhortation.* "See that ye refuse not him that speaketh" (12:25a). "God . . . hath . . . spoken"—that's how this epistle begins. We had better listen. The higher a speaker's rank and dignity, the more weight we should attach to his words. Little weight is attached to a child's prattle; but if a policeman speaks, we listen because of the authority vested in his position; and if a king or president speaks, we pay attention still more because his words affect our way of life. When *God* speaks, let all keep silent and pay earnest heed.

The exhortation is backed up by *an example* with a twofold thrust. There is, first, *the danger of insulting God's Person*. In Old Testament times there was no escape for those who refused to listen when God spoke in government. "They escaped not who refused him that spake on earth" (12:25*b*). Any person present at the giving of the law, who pressed forward onto the mount when expressly commanded to stand back, was summarily executed by divine decree. There was no escape from the full weight and penalty of God's wrath.

In New Testament times there is no escape for those who hang back when God urges them to go forward. Now He speaks in grace. "Much more shall not we escape, if we turn away from him that speaketh from heaven" (12:25*c*). For a person to turn his back deliberately upon a ruler, speaking in grace but from a seat of power, would be to invite righteous indignation and wrath. How much more serious an offense is it to turn one's back upon God when He speaks in grace and offers the highest of all possible positions and privileges! It is an offense of the most serious kind.

In addition to offering insult to God's person by turning away from Him, there is *the danger of ignoring God's power*. Again a comparison is made between Old Testament and New Testament times (12:26-27).

Going back to the Old Testament, the writer warns of *what God demonstrated so fearfully then*. He was the God "whose voice then shook the earth" (12:26*a*). The very earth trembled when God spoke of old, for it heard and recognized the voice of its Maker. If the dumb, inanimate creation trembled, how much more should sinful men?

Coming back to New Testament times, the writer warns of *what God declares so forcibly now*. "Yet once more I shake not the earth only, but also the heaven. And this word, yet once more, signifieth the removing of those things that are shaken, as of things that are made, that those things which cannot be shaken may remain" (12:26*b*-27). In a coming day, all that has been created is to be demolished. Man's defiance under grace makes this inevitable. The day is coming when this world will see such a demonstration of God's power as will leave nothing standing at all, except what is founded on His grace.

Here, then, is the appeal. God spoke in the Old Testament at Sinai, and those who ignored His voice and deliberately pushed onto the mount, when expressly commanded to stand back, paid for their presumption with their lives. God has spoken again in His Son and in sovereign grace. Those who refuse to heed His voice and purposely draw back when expressly commanded to go on will bear the penalty. They will be summoned before the great white throne to answer for the worst of crimes: willful apostasy against God's Son. It is a warning to those contemplating apostasy.

b. THE APPLICATION (12:28-29)

True believers are to *be moved by a glorious fact;* they have received "a king-dom which cannot be moved" (12:28*a*). Judaism, after all, was but a temporary thing. It has served its purpose and has been shaken to its very foundation. It will be revived, of course, during the Millennium, but even the millennial age will be temporary and its kingdom transient. In contrast to that, believers have a place in God's ultimate kingdom, a kingdom that cannot be shaken at all. The relation of the *eternal* kingdom to the *millennial* kingdom is symbolized in Revelation by the relation of the *New Jerusalem* to the *earthly Jerusalem.* The heavenly Jerusa-lem hovers in space over the earthly Jerusalem. The one is heavenly, but the oth-er earthly; the one eternal, the other destined to be burned up at the end of the Millennium. Believers, in the heavenly Jerusalem, will "reign with Christ" and have jurisdiction over the earth during the Millennium; their place and privilege is determined by their faithfulness on earth in this life.[1] We should be moved by this glorious fact.

Moreover, we should be *moved by God's gracious favor.* "Let us have grace, whereby we may serve God acceptably" (12:28*b*). Out of a deep sense of the favor bestowed upon us by God, we should give Him back joyful service.

Far from sitting on the fence, as many of the Hebrews were doing, we should be flinging ourselves wholeheartedly into God's work, moved not only by God's gracious favor but *moved by a godly fear* as well. We should serve "with rever-ence and godly fear: for our God is a consuming fire" (12:28*c*-29). Grace gives us no license to forget God's holiness. He is our Father, but He is also a consuming fire. In the Old Testament, God put distance between the sacred Ark of the Cove-nant and the rank and file of the people even when the camp was on the march. The distance has now been removed, but the burning holiness remains.

Thus ends the last warning in the book. For a Hebrew believer to go back to Judaism in the light of all that has been said would simply prove that he is an apostate and not a regenerate person at all.

---

1. See John Phillips, *Exploring Revelation,* rev. ed. (Chicago: Moody, 1987).

IX

The Way of Love (13:1-17)

A. Christian Compassion (13:1-3)
    1. To Be Shown to Saints (13:1)
    2. To Be Shown to Strangers (13:2)
    3. To Be Shown to Sufferers (13:3)
B. Christian Chastity (13:4)
C. Christian Contentment (13:5)
D. Christian Courage (13:6)
E. Christian Consideration (13:7)
    1. For What Christian Leaders Have Taught (13:7a)
    2. For What Christian Leaders Have Wrought (13:7b)
F. Christian Consistency (13:8)
G. Christian Conviction (13:9)
H. Christian Communion (13:10-14)
    1. The Principle of Communion (13:10-12)
        a. The Fruit of Calvary (13:10)
        b. The Fact of Calvary (13:11-12)
    2. The Place of Communion (13:13)
    3. The Prospect of Communion (13:14)
I. Christian Consecration (13:15-16)
    1. Spiritual Worship: Praising God (13:15)
    2. Spiritual Works: Pleasing God (13:16)
J. Christian Concern (13:17)
    1. Rule of the Elder (13:17a)
    2. Responsibility of the Elder (13:17b)
    3. Reactions of an Elder (13:17c)

IX

The Way of Love (13:1-17)

The Christian life is a practical life, and the driving force behind everything is love. Love first conceived salvation's plan in a past eternity. Love brought the Son of God from heaven to die for sinners on the cross. Love is shed abroad in the hearts of believers by the Spirit of God. Love led the writer of this letter to take his pen and pour out his heart, urging, pleading with those professing the Christian faith to prove their profession to be real by going on. Now he spreads wide the net of love and shows how it embraces the various functions of the Christian life.

Some believe that this chapter (Heb. 13) is a covering letter that accompanied the treatise. If so, and if it stood alone, no one would ever doubt that it had come from the pen of Paul. The presumption, in this case, is overwhelming that the one who penned the letter also penned the book. Verse 22 refers to a "letter in few words," which lends credence to the idea that chapter 13 was the covering note for the whole epistle.

A. Christian Compassion (13:1-3)

"Let brotherly love continue" (13:1) is the first urging of love.

1. TO BE SHOWN TO SAINTS (13:1)

One evidence of genuine conversion is genuine love for God's saints. John, the great apostle of love, wrote, "We know that we have passed from death unto life, because we love the brethren" (1 John 3:14). It is sad that words such as these could be penned:

> To dwell above, with saints in love
> That will indeed be glory;
> To dwell below, with saints we know—
> Well, that's another story!

We are to love those who are fellow members of the Body of Christ.

2. TO BE SHOWN TO STRANGERS (13:2)

Christian compassion reaches out, not only to the saints in the local fellow-ship but also to strangers. "Be not forgetful to entertain strangers: for thereby some have entertained angels unawares" (13:2). This was literally true in the ex-perience of Abraham. The three wayfaring men visited him; two were angels, and the other was the Son of God Himself. "I was an hungered, and ye gave me meat," the Lord will say to some at that great assize of the nations. "Then shall the righ-teous answer him, saying, Lord, when saw we thee an hungered, and fed thee? or thirsty, and gave thee drink? When saw we thee a stranger, and took thee in? . . . And the King shall answer and say unto them, Verily I say unto you, Inas-much as ye have done it unto the least of these my brethren, ye have done it unto me" (Matt. 25:35, 37-38, 40).

3. TO BE SHOWN TO SUFFERERS (13:3)

Christian love embraces sufferers too. "Remember them that are in bonds, as bound with them; and them which suffer adversity, as being yourselves also in the body" (13:3). Some of the Hebrew believers were suffering for the cause of Christ. The professing Hebrew Christians, those still sitting on the fence, would naturally draw back from helping those being persecuted for the cause of Christ, because they would be afraid of guilt by association. Thus Peter denied the Lord in Caiaphas's yard. In contrast with that, Paul praised the boldness of Onesipho-rus. He was "not ashamed of my chain," he said (2 Tim. 1:16*b*). Nero was then on the rampage, and it was a dangerous thing indeed to be a known associate of a Christian.

B. CHRISTIAN CHASTITY (13:4)

A tremendous attack is being mounted upon chastity today by the forces of evil. Permissiveness is the rule, and every moral restraint is being attacked and set aside. The marriage bond is being regarded as archaic and, even if valid, only to be entered into after a period of promiscuity and experimentation and with the reservation that easy divorce can soon untie the knot. Pornographic literature and X-rated films are fanning the flames of lust, making explicit and unrestrained sex appear the norm.

But God's Word has not altered. "Marriage is honourable in all, and the bed undefiled; but whoremongers and adulterers God will judge" (Heb. 13:4). God's moral laws have not changed. Horrible consequences await those who abandon His standards of sexual purity. Disease, guilt, psychological disturbances, insanity, and even suicide lurk in the way of those who abandon His codes. For a profess-ing believer to indulge in wrongful sexual activity is to invite God's inescapable judgment. David is an example of that. Because of his seduction of Bathsheba,

David was bereft of his power, and from that day on he had trouble in his family and upheavals in his kingdom. And though God removed the guilt of David's sin, He never removed its temporal consequences.

C. CHRISTIAN CONTENTMENT (13:5)

The next great principle of the Christian life is contentment. "Let your conversation be without covetousness; and be content with such things as ye have: for he hath said, I will never leave thee, nor forsake thee" (13:5). God is the ultimate Provider. He feeds the birds and the beasts, sends springtime harvest and soft, refreshing rain. Our ability to work and our temporal employment are of His providing. God knows our needs, our circumstances, and all about us, and He has pledged Himself to take care of us.

The Lord Jesus gave an interesting illustration of this when He said, "Are not two sparrows sold for a farthing [penny]? And not one of them shall fall on the ground without your Father" (Matt. 10:29). "Are not five sparrows sold for two farthings? And not one of them is forgotten before God" (Luke 12:6). Did you notice that? *Two* sparrows for a penny, *five* sparrows for two pence. Now look at that odd sparrow, the one with no value, tossed in to make a bargain. Even its affairs are God's concern! How it must grieve Him when we distrust Him, when we are greedy, materialistic, and filled with a love for money.

D. CHRISTIAN COURAGE (13:6)

Next comes Christian courage. "So that we may boldly say, The Lord is my helper, and I will not fear what man shall do unto me" (Heb. 13:6). The Hebrews were facing persecution from family, friend, and foe alike. God was using that very persecution to separate the wheat from the chaff, those who were merely professing Christianity from those who were genuinely saved, those who were drawing back from those determined to press on at all costs. What needed was courage, courage born of a dynamic faith in the Lord Himself, courage before which the fear of man would melt as the snow before the noonday sun. Men can be cruel, and the fear of man is a real snare for the soul. None of us can say for sure how he would react when faced with torture, prison, and the stake. But God gives grace to help in time of need.

There is, of course, a false courage based on too great an estimate of one's own fortitude. This was the kind of courage Peter had when he blustered that, though all the other disciples were to forsake the Lord, he never would. He was to find out within a few short hours that he himself was capable of denying the Lord before a mere girl, plus adding oaths and curses to his denial. There is true courage, born of a growing faith, a deepening love, and a hope beyond the veil. This is the kind of courage Peter displayed later on. According to tradition, when Peter was led forth to his death, he asked to be crucified upside down because he was not worthy to be crucified the same way as his Lord.

E. CHRISTIAN CONSIDERATION (13:7)

1. FOR WHAT CHRISTIAN LEADERS HAVE TAUGHT (13:7a)

We are to respect those whom God entrusts with positions of leadership among His people. We must pay attention to what they teach from the Word of God. God would have them reign in the affections of His people. Solomon said, "I the Preacher was king over Israel in Jerusalem" (Eccles. 1:12). That, of course, was literally true, for he was firmly seated upon David's throne, but it was also symbolically true. Those who faithfully minister God's Word to His people are always enthroned in their love. A person who handles the Word of God with skill and in the power of the Holy Spirit is engaged in the highest and noblest profession on earth.

2. FOR WHAT CHRISTIAN LEADERS HAVE WROUGHT (13:7b)

Then, too, Christian leaders are to be given every consideration for what they have wrought. We are to consider "the end of their conversation" ("the issue of their life") and imitate their faith (Heb. 13:7). The writer of Hebrews has already given his readers numerous examples of the kind of thing he has in mind. He has devoted a whole chapter to the great Old Testament heroes. The church is daily adding new, illustrious names to the list of faith's heroes. The lives of God's mighty men are set up as beacons along the way. They are shining examples, and we should imitate them.

F. CHRISTIAN CONSISTENCY (13:8)

Next comes Christian consistency as exemplified for us in the person and life of the Lord Himself: "Jesus Christ the same yesterday and to day, and for ever" (13:8). He is One who never wavers, never changes. Men are fickle and changing, and even the best of them are not always the same from one meeting to the next, but He is. He is always the same.

Look at Him when the pressures of life crowded in upon Him, when the multitudes thronged Him, pushed and surged around Him, each person eager to get close to see Him, to touch Him. Look at Him reclining at ease in the home of Lazarus at Bethany. Look at Him talking to His friends. Look at Him in the heat of debate with accusation, slander, and loaded questions coming at Him from every side. Look at Him at supper in the upper room.

Look at Him when faced with the red-hot hatred of His foes in the high priest's palace, when confronted with mob violence in Pilate's judgment hall, when encountering contemptuous scorn in Herod's court. Look at Him when talking to cultured, moral, upright Nicodemus, when talking to the sin-laden woman at the well, when faced with a bereaved widow's grief, when greeting the exuberant disciples who were flushed with their recent victories over demons and disease.

Look at Him as a boy of twelve, as a candidate for baptism at John's hands, as an itinerant preacher riding the crest of His fame, as a lonely sufferer in the Garden. He is always the same, never ruffled, never complaining, never at a loss for words, never wondering what to do, never wrong, never needing to apologize, never hesitating for a moment, never out of communion with God. He was always the same, as He is still the same today. This is the quality of life He would impart to us.

He knows well the problems and perplexities of life, its trials and testings, its fierce temptations. He has been this way. He knew and understood those Hebrew Christians of old, with all Judaism ranged against them, even as He knows and understands His people today in lands where intolerance reigns and His struggling saints are facing dangers and difficulties on every hand. He is the same today as yesterday, able to meet every need we have.

G. CHRISTIAN CONVICTION (13:9)

Another basic factor of Christian life is conviction. We are not to be "carried about with divers and strange doctrines" (13:9a). Such instability is set in contrast with the immutability of Christ. Any doctrine that is not true to the person and work of Christ is "strange" or alien. The reference here is primarily to Judaism with its fatal allurement for the unwary Hebrews. By its rejection of Christ, Judaism had become as foreign as any other wrong teaching. Christians are to have conviction about the great truths of the faith and not trade them for comfort or convenience. "It is a good thing that the heart be established with grace; not with meats, which have not profited them that have been occupied therein" (13:9b). Grace is so much more virile and glorious a principle than law. Notice that the writer's appeal is to the *heart*. For the most part, error appeals to the mind. The Hebrews were being warned not to try some form of compromise with Judaism. "Meats" (that is, the ceremonial law) could profit them nothing. The entire Judaistic system had been rendered bankrupt by Calvary. Jewish ritual was a rival to grace and must be recognized as such.

H. CHRISTIAN COMMUNION (13:10-14)

An important part of Christian living is communion. *The principle of communion*, upon which all Christian communion is based, is Calvary (13:10-12).

We are to think first of *the fruit of Calvary*. "We have an altar, whereof they have no right to eat which serve the tabernacle" (13:10). There are some four hundred references to the altar in the Old Testament. The altar is rarely mentioned in the New Testament except in reference to the Old Testament. The great brazen altar, in the Temple court, still beckoned to the Hebrews. But no matter how attractive the symbol seemed, with its appointed priests performing a divine service originally divinely ordained and hallowed by the custom of centuries, the Christian had no part in that altar. It was obsolete. To go on offering the blood of bulls and goats to God, after the shedding of Christ's blood, was an insult, not an inspiration. Believers have a better altar, a better sacrifice. The writer has just warned against trading grace for the "meats" of the Judaistic system. Many of the Old Testament sacrifices were used as food for the priests. Having served their purpose on the altar, they became the basis for a communion feast. Calvary did away with all that. We feast now upon Christ, and our communion is with Him. This is the fruit of Calvary. To go back to Judaism would be to forfeit forever this higher, holier, spiritual communion of which the feasts connected with the Old Testament altar were but a feeble picture. To go back to those feasts would be to deny the reality in Christ. It would mean that the person who did this was never really saved at all and that, by proving himself an apostate, he would never be able to partake of Christ.

The writer pursues his theme by emphasizing *the fact of Calvary*. "For the bodies of those beasts whose blood is brought into the sanctuary by the high priest for sin, are burned without the camp. Wherefore Jesus also, that he might sanctify the people with his own blood, suffered without the gate" (13:11-12). The Old Testament offerings were of two kinds. There were the sweet-savor offerings, already referred to by the writer of Hebrews, which became food for the priests. Then there were the sin offerings, and there was no feasting on those. The Lord Jesus is not only the sweet-savor offering upon which we feed; He is also the sin offering and, as such, establishes the principle upon which all communion rests. The sin offerings were always burned outside the camp. What the camp was to the Israelite in the wilderness, Jerusalem was to the Jew of Jesus' day. He was slain outside the city's walls on a hill of shame. There He was made a sin offering by God. This is the principle upon which communion is established.

The next thing to consider is *the place of communion*. "Let us go forth therefore unto him without the camp, bearing his reproach" (13:13). The Jews had rejected Christ and cast Him "outside the camp." The Temple and all it stood for still remained inside Jerusalem (the "camp" of Israel). Since Christ was outside the whole thing, there could be no communion with Him inside the Judaistic system. The place of the Hebrew believer was with Christ, outside all that Judaism stood for. To go back to Judaism would be tantamount to forsaking Him and giving the right hand of fellowship to the system that had cast Him out. True, to share His place "outside the camp" would be to share His rejection, but nothing else was possible. The very essence of Christianity is that we bear His reproach.

Of course, while the entire argument has particular force for those living in the first century of the Christian era when the Temple and its sacrifices were still a powerful magnet to the Jewish Christian, the principle can be applied today. Many have been brought up in Christ-dishonoring religious systems, some of them professedly Christian. The true believer must not go back into these religious systems that cast Christ out. Instead, he must share Christ's reproach and meet Him on the ground He himself has chosen "outside the camp."

Best of all, the Christian has *the prospect of communion*. "For here have we no continuing city, but we seek one to come" (13:14). All our prospects are heavenward, not earthward; not the earthly Jerusalem but the heavenly; not the Jewish Temple but Christ (for in the New Jerusalem there is no temple). Christ is the sum and center of our communion. So the Spirit urges the believers to go on, to keep things in proper perspective, to look beyond earth's scenes to the glory land. Thus, now with warnings, now with wooings, he keeps pressing home the burden that has been ever before him from the very first word in his letter.

I. CHRISTIAN CONSECRATION (13:15-16)

Another fact of the Christian life is consecration, the setting apart of oneself for the Lord. This calls for *spiritual worship*, for a life of praising God. "By him therefore let us offer the sacrifice of praise to God continually, that is, the fruit of our lips giving thanks to his name" (13:15). That is all God wants from us, and it is all we can give to Him. The animal sacrifices of a dead and outmoded religion are not for us; ours is the sacrifice of praise.

And is that a cheap or a costly offering? David vowed he would not offer the Lord that which cost him nothing. Can we praise God without cost to ourselves? For these hesitant Hebrews to lift up their voices in praise to the Lord Jesus meant the fierce hatred of their fellows. For many in the world today it means the same. For everyone it means the investment of time, to say the least. How many hours, one wonders, did David spend perfecting the words of his psalms? How long does it take to perfect praise, to soberly think through the immense realities of the grace and the goodness and the glory and the government of God? Is praise the glib singing of a chorus, or is it hours spent in God's presence with heart uplifted in awe and worship at the wonders of His person and His works? Is praise the thoughtless line or two of a hymn sung with others at a worship service, or is it the voice of testimony raised among people in glory to God at home, at work, at play?

Along with spiritual worship, lips used to glorify God, there must be *spiritual works*, a life spent for God's glory. "But to do good and to communicate forget not: for with such sacrifices God is well pleased" (13:16). Good works are not offered as an inducement to God to have mercy upon us; they are the response of a heart filled with gratitude to God for His Son. Praise is *Godward;* good works are *manward*. The Christian life must be marked by the willing sacrifice of money, time, and ability poured out for Christ and His cause. And with such a life God is well pleased. When His Son lived on earth, God opened heaven more than once to say, "This is my beloved Son, in whom I am well pleased" (e.g., Matt. 3:17; 17:5). If He does not open heaven now to express the same joy in consecrated lives lived in the power of the Spirit of God for His glory, it is because He is treasuring up such high commendation to be expressed at the judgment seat of Christ.

J. CHRISTIAN CONCERN (13:17)

This long section on the way of love ends with a word on the ministry of an elder and the obligation of the believer to recognize the elder and his work.

The *rule of the elder* must be acknowledged. "Obey them that have the rule over you, and submit yourselves" (13:17a). The Christian community is not a democracy where the majority rules, nor is it anarchy where every man does whatever pleases him; it is a theocracy over which God rules through elders. An exhortation such as this is greatly needed today when resentment and rebellion against authority are so commonplace in the world. In the church, no such carnal and satanic spirit must prevail. Those whom God has raised up and gifted to be spiritual leaders must be obeyed. The rule of the elder must be acknowledged.

The *responsibility of the elder* must be recognized too. "They watch for your souls, as they that must give account" (13:17b). They are not lords over God's people. Their position is not that of a worldly prince. They minister, with an eye fixed firmly on the judgment seat of Christ at which they, too, must appear to give account of their work. They must shepherd the flock, know those entrusted to their care, provide spiritual food, hasten after those who are going astray, exhort those who are growing cold, encourage the weak, visit the sick, urge the development of spiritual gifts in those to whom they minister, give help to all, and be hospitable and exemplary in their own lives. Elders' responsibilities are heavy, and those over whom they rule must recognize that.

The *reactions of the elder* must also be considered. Those are of two kinds. What they do, they do either with joy or with sorrow. The writer of Hebrews urges his readers to make the task of the elders easy, in order that "they may do it with joy, and not with grief: for that is unprofitable for you" (13:17c). At the judgment seat of Christ, the joy or sorrow of the elder will be reflected in the gain or loss of the believer. What a tragedy to be truly saved but to appear at the judgment seat of Christ as "unprofitable"! Love would guard against any such thing.

X
Conclusion (13:18-25)

A. A Word of Exhortation (13:18-19)
 1. The Request for Prayer (13:18*a*)
 2. The Reason for Prayer (13:18*b*-19)
B. A Word of Benediction (13:20-21)
 1. The Glory of His Person (13:20*a*)
 2. The Glory of His Provision (13:20*b*)
 3. The Glory of His Power (13:21*a*)
 4. The Glory of His Praise (13:21*b*)
C. A Word of Supplication (13:22)
D. A Word of Information (13:23)
E. A Word of Salvation (13:24-25)

X

Conclusion (13:18-25)

It only remains now for the writer to make his concluding remarks. What more can he say? He has roamed the Old Testament for illustrations, examples, and verses to support his warnings and pleas. He has appealed to the conscience, the intellect, the emotions, and the will. He has urged the horrors of apostasy and the bright hopes of heaven. He has balanced the sufferings of his present time against the glory that is to be revealed. All that remains is to draw together a few of the threads and make a few personal remarks.

A. A WORD OF EXHORTATION (13:18-19)

He begins with *a request for prayer*. "Pray for us" (13:18a), he says. So whoever he was, evidently the writer was well known to his readers, and his circumstances were known. He felt sufficiently close to them that he could not only write the way he did but could also solicit their prayers. Ordinarily we request prayer only from those we know are interested in us and sympathetic toward us.

Next he gives *the reason for prayer*. "For," he says, "we trust we have a good conscience, in all things willing to live honestly" (13:18b). Wrong motives and sin in the life are both hindrances to prayer. The writer knew that his life was clean and that he harbored no hindrances to prayer. He had a good conscience. Nothing hinders prayer as much as dishonesty. The Lord Jesus said to the woman at the well, "God is a Spirit: and they that worship him must worship him in spirit and in truth" (John 4:24)—in spirit because of what He is and in truth because of what we are.

"But," continues the writer, "I beseech you the rather to do this, that I may be restored to you the sooner" (13:19). Evidently prayer does change things. Prayer and its attending forces are as much a part of the universe as are the forces of gravity and magnetism. In some mysterious way, not fully explained to men, prayer has an effect upon what happens in life. The writer seemed to have no doubt that he would eventually be able to visit his readers. However, their prayers would work upon his circumstances so that it might be "the sooner." Is there something that needs to be changed in your life's situation? A loved one who needs to be saved, or something else clearly within God's will? Pray, and get others to pray! Things will happen sooner that way. God is willing to work, but often He waits for us to get earnest about the matter ourselves. In any case, prayer is one of the forces of the universe, and it is a force we can set in motion if we will.

B. A WORD OF BENEDICTION (13:20-21)

The writer now has a fourfold benediction to offer his readers. First, he offers praise and brings glory to God for *His person*. He is "the God of peace" (13:20*a*). War with God was begun, as far as man is concerned, in the Garden of Eden. Peace means that the war is over. God is the God of peace; only He can bring peace to the troubled heart and to a warning world. To turn one's back upon Christ is to turn away from any hope of peace, for the Lord Jesus is "God's great peace offer to men" (Luke 2:14). Here, incidentally, is another oblique warning to the Hebrews not to turn away from God's Son and thus reject His offer of peace.

Next, the writer brings glory to God for *His provision*. He is the God who "brought again from the dead our Lord Jesus, that great shepherd of the sheep, through the blood of the everlasting covenant" (13:20*b*). Thus we have in Christ and His work an everlasting Shepherd and an eternal shelter. The Lord Jesus lives forever in the power of an endless life, and, as a living Shepherd in glory, He cares for His sheep.

In His discourse on the good shepherd, the Lord Jesus said, "I lay down my life for the sheep. And other sheep I have, which are not of this fold: them also I must bring, and they shall hear my voice; and there shall be one fold [flock] and one shepherd" (John 10:15*b*-16). The fold characterized the Old Testament; it is marked by a circumference, by the wall all around it. The nation of Israel was the Old Testament fold. The flock characterizes the New Testament; it is marked by a center, by the Shepherd in the midst of His sheep. The Hebrew believers had been called out of the Jewish fold and had been gathered to the Shepherd, whose task it is to protect and provide for His sheep and to see them safely home.

The assurance of the true believer's security is based on the blood of the eternal covenant. The writer cannot forget the shifting shadows in the background, those wavering Hebrews who were professing Christianity, but who, at heart, preferred the imagined security of the fold of Judaism to the real security provided by the Good Shepherd. A fold without a shepherd is, after all, a desolate and unsafe place.

The writer's benediction next embraces the glory of *His power*. The Lord Jesus is able to "make you perfect in every good work to do his will, working in you that which is well-pleasing in his sight, through Jesus Christ" (13:21*a*). The statement begins with a reference to the "Lord Jesus" and ends with a reference to "Jesus Christ." The names and titles of the Lord are used discriminately throughout the Scriptures. He is "the Lord Jesus"; that refers to His position, to His coming out of eternity into time to take upon Himself humanity. He is "Jesus Christ" through human life and who now occupies a position as the great High Priest in glory. He and He alone can perfect God's work in us. His mighty power alone can enable us to live in a way pleasing to God.

Finally, the writer's benediction embraces the glory of *His praise*. "To whom be the glory for ever and ever. Amen" (13:21*b*). The great need was for the Hebrews to get their eyes off their circumstances and themselves and onto Christ. When Peter tried walking on the water, he did well as long as his eyes were on the Lord; but the moment he began to look at the waves and listen to the wind, he began to sink.

The Hebrews were filled with memories of the splendid Temple, the gorgeous rituals, the priests' rich and costly vestments, the magnificent choirs, the orchestras, the music of Judaism. All this they had to give up for a place "outside the camp" with the despised Nazarene, meeting in homes and hideouts, without any of the rich trappings of their former religion. What they needed more than anything else was to look up and see beyond the present age and beyond the temporal things to the eternal realities in heaven.

Why trade the splendid Temple for Christ? Because all glory belongs to Him. True glory did not reside in a Temple that, within a few years, was to be reduced to charred timbers and smoke-blackened ruins. True glory was worn by the risen, ascended Christ like a shimmering robe of light. If they looked to Him they could never sink!

C. A WORD OF SUPPLICATION (13:22)

"And I beseech you, brethren, suffer the word of exhortation: for I have written a letter unto you in few words" (13:22). The writer—especially if it was the apostle Paul—could well visualize the bristling and hostility with which his epistle would be received by some. It struck so hard at Jewish prejudice. He pleaded for a fair hearing. After all, while he had covered the ground, there remained so much more that could have been said. He had already mentioned this when speaking of Melchizedek (5:11). His letter is brief compared to the dimensions of its theme and the seriousness of its implications.

D. A WORD OF INFORMATION (13:23)

Timothy was free! The writer had this important piece of news for the Hebrew church. Whatever may be the thoughts of some, the praise of Timothy was in all the churches (2 Cor. 8:18). In this reference to Timothy, many have seen proof that the apostle Paul wrote the epistle. Whoever the writer was, he obviously stood in good relation to Timothy, for not only did he look forward to seeing him soon but also to coming with him to visit those to whom he has been writing.

E. A WORD OF SALUTATION (13:24-25)

The writer closes by greeting the shepherds of the flock and the saints in general. He also sends greetings from the brethren in Italy with whom he was in touch. It is wonderful how Christ binds brethren together in bonds of love. In the world of that day, Hebrew and Italian, Jew and Roman, would be at each other's throats. In Christ they were one. It is grace that makes it possible. Grace brings us together in the family; grace keeps us moving forward in the faith. Grace! "Grace be with you all. Amen" (13:25).

Moody Press, a ministry of the Moody Bible Institute, is designed for education, evangelization, and edification. If we may assist you in knowing more about Christ and the Christian life, please write us without obligation: Moody Press, c/o MLM, Chicago, Illinois 60610.